SO-CTK-292

DA990.U46D66 1985

DOUMITT
CONFLICT IN NORTHERN I

DATE DUE

DATE DUE			
JUN 3 '87			
JUN 8 '88			
MAY 16 '89			
6/5/03			
MAR 11 '04			
MAY 05 '04			
DEC 1 3 2006			

Conflict in Northern Ireland

343
11

American University Studies

Series IX
History

Vol. 5

PETER LANG
New York · Berne · Frankfurt am Main

Donald P. Doumitt

Conflict
in
Northern Ireland

The history, the problem
and the challenge

PETER LANG
New York · Berne · Frankfurt am Main

Library of Congress Cataloging in Publication Data

Doumitt, D. P. (Donald P.), 1926–
Conflict in Northern Ireland.

(American University Studies. Series IX, History;
vol. 5)
Bibliography: p.
1. Northern Ireland – History. 2. Northern Ireland –
Politics and government. 3. Northern Ireland – Social
conditions. I. Title. II. Series.
DA990.U46D66   1985   941.60824   83-49030
ISBN 0-8204-0068-8 (pbk.)
ISSN 0740-0462

CIP-Kurztitelaufnahme der Deutschen Bibliothek

Doumitt, Donald P.:
Conflict in Northern Ireland: the history, the
problem and the challenge / Donald P. Doumitt. –
New York; Berne; Frankfurt am Main: Lang,
1985.
(American University Studies: Ser. 9,
History; Vol. 5)
ISBN 0-8204-0068-8
ISBN 0-8204-0102-1

NE: American University Studies / 09

Illustration of the cover:
IRA Volunteer (© An Phoblacht / Republican News)

© Peter Lang Publishing, Inc., New York 1985

Printed by Lang Druck, Inc., Liebefeld/Berne (Switzerland)

TO THE PEOPLE OF NORTHERN IRELAND:

MAY THE GOD THEY HOLD IN COMMON
LEAD THEM TO THE PEACE THEY SEEK

Acknowledgements

I wish to extend my thanks to the many people who have assisted me in the course of my work, especially to Dr. James J. O'Connor, Director of Liberal Arts, Oregon State University, Dr. Thomas C. McClintock, Chairman of the Department of History, Oregon State University, and to Dr. Ronald O. Clarke, Department of Religion, Oregon State University. I wish to also thank Ruth L. Lindsey, who worked diligently as my typist; the library staffs of Clatsop College and University College, Cork; and my wife, Suzanne, who courageously perservered.

Table of Contents

Illustrations

List of Tables

Map of the Republic of Ireland and Northern Ireland

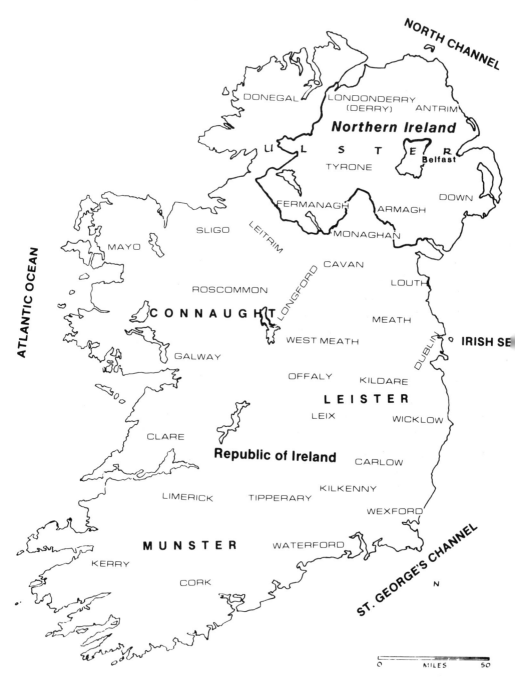

(Benedictine Press, Mt. Angel Abbey, St. Benedict, Oregon 97373 USA)

Demographic Map

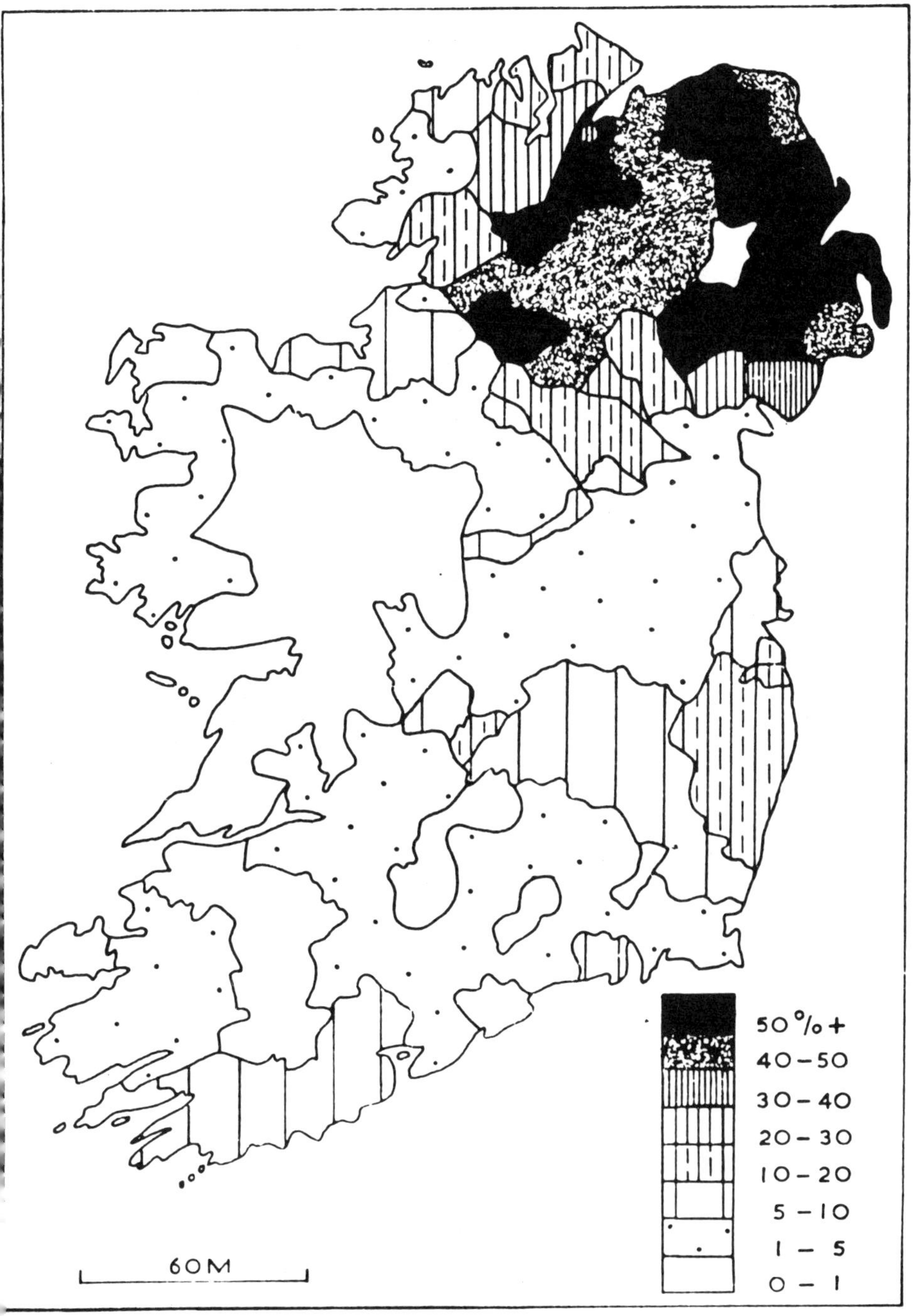
50%+
40-50
30-40
20-30
10-20
5-10
1-5
0-1
60M

Source: T. W. Freeman. *Ireland: A General and Regional Geography*. London: Methuen and Co. Ltd., 1972. Percentage of Protestants throughout the 32 counties showing a majority in most of Ulster except in some rural districts.

Districts of Belfast

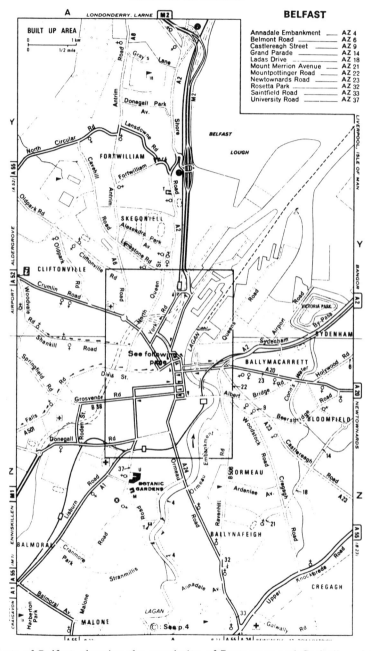

Parts of Belfast, showing the proximity of Protestant and Catholic neighborhoods along the Shankill and Falls Roads. Reproduced with the permission of the Michelin Tyre Public Limited Company from their publication 'Great Britain and Ireland' 1980, p. 528.

CHAPTER I

Introduction

This study has three objectives: (1) to analyze the intellectual influences on the rise of Ireland's national consciousness from 1890 to 1981, (2) to clarify the social and psychological tensions in Northern Ireland, and (3) to explore the means of a possible resolution of the present civil war.

The importance of the study is that it identifies Northern Ireland's present multi-faceted political character and social polarization which stunted her political development. It focuses on the attitudes of prejudice, religious bigotry, and exaggerated fears and social paranoia endemic to that area. These character traits contribute to the enmity found between Protestant and Catholic and perpetuate the present societal divisions.

The Problem and Delimitations

This study analyzes the problem of violence, the use of power tactics of competitive groups to manipulate the working class and explores the behavior on the part of Ulster's populace in spite of the information available to them. Probing these problems allows the researcher to explore new ideas in search of a peaceful solution.

Delimitations

The study is confined to the years 1890 to 1981.
No attempt is made to probe deeply into the history of Irish politics or individuals and events that shaped Irish nationalism during the seventeenth and eighteenth centuries.
The research does not cover in detail the organization and leadership of the Irish Republican Army.
The structures of the Orange Order and other Protestant parties are not discussed in detail.

For a comprehensive study of these areas the following sources are recommended:

Bell, J. Bowyer. *The Secret Army: The IRA, 1916 - 1974.* Cambridge, Mass.: The MIT Press, 1974.

Bowden, Tom. "The IRA and the Changing Tactics of Terrorism," *Political Quarterly.* n.v. October-December, 1976.

Coogan, Tim Pat. *The IRA.* London: Pall Mall Press, 1970.

Coogan, Tim Pat. *On the Blanket: The H-Block Story.* Dublin: Ward River Press, 1980.

Gray, Tony. *The Orange Order.* London: Bodley Head, 1972.

Kee, Robert. The Green Flag: *The Turbulent History of the Irish Nationalist Movement.* New York: Delacorte Press, 1972.

Mansergh, Nicholas. *The Irish Question.* 3rd ed. London: George Allan and Unwin, Ltd., 1975.

McCaffrey, Lawrence J. *Ireland from Colony to Nation State.* Englewood Cliffs, N. J.: Prentice-Hall, Inc., 1980.

CHAPTER II

Definitions of Terms Used

The following definitions and clarifications are used in this study:

Alliance Party. A non-sectarian coalition of moderates formed in Northern Ireland in 1969 that favors continued political ties with Britain.[1]

Ascendancy Class. The ruling Irish and Anglo-Irish Protestants, mainly Episcopalians in communion with the Church of England (Anglican) but also includes some Presbyterians. Throughout the nineteenth century they were the majority of Irish landlords and landed aristocracy.[2] Presently they are considered an influential part of the political-economic establishment in Ulster.

"B Specials." A category of the Ulster Special Constabulary (USC), a Protestant force founded in 1920. The "B Specials" became a contingent of the USC in 1969 to protect Protestant interests.[3] The force grew to 50,000 men and had full discretion under the Special Powers Act of 1922.[4]

Cameron Commission. An investigative body created by the British Government in 1969, which documented the political and economic discrimination against Roman Catholics of Northern Ireland.[5]

Church of Ireland. The Episcopalian body found in the Republic of Ireland and Northern Ireland with a membership of approximately 500,000.[6]

---

1 "The Moderate Voice," *Peace By Peace* (September 18,1981), 4.
2 Nicholas Mansergh, *The Irish Question: 1840-1921,* 3rd ed. (Toronto: George Allen & Unwin, Ltd., 1975), pp. 5, 31.
3 Roger H. Hull, *The Irish Triangle: Conflict in Northern Ireland* (Princeton University Press, 1978), p. 37.
4 Public Information Office, *Northern Ireland Report-1975,* Belfast: n.p., p. 4. (Hereafter cited as Northern Ireland Report-1975).
5 "Modern History Background," *Christian Century,* 88, (February, 1971), 170.
6 Lawrence J. McCaffrey, *Ireland From Colony To Nation State* (Englewood Cliffs, N. J.: Prentice-Hall, Inc., 1979), p. 85.

Direct Rule. Northern Ireland is ruled directly from Westminister Parliament in London. This came in response to the spread of violence in Ulster, which led in 1972 to the suspension of the Stormont Parliament. It was imposed in 1974 again in response to an escalation of violence by the IRA and a variety of Protestant groups. It introduced stronger military security and is still in force.[7]

Downing Street Declaration. A directive promulgated by James Chichester-Clark, Prime Minister of Northern Ireland, and three ministers in 1969. It declared that Unionists would be responsible for their actions in Northern Ireland. The statement directed Unionists to end political and religious discrimination in public housing, investigate the problem and provide fair representation for minorities in elected offices by fair electoral laws.[8]

European Economic Community. (EEC, also called Common Market). A co-operative economic organization of western European countries established in 1957 by the Treaty of Rome. Its purpose was to create a single market economy by removing trade barriers among member states, to coordinate trade, transportation, and agriculture and to provide employment for people from other Common Market countries.[9]

Fair Employment Agency. (FEA). A British Government agency formed in 1976. Its purpose is to promote equality of opportunity and work to eliminate discrimination in Northern Ireland because of differences in religious belief or political opinion.[10]

Fenians. A secret revolutionary organization founded in Ireland and in New York in 1858 almost simultaneously. The Fenians' aim was the creation of an independent Irish Republic. The Fenians were the forerunners of the Irish Republican Army (IRA) and the

---

7 *Ibid.,* pp. 182 - 183.
8 Edward Vincent Feeney, "From Reform to Resistance: A History of the Civil Rights Movement in Northern Ireland" (Ph. D. dissertation, University of Washington, 1974), p. 190.
9 Alvin J. Cottrell and James E. Dougherty, *The Policies of The Atlantic Alliance* (London: Frederick A. Praeger, 1964), pp. 134 - 144.
10 Fair Employment Agency For Northern Ireland, *An Industrial and Occupational Profile of the Two Sections of the Population of Northern Ireland: An Analysis of the 1971 Population Census,* p. 1 (Hereafter cited as FEA).

18

Republican movement.[11] They led a revolt against Britain in 1867. Fenians were banned by the Catholic Church in 1870 because they were viewed as an equivalent to the Italian revolutionary movements that were anti-clerical and threatening the papal states in central Italy. Fenians were similar to other nineteenth century European nationalists in that they used violence to achieve their objective.[12] The Church banned its members from receiving absolution, but the ban was disregarded by many priests.[13]

Fianna Fáil. ("Soldiers of Destiny"). One of the major political parties in Eire founded by Eamon de Valera, President of the Irish Free State, 1932 - 1937. It is reputed to be the heir to the Republican movement that rejected the Free State Government of twenty-six counties established in 1921 and is believed to still hold IRA sympathies.[14]

Fine Gael. Another of the major parties that made up a coalition government with the Labour Party and other groups in opposition to *Fianna Fáil* in 1976. The coalition government favored greater autonomy from Britain and collaborated with *Fianna Fáil* to protect the Republic's economy from foreign competition and to expand the industrial sector.[15]

Humanae Vitae. ("Concerning Human Life"). An encyclical letter issued July 25, 1968 by Pope Paul VI. It speaks to problems concerning birth control and human sexuality. The encyclical's importance was its restatement of the Catholic Church's right to pass final judgment on moral problems.[16]

11 Richard W. Mansbach, ed., *Northern Ireland: Half a Century of Partition* (New York: Facts On File, Inc., 1973), p. 3.
12 *Ibid.*
13 Edgar Holt, *Protest In Arms: The Irish Troubles, 1916-1924* (New York: Coward-McCann, 1961), pp. 66-67.
14 T. E. Utley, *Lessons of Ulster* (London: J. M. Dent & Sons, 1975), p. 56.
15 Republic of Ireland; Department of Foreign Affairs, *Facts About Ireland* (Dublin: Irish Printers, Ltd., 1978), pp. 45-46. (Hereafter cited as *Facts*).
16 *Report on Sex in Marriage: Love-Giving, Life-Giving*, Washington, D. C.: Archdiocese of Washington, 1968.

Irish Republican Army (IRA). Formerly known as the Irish Volunteers which in 1919 was reconstituted into the Irish Republican Army. The IRA waged a guerilla war against British forces during the Anglo-Irish War (1919 - 1921).[17]

Mater et Magistra. ("Mother and Teacher"). An encyclical letter issued in 1961 by Pope John XXIII. It reviews past encyclicals and speaks to problems of social justice, relationships in social and economic life and responsibilities of affluent nations toward the developing nations.[18]

Nationalist Extremists. Pertains to Catholic groups in the north such as the Irish Republican Army and Irish National Liberation Army which are committed to unite Ulster with the Irish Republic. They claim the right to determine their own political goals and to use violence in achieving their objectives.[19]

Northern Ireland Civil Rights Association (NICRA). A non-sectarian organization founded in 1964 to demonstrate against unfair housing and to expose the sectarian nature of society in Northern Ireland.[20]

Official and Provisional IRA Schism. The Irish Republican Army (IRA) split into "Officials" and "Provisionals" in 1969 because of ideological differences. The Officials are amenable to some participation within the political process and are often described as envisioning a united Ireland with Marxist economics.[21] The Provisionals (called "Provos") will not participate in the present government which it contends is illegal. Its mission is to expel the British from Ulster and achieve political unity with the Republic by any

---

17   Patrick Buckland, *Irish Unionism: Two* (Dublin: Gill and MacMillan, 1973), pp. 114 - 115.
18   *Encyclical Letter: Mater et Magistra, Christianity and Social Progress,* by Pope John XXIII, trans. W. J. Gibbons, S.J. (Glen Rock, N.J.: Paulist Press, 1962).
19   Enda McDonagh, "Violence and Political Change," *Furrow,* 29 (February, 1978), pp. 86 - 87.
20   Liam De Paor, *Divided Ulster* (Baltimore: Penguin, 1970), pp. 165 - 166.
21   Tom Bowden, "The IRA and the Changing Tactics of Terrorism." *Political Quarterly,* 47 (October-December, 1976), p. 427. (At the time of this writing, Bowden was a Senior Lecturer in Politics at the Manchester Polytechnic School).

means possible. It describes itself as socialist rather than Marxist and similar to western European democratic socialism.[22]

Orange Order. A semi-secret order founded in 1795, through collaboration of Episcopalians and conservative Presbyterians. Its ideology today is to defend Ulster and the British Crown against Catholicism, with primary loyalty to Protestantism.[23]

Pacem in Terris ("Peace on Earth"). An encyclical letter issued in 1964 by Pope John XXIII. It discusses the arms race, maldistribution of the world's resources, and problems concerning world peace.[24]

Peace People Community. The community formed in Ulster in 1976 as a non-sectarian movement. Its purpose is to contribute to better relations between Protestants and Catholics and to end sectarianism in Northern Ireland.[25]

Penal Laws. The laws that reinforced the 1689 English Bill of Rights, making allegiance to England conditional on the profession of Protestantism. The purpose of the Penal Laws was to prevent the re-emergence of a Catholic property-owning class in England or Ireland.[26]

Republicanism. Ideology of Irish nationalism which advocates complete British withdrawal from Northern Ireland and political union with the Irish Republic.[27]

Royal Ulster Constabulary (RUC). A 3,000-man military force which was formed in 1922 to maintain security in Northern Ireland; ninety percent of its members were Protestant. The RUC had authority under the Special Powers Act to arrest and detain anyone

---

22 Interview with Richard McAuley, Provisional Sinn Fein Headquarters, Falls Road, Belfast, May 11, 1979. (Hereafter cited as McAuley interview).
23 McCaffrey, p. 21.
24 *Encyclical Letter: Pacem in Terris, Peace on Earth.* By Pope John XXIII, Trans. by Vatican Polyglot Press, Washington, D. C.: National Catholic Welfare Conference, 1963.
25 Steve McBride, "Six Years On . . . ", *Peace By Peace* (August 20, 1982), p. 2.
26 Gary MacEoin, *Northern Ireland: Captive of History* (New York: Holt, Rinehart, & Winston, 1974), p. 124.
27 McCaffrey, pp. 124, 162-165.

whom it suspected to be an enemy and to do this outside ordinary constitutional rights.[28]

Shankill and Falls Roads. Two ghettos in Belfast. The Protestant Shankill Road and the Catholic Falls Road are known for their high rate of unemployment and scenes of social unrest. The "Protestant Shankill" and "Catholic Falls" were for a time separated by barbed-wire. Today cement posts mark a "peace line" blocking streets that cross from one neighborhood to the other.[29]

Sinn Fein ("We Ourselves"). A term signifying a commitment to revive the Irish language and culture.[30] It was established in 1905 as a political organization but became illegal in 1919.[31] In 1922, *Sinn Fein* opposed Dominion status and favored complete independence for Ireland.[32] Today it is legal and free to function in both north and south. Acting as political spokesman for the IRA, the *Sinn Fein* split into Officials and Provisionals who presently support both IRA's.

Social Democratic Labour Party (SDLP). The party was formed in 1970 by six members of the Stormont Parliament. The SDLP speaks for the Catholic community in the north. The party wants a reformist solution to the Ulster conflict and is no longer stressing unification, but greater political participation in the government of Northern Ireland.[33]

"Special Category." A special status which became available to convicted prisoners in June, 1972, following a hunger strike at Crumlin Road Prison in Belfast. This meant that a person who was sentenced to more than nine months imprisonment, who claimed

---

28 *Ibid.*, pp. 180-181.
29 MacEoin, p. 17.
30 *Ibid.*, p. 138.
31 George Dangerfield, *The Damnable Question: One Hundred and Twenty Years of Anglo-Irish Conflict - A Study in Anglo-Irish Relations* (Boston: Little, Brown & Co., 1976), pp. 287-294.
32 Mansergh, p. 23.
33 Eamonn McCann, *War in an Irish Town* (Middlesex, England: Penguin Books, Inc., 1974), p. 249.

political motivation and was acceptable to a compound leader at the Maze Prison, would be able to wear his own clothes and be exempt from having to work. The special category status was terminated in 1974.[34]

Special Powers Acts of 1922, 1933. This legislation was enacted in 1922 and became a permanent law in 1933. It provided the Minister of Home Affairs or a policeman with the authority to arrest and intern anyone without a warrant or having to present the person with charges.[35]

Stormont Parliament. Stormont Castle is the site of the parliament of Northern Ireland in Belfast.

Sunningdale Agreement of 1973. This was the result of a conference in Sunningdale, England in which Britain, the Republic of Ireland and the Government of Northern Ireland agreed to establish a power-sharing for the Catholic community of Ulster. The agreement also accepted the formation of a Council of Ireland which would act as a vehicle for cooperation between the north and south. The Council would also act as a forum for the expression of Irish nationalist aspirations.[36] It would be composed of fourteen members who represented Northern Ireland, the Republic of Ireland and Britain. Council members would be elected by citizens of the north and south based on proportional representation. The Council would recognize Britain as having sovereignty over Northern Ireland, but opened the way to Irish unity through popular consensus in Ulster. The Sunningdale Agreement was never implemented because it produced violent Protestant and IRA opposition.[37]

Unionist Party. The party was formed in 1885 in opposition to Home Rule which would have provided colonial self-rule for Ireland. The Unionists associated Home Rule with "Rome Rule," using sectarian politics to assure Ulster's union with Britain and a separate parliament.[38] The Unionist Party receives support from

34   McAuley Interview.
35   Hull, p. 37.
36   McCaffrey, p. 185.
37   *Ibid.*
38   Hull, p. 23.

the wealthy business class, the Protestant urban proletariat, and farmers.[39]

Ulster Defense Association (UDA). The largest Protestant para-military group in Ulster claiming a membership of 50,000. Formed in 1972 as a legal entitiy, the UDA today advocates separation from Britain in an independent state of Ulster, and recommends power-sharing with the Catholic minority. Its primary loyalty is to Northern Ireland rather than to Protestantism.[40]

Ulster Freedom Fighters (UFF). A fictitious name invented by the Ulster Defense Association in the early 1970's as a suitable cover for the UDA. The cover name was used to deflect blame for sectarian murders and to mislead British authorities from moving against the UDA as a source of Protestant terrorism.[41]

Ulster Volunteer Force (UVF). An illegal Protestant paramilitary group which was formed in 1966. It is described as the Unionist counterpart to the Irish Republican Army with the avowed pupose to defend the constitution of Northern Ireland.[42]

White Paper of 1973. This document came out of the Sunningdale Agreement and was entitled *Northern Ireland Constitutional Proposals*. It recommended the following:

1. Power-sharing in an Executive Committee with Catholic participation.
2. An eighty-three-member Assembly elected by proportional represent-ation.
3. British responsibility for police power.
4. An Irish Council composed of representatives from Britain, Northern Ireland and the Republic of Ireland for the resolution of mutual pro-blems.
5. Guaranteed civil rights for Catholics in voting, local government, employ-ment, housing and education.
6. The possibility of achieving political unity by means of mutual consent and negotiation.[43]

---

39 McCaffrey, pp. 11, 177.
40 Tony Gray, *The Orange Order* (London: The Bodley Head, 1972), pp. 276-277.
41 Jack Holland, *Too Long a Sacrifice: Life and Death in Northern Ireland Since 1969* (New York: Dodd, Mead and Company, 1969), pp. 92-96.
42 *Ibid.*, pp. 244-246.
43 McCaffrey, p. 184.

24

CHAPTER III

Historical Background

The six northern counties of Ireland, known as Ulster, provide a classic example of social and political hatred. Jill and Leon Uris describe the several centuries of British rule as a murderous historical episode:

> Ireland has been cruelly and shamefully persecuted with every sort of indignity brought to bear. The most wanton penal laws legislated by a civilized western nation denied the Irish Catholics every human and material right. In the mid-nineteenth century the great famine was little more than a subtle exercise at gentlemen's genocide.[1]

Although the English have been in Ireland for 800 years, the present Ulster conflict began in the sixteenth century when the Irish resisted becoming an English colony.[2] At this time England's monarchs Henry VIII and his daughter Elizabeth I mandated Protestantism as the religion of the realm. Oliver Cromwell's invasion and subsequent devastation of the Irish countryside in 1649 intensified Irish hatred of the English. The Irish sense of despair was further deepened when Protestant forces under William of Orange defeated the Catholic army of James II in 1690 at the Battle of the Boyne River.[3] Thereafter a minority Protestant business class dominated political and economic life throughout the island.

This development was accompanied by the migration of large numbers of Scottish Presbyterians into Northern Ireland in the seventeenth century. Oliver Cromwell's immigration policy was to remove

---

1 Jill and Leon Uris, *Ireland, A Terrible Beauty* (New York: Bantam Books, 1978), p. 11.
2 McCaffrey, pp. 1-34.
3 Gary MacEoin, *Northern Ireland: Captive of History* (New York: Holt, Rinehart & Winston, 1974), p. 122. (MacEoin describes the Battle of the Boyne as a successful rear-guard action. The decisive defeat of Catholic forces took place a year later at the Battle of Aughrim).

the native Irish from the more productive lands to the less productive areas. The Irish historian Sean MacManus has written:

> The lands of six counties of Donegal, Derry (then called Coleraine), Tyrone, Fermanagh, Caven and Armagh - - four million acres were confiscated. (The lands of the three remaining Ulster counties, Antrim, Down and Monaghan were bestowed upon Britons at other times). The true owners, the natives, were driven like wild fowl or beasts, from the rich and fertile valleys of Ulster, which had been theirs from time immemorial, to the bogs and the moors and the barren crags where it was hoped they might starve and perish.[4]

Donegal, Monaghan and Caven were included in Ulster until 1922, when they became part of the Republic.

The eviction of the native populace and the plantation system settled by immigrants gave rise to a new population whose sole loyalty was to the Crown. The Protestants soon developed an attachment to the land as intense as that of the dispossessed Irish. As a result, the newly created settlements became permanent institutions. Land claims became not only a matter of legal principle guaranteed by the Crown but a moral imperative ensuring Britain a permanent presence in Irish affairs. These Protestant attachments to Ulster and the English throne ignored the possibility of a conflict that would result when the original Irish populace sought to reclaim the land.

Britain's policy of moving people into a hostile land was to assure that her political and economic interests could best be served in the hands of a frugal, hard-working and loyal Protestant population. Though a minority in relation to their numbers throughout Ireland, Protestants soon became a majority in the six counties of Ulster, where their increasing numbers made it easier to resist any future attempts to expel them. In succeeding periods Prostestant Ulster successfully resisted native Irish pressures to reclaim the whole of the island.[5]

The modern concept of "settler nationalism" carried with it a conviction that Protestants built the economic base and considered it

---

4 Sean MacManus, *The Story of the Irish Race: A Popular History of Ireland* (New York: The Devin-Adair Co., 1967), p. 405.
5 MacEoin, pp. 130-133.

their own domain. This attitude is similar to that of the French *Colons* in Algeria and the Zionist pioneers in Palestine.[6] In each case the settlers considered commercial-industrial development as having come from their own work and sacrifice. This, they believed, gave them a special claim to the land.[7] The emergence of Northern Protestant loyalism corresponded to the rise of Irish Republicanism during the time period under study. Recognition of these two emergent and concurrent nationalisms is crucial to an understanding of the conflict.

Protestant nationalism and loyalty to England are long-established realities in Ireland's modern history and are best expressed in a poem written prior to World War I. One notes the siege mentality linked to a sense of duty in which the defense of Ulster is deep, unwavering, and passionate:

> "Tis the voice of Ulster calling, and the hand of Ulster too
> Hold on high the flag of England, bids it flutter to the blue.
> Will you tear it from her fingers, will you drag the banner down,
> And unfold instead the Emblem of the Harp without the Crown?
>
> "Tis the voice of Ulster calling: shall her cry be in vain?
> Shall the Union bonds be broken and the One be henceforth twain?
> "Tis the voice of Ulster calling, in the crisis of her fate:
> Ye will bear it, oh my brothers, ye will hearken ere too late.[8]

Protestant nationalism, as exemplified by the preceding poem, intensified as a reaction to the nineteenth century Fenian revolts whose

6 During the nineteenth century, French policies in Algeria were to occupy the land with French people. These "Colons" strengthened the French position in the face of hostile native Algerian *Piednoirs* (translated 'black feet'), a name given to the dark-skinned, bare-footed natives. Similiarly, the Jewish national movement known as Zionism had as its goal the creation of a Jewish state in Palestine. The settling of Zionist pioneers into Palestine generated resistance from displaced Palestinians during the 1920s until the present day. See: Walter Z. Laqueur, ed., *The Middle East in Transition: Studies in Contemporary History* (New York: Frederick A. Praeger, 1958) pp. 232-255.
7 William Kingston, "Northern Ireland — If Reason Fails", *Political Quarterly* 44 (1973); 32. For a study of the emergence of modern Zionist nationalism, see: Theodor Herzl, "The Rise of Israel", in *The Middle East: Selected Readings*, Ed. Don Peretz, (New Jersey: Houghton Mifflin Co., 1973), pp. 197-225.
8 "The Voice of Ulster", *Orange Standard*, May, 1979, p. 8.

participants sought to alter their subservient connection with Britain. The attempts were crushed, but they did result in some easing of Britain's controls in the form of economic and political concessions.[9]

Karl Marx, commenting on the Irish Rebellion of 1845, noted close similarities in the character of the Irish and that of Latin nationals, most notably the French and Italians. He explained that in each of those nations feelings and passions predominated over reason and quiet reflection. Thus, the uneducated Irish farmers' traditional reaction to the crime of injustice was to inflict physical violence upon ". . . their most immediate enemies, the landlords' agents, or their obedient servants, the Protestant intruders whose large farms are made up of potato patches of hundreds of rejected families."[10]

Over time, however, Ulster's Protestant leaders developed their own habit of using force rather than granting concessions in dealing with the Catholic minority.[11] This grew out of the issue of Home Rule prior to World War II, which would have granted considerable autonomy to Ireland in domestic matters except internal security and maritime activities yet kept it an integral part of the British Empire. Protestant conservatives opposed Home Rule because they saw it as a major step toward unity with the Catholic south. They, therefore, encouraged extremism as a necessary and inevitable way to resist it. In 1912, Andrew Bonar Law, the Unionist party leader, saw Home Rule as a papal conspiracy. The slogan "Home Rule is Rome Rule"[12] became common, and the Unionists threatened civil war should Home Rule pass the House of Lords.[13]

One result of this divisiveness is that politicians have exploited Northern Ireland's political climate, encouraging an attitude that societal turmoil and cold-blooded murder are plausible methods for defending one's interests. The history of Ulster politics has

9 Eric Strauss, *Irish Nationalism and British Democracy* (New York: Columbia University Press, 1951), pp. 68, 163.
10 Karl Marx and Friedrich Engels, *Ireland and the Irish Problem: A Collection of Writings* (New York: International Publishers, 1945), pp. 41 - 42.
11 McCaffrey, p. 112.
12 De Paor, p. 73.
13 McCaffrey, p. 112.

shown this to be the case even when it meant countermanding Westminister's constitutional authority and the democratic, parliamentary process.

This propensity for extremism is seen in the historian Lawrence McCaffrey's comment about Lord Milner, "Pro-Consul" of the British Empire in 1912, who . . . pleaded with Sir Edward Carson, head of Ulster's provisional government, to "start the shooting" and encouraged Ulster politicians who were ". . . making treason to be the fashion." Even A.V. Dicey, a distinguished Oxford scholar, excused Ulster's revolt against the Home Rule Bill of 1912.[14]

Historically, the rigidity of Ulster's politicians was based on "defending democracy," but it did little to promote the growth of a pluralistic spirit. This was countered by the Celtic Renaissance whose writers, Padraic Pearse, George Bernard Shaw, Sean O'Casey, W. B. Yeats, and others inflamed modern nationalists to defy British authority and inspired the 1916 Easter Rising in Dublin. The rebellion was defeated by an overwhelming British force, yet the event marked the beginning of a new consciousness of open resistance, an important chapter in Ireland's effort to liberate the whole island.

Ulster Protestants feared becoming a minority in a Catholic state and thereby losing their privileged status. To prevent this possibility, the Protestants threatened the use of force to preserve their ties with the United Kingdom.[15] Republicans, on the other hand, demanded no borders separating the north and south in a united nation and waged a two-year guerilla war against British forces. Their tactics hastened the collapse of Britain's Royal Irish Constabulary (RIC), giving the Irish Republican Army (IRA) a free hand in large areas.[16] "With their strength in ambush," comments the writer, Bill Severn,

---

14 *Ibid.,* p. 139. (Sir Edward Carson was a founder and leader of the Unionist Party in 1912 and co-founder of Northern Ireland). See: Nicholas Mansergh, *The Irish Question, 1840 - 1921* (Toronto: University of Toronto Press, 1975), pp. 19 - 20, 219 - 224.

15 Trevor Beeson, "Northern Ireland: Can Order Come Out of the Chaos?" *Christian Century* 91 (July 17, 1974), pp. 720 - 724. (Hereafter cited as Beeson, "Can Order Come?").

16 McCaffrey, p. 146.

" . . . volunteers fought a guerilla war that shattered England's poise before the world of merely trying to 'pacify' the Irish people."[17]

The Anglo-Irish Treaty of 1921 provided for an Irish Free State as a dominion of the British Commonwealth. The earlier Government of Ireland Act passed by the British Parliament in 1920, allowed for a majority opinion in Ireland to decide on a future union with Ulster unless the Ulster Parliament voted to sever itself permanently from Dublin's jurisdiction:[18]

> Northern Ireland remains part of Her Majesty's Dominions of the United Kingdom. And it is hereby affirmed that in no event will Northern Ireland or any part thereof cease to be part of Her Majesty's Dominions and United Kingdom without the consent of the Parliament of Northern Ireland.[19]

Republicans led by President Eamon De Valera rejected the Anglo-Irish Treaty as treasonous. Especially unacceptable were two of its provisions which permitted permanent partition of Ireland and required elected officials to take an oath of allegiance to the Crown.[20] But the Irish Parliament accepted the treaty by a vote of 64 to 57 after heated debate. This action triggered a two-year civil war in which anti-Free State Republicans failed to repudiate the treaty.[21] By 1925, Republican strategy called for working within the system and electing members to the Free State *Dail* (Parliament). *Sinn Fein,* the Republican political arm, strove to outnumber parliamentary opponents in Dublin in order to re-establish the Republic which had been proclaimed in 1916 during the Easter Rising.[22]

A year later, De Valera organized a new party called *Fianna Fáil* ("Soldiers of Destiny") whose objectives were to remove the oath of allegiance and work toward the unification of Ireland.[23]

---

17 Bill Severn, *Irish Statesman and Rebel: The Two Lives of Eamon De Valera* (New York: Ives Washburn, Inc., 1970), p. 72.
18 MacEoin, p. 55.
19 Tim Pat Coogan, *The IRA* (London: Pall Mall Press, 1970), p. 262. (Hereafter cited as Coogan, *IRA*).
20 MacEoin, pp. 181 - 182.
21 *Facts,* p. 42.
22 MacEoin, p. 180. (See *Sinn Fein* in Definition of Terms).
23 *Ibid.,* pp. 182 - 183.

Conservative support for the Free State government came from the Protestant-dominated business community and the Catholic Church. This was largely in response to the IRA and the *Fianna Fáil* Party, whose socialistic leanings appeared to threaten the Free State.[24] During the general election in 1932, both the Church and government reaffirmed their opposition to all radical movements which were considered dangerous to the class order "ordained by Providence." Prior to the elections Catholic bishops issued a statement condemning all radical organizations as " . . . sinful and irreligious . . . No Catholic can lawfully be a member of them."[25] Irish politics, according to the Irish historian, Gary MacEoin, seemed to move further to the right:

> The government for its part, lost no opportunity to identify *Fianna Fáil* with organizations condemned by bishops, thereby hoping to detach enough support to swing the upcoming elections. As soon as the constitutional amendment became effective, it banned not only *Saor Eire* and the IRA but a dozen related organizations such as the Friends of Soviet Russia and Workers' Defense Corps.[26]

In spite of these denunciations, large numbers of people sympathized with leftism during the thirties out of conviction that capitalism had failed them during the depression.[27]

Sensitive to the political mood, De Valera put forward a moderate position and, in so doing, gained enough support from conservatives to defeat Prime Minister William Cosgrave's *Fine Gael* (United Ireland) party.[28]

As Prime Minister, De Valera eliminated all British authority over the Free State Constitution and renounced the Anglo-Irish Treaty. Ireland ". . . ceased to be one of His Majesty's Dominions."

24 *Ibid.,* pp. 190 - 191.
25 *Ibid.*
26 *Ibid.,* pp. 187, 192, 197. (*Saor Eire,* translated, "Free Ireland," was an organization which came out of the radical wing of the IRA, and became its political spokesman. Its members, mostly workers and farmers, opposed British imperialism and Irish capitalism).
27 *Ibid.,* p. 193.
28 Patrick O'Farrell, *Ireland's English Question* (New York: Schocken Books, 1971), p. 296.

It became an Associated State, republican in form, with King and Crown finally removed.[29] On April 18, 1949, the *Fianna Fáil* and the *Dail* formally declared that Ireland was a republic. These actions were momentous for Ireland, but they were no less important than De Valera's goal of eliminating the partition of Ulster from the rest of Ireland.[30]

So long as the Free State remained within the British Commonwealth, Ulster Protestants had no reason to feel the danger of southern encroachment. But Ireland's break with the Commonwealth caused renewed apprehension in the north concerning Ulster's political status. Unionist pressures on the Westminister Parliament caused it to reaffirm Britain's earlier commitments to the northern six counties.[31]

The original Government of Ireland Act of 1920 assured a majority status for Unionists who controlled the Northern Ireland Parliament at Stormont. Essentially the Act provided a British guarantee to Unionists that Northern Ireland would remain a part of the United Kingdom unless the Parliament of Northern Ireland voted otherwise. John Hume, Deputy Leader of the Social Democratic Labour party in Northern Ireland and elected to the Parliament of the European Economic Community in 1979, asserted that the guarantee was a tragic mistake as it has remained a key bone of contention for Ulster Catholics:

> The 'British Guarantee' . . . proved to be a guarantee to permanent exclusive power to one side, the Unionist, and a guarantee of exclusion from power to the other, the Catholic minority. Its existence undermined any hope of political negotiation between the two sides in Northern Ireland. . . . While the guarantee exists there is no incentive for Unionists to enter into genuine dialogue with those with whom they share the island of Ireland.[32]

29 Severn, pp. 154 - 155.
30 *Ibid.*, p. 169.
31 *Ibid.*
32 John Hume, "The Irish Question: A British Problem," *Foreign Affairs.* 48 (Winter, 1979 - 1980), p. 303. (Hereafter cited as Hume: "The Irish Question").

The creation of a permanent border between the north and south was Britain's answer to Unionist demands. But it did not solve the problems of growing Catholic *versus* Protestant hatred and the ensuing violence.[33]

While the problems that arose out of a divided Ireland were many, the most divisive and difficult was that of sectarian antagonism. Partition had given Unionist extremists opportunities to use religious hatred for political gain. They associated Catholicism with Gaelic-Irish nationalism and Fenian disloyalty whereas they linked Protestantism with loyalty and union with England.[34]

William Kingston, a McConnell Research Fellow at Trinity College in 1972, analyzes what he calls a deeply-rooted paradigm that has long formed a part of the intellectual consciousness of the Ulster Protestant community. It is that Catholics are inferior, superstitious and intolerant. Priests are viewed as symbols of inquisitions and the Roman Catholic Church as the enemy of humanity. Ulster Catholics are described as determined to "outbreed" their Protestant neighbors and eventually catch up with them in population. It is argued that this might even significantly dilute the clear two-thirds majority and privileged position of the Protestant population. Such a prospect continues to be alarming to Protestants who have traditionally controlled political and economic life. Ulster Catholics are viewed as an "aggressive minority", no longer willing to remain quiet in the face of their inferiority. Since they are regarded as quasi-citizens, their loyalty to the Crown remains highly suspect because they continue to look to the Republic for encouragement and eventual union.[35]

Ulster's significant minority of Roman Catholics became an unhappy and infuriated group that rejected the Government of Ireland

33 Coogan, IRA, p. 263
34 Michael McDowell, "Northern Ireland: A Protestant Perspective," *Visiter* (February 3, 1980), p. 6. (McDowell is a journalist from Belfast, a Senior Associate with the Carnegie Endowment for International Peace, and a Fellow at Harvard University. Also see: "London and Northern Ireland," *Peace By Peace,* August, 1980, p. 6).
35 William Kingston, "Northern Ireland – The Elements of a Solution," *Political Science Quarterly* 43 (April - June, 1971), p. 202. (Hereafter cited as Kingston, "Elements").

Act. They had no desire to be a permanent part of the United Kingdom and be subservient to a Unionist-dominated government. The Act concretized Catholics as second class citizens.[36]

Kingston explains that the "Protestant paradigm" developed " . . . a low minority tolerance factor" which Protestants seem incapable of altering.[37]

Northern Ireland's political life remained divided between Republican nationalists and Unionists. But from the 1920s until 1972, Unionists remained in firm control of government. Yet every administration faced inter-communal turmoil.[38] Because of persistent discrimination, Catholics began a series of civil rights demonstrations in 1968, demanding electoral rights and administrative changes. This resulted in the Downing Street Declaration of 1969 which included reforms in the electoral system, local government, police force, the Northern Ireland government and several other areas to end discrimination.[39]

The new program was implemented in 1969, but the IRA was not pacified and that organization began a campaign of violence in Londonderry (Derry) and Belfast. This was countered by the Royal Ulster Constabulary (RUC) and the Ulster Constabulary known as the "B Specials."[40] The IRA viewed reforms as too little and too late to handle the massive unemployment in the ghettos of Belfast and other cities.[41] It contended that the only true solution to the Irish question was British withdrawal and union with the Republic.[42]

According to the National Council for Civil Liberties, even the implementation was hampered by a contradiction within the decision-making process. In that organization's open letter to Prime

36 Michael McDowell, p. 6.
37 Kingston, "Elements," p. 202.
38 *Facts,* p. 75.
39 Richard Rose, "On Priorities of Citizenship in the Deep South," *Journal of Politics* 38 (May, 1976), p. 260. (Hereafter cited as Rose: "Priorities").
40 British Information Services, *Northern Ireland.* London: Central Office of Information, May, 1975, p. 8. (Hereafter cited as British Information, *Northern Ireland*).
41 *Ibid.,* p. 5.
42 National Council for Civil Liberties of Great Britain, *Bulletin of Peace Proposals,* September 29, 1971, p. 53. (Hereafter cited as National Council for Civil Liberties).

34

Minister Edward Heath in 1971, the Council explained the underlying reasons why reforms had failed to produce anything worthwhile. Government promises for reforms were never matched by its willingness to carry them out. The government was caught between pressures of the Catholic minority and Protestant organizations.[43]

The Council's report further outlined a kind of tautology operating within the social structure where failure to establish civil liberties served only to further alienate the Catholic minority. To handle the anticipated disorder, the police and military acted upon the measures permitted by the Special Powers Acts of 1922 and 1933, the Public Order Act and the Criminal Justice Amendment Act of 1970. These statutes allowed the police and military a legal base for violations of personal privacy and its attendant rights. People were stopped on the street whenever they were suspected of terrorist involvement.[44] This was far more frequent in the Catholic areas, thus allowing a double standard of justice. The same was also true in the search and seizure of weapons and subsequent court sentencing.[45]

Yet the Report of the National Council was largely ignored by British authorities. Their response to civil disorders was to continue to rely upon emergency legislation and to superimpose order by means of more military strength.[46]

In the face of continued strife Britain dissolved the Northern Ireland Parliament at Stormont in 1972 and ruled directly from Westminister via the Foreign Secretary's office in Belfast. Direct Rule was considered only a temporary emergency measure in order to cope with the conditions which had spawned political and social tensions. It was intended to prevent an open and bloody confrontation between the Protestant and Catholic populations. This arrangement would continue until the two communities reached some agreement on workable solutions toward peace.[47] So far, this has not

---

43   "Ireland," *Political Quarterly* 43 (April - June, 1972), p. 141.
44   National Council for Civil Liberties, p. 54.
45   *Ibid.*
46   *Ibid.*
47   Jonathan Power, "Can The Peace People Bring an Irish Peace?" *Encounter* 48 (March, 1977), p. 16.

happened, and many of the conditions that have exacerbated communal strife remain.

Summary. Tensions between Protestant and Catholic are rooted in conflicting claims to land and subsequently to issues relative to fair participation within Ulster's politics and a united Ireland. Politicians historically encouraged tensions by exploiting political-religious differences. The Government of Ireland Act and Anglo-Irish Treaty satisfied Ulster's Protestant majority. Loyalists, who were assured a monopoly of power, could effectively prevent unity with Catholic Ireland. This and frustration out of failure to achieve reforms in electoral laws and discriminatory allocation of jobs and housing contributed to Catholic alienation and sectarian conflict.

To understand the intensity of feeling of the Irish on these matters, one must study the literary movement of the late nineteenth century. Nothing clarifies better how the Irish felt about themselves in relation to the English, and it presents insight into what Irish intellectuals were expressing through the "Celtic Renaissance."

CHAPTER IV

The Influence of the Celtic Renaissance on Irish Nationalism

Ireland's literary heritage is important in that it focused on Irish national consciousness and the resultant frustration under British rule. Such feelings were expressed in eighteenth and nineteenth century writings, examples of which would include *The Wearin' O the Green* by Oliver Goldsmith; *Dear Harp of My Country* by Thomas More; and *To My Native Land* by James Clarence Mangan.[1] The late nineteenth century phase of this movement became known as the "Celtic Renaissance" and amplified that consciousness as well as creating a new awareness about national political independence. Many of the intellectuals writing at this time were ambivalent about Ireland and the course it would take. William Butler Yeats, Joseph Plunkett, Terence MacSwiney, Padraic Pearse and James Connolly raised the question of Irish independence from Britain, but appeared to be indifferent to Ulster Protestants who were determined to remain part of the United Kingdom. This attitude toward Protestant nationalism in Ulster set the two entities of the north and south on a collision course.

The literary historian Herbert Kenny cites the creation of the Gaelic League in 1893 as the beginning of Ireland's literary revival. It was established by Douglas Hyde, later to be President of Eire; Eoin MacNeill, Professor of Irish history at University College in Dublin; and the Reverend Eoghen O'Growney, who taught Gaelic at the Catholic seminary in Maynooth.[2]

The League's goal was to revive Gaelic, which had fallen into disuse during the British presence. Mansergh noted that the language had long been on the decline and was rapidly dying out by the 1880s,

---

1 D. J. O'Donaghue, Ed., *Poems of James Clarence Mangan*, Century Edition (London: A. H. Bullen, 1972), p. 107.
2 Herbert A. Kenny, *Literary Dublin: A History* (Dublin: Gill and MacMillan, 1974), p. 179.

particulary in the urban centers of Dublin and Belfast.[3] Gaelic was not even taught in the schools, although the seminary at Maynooth was an exception. "In Dublin," according to Kenny, "a person could spend half a lifetime and never hear a word of Gaelic . . . The situation was so bad that the Irish tongue as a spoken language was in danger of disappearing altogether."[4]

The Irish writer Richard Loftus considered the revival of the ancient Gaelic the important beginning for renewing Ireland's cultural identity.[5] Hyde put it even more succinctly, envisioning that the purpose of the Gaelic League was " . . . to cultivate everything that was most racial, most Gaelic, most Irish."[6]

A noted writer and critic of the 1920s, George Moore, cited restoration of the Irish language as central to discovering Ireland's heritage. Although non-Gaelic-speaking himself, he saw in its revival the hope of preserving the language. He believed its rejuvenation would be like a spiritual renewal allowing Ireland to rediscover its soul. Like many intellectuals of the time, Moore associated the English language with English vulgarity, materialism and perhaps symbolizing England's control of Ireland. That tongue had been corrupted and polluted by British urban materialsm.[7]

Padraic Pearse, who later became the first President of the Provisional Irish Republic, joined the Gaelic League in 1899 and taught Irish linguistics. His ambition was to restore an appreciation for Ireland's past and recapture her traditions in the context of his time.[8] Pearse became editor of the League's official newspaper whose Gaelic title was *An Claidheamh Soluis,* or *The Sword of Light.* Its function was to counteract English cultural influences, which

3 Mansergh, p. 100.
4 Kenny, p. 179.
5 Richard J. Loftus, *Nationalism in Modern Anglo-Irish Poetry* (Madison and Milwaukie: University of Wisconsin Press, 1964), pp. 125 - 126.
6 *Ibid.,* p. 6.
7 George Moore, "Literature and the Irish Language," in *Ideals in Ireland,* Ed. Lady Augusta Gregory (New York: Lemma Publishing Corporation, 1973): 45 - 51.
8 Francis P. Jones, *History of the Sinn Fein Movement and the Irish Rebellion of 1916* (New York: P. J. Kenedy, 1921), p. 152.

38

were considered to be " . . . an insidious conquest of Ireland's mind and spirit."[9]

Pearse assessed the language movement as having the most lasting effect on the Irish national conscience. He believed the inception and proliferation of various branches of Gaelic Leagues throughout the country marked the real beginning of the Irish revolution. Within it was contained " . . . the germ of all future Irish history."[10]

Poetry and the Shaping of National Feeling

The poetry written during the Celtic Renaissance contained references to concepts of race and blood, honor and soul, love, beauty, truth and God. The Irish poets were exemplars in their sensitive and powerful use of symbols in language and poetry. This resulted in the transformation of the idea of an Irish national state into a holy crusade. The dream of political freedom seemed to require that violence be used to achieve that goal. The psychology of passionate nationalism found in Pearse's *Songs of Irish Rebels* supports this attitude even to the present day. The highest virtues of heroes and sainthood were embodied in the ultimate act of sacrifice.[11]

Loftus points to this fusion of spirituality and the attendant concepts of good and evil in the works of many Irish writers. One example was Pearse's poem, *The Fool,* treating the nationalist as an innocent victim of evil men. Irish nationalists were discredited and persecuted as was Christ before his crucifixion. Pearse implied that the victim's ambitions for political freedom were reasonable and justified the use of violence:

---

9 Loftus, pp. 124 - 125.
10 Goddard Lieberson, *The Irish Uprising, 1916 - 1922* (New York: MacMillan Co., 1960), p. 12.
11 Loftus, p. 133.

The lawyers have sat in council, the men
    with the keen, long faces,
And said, "This man is a fool," and others
    have said, "He blasphemeth,"
And the wise have pitied the fool that hath
    striven to give a life.
What if the dream come true? and if
    millions unborn shall dwell
In the house that I shaped in my heart, the
    noble house of my thought?
Lord, I have staked my soul, I have staked
    the lives of my kin.[12]

The number of writers is impressive and all of them, including Yeats, Joyce, O'Casey and others, seem to envision what their nation could become. They expressed the nationalistic struggle against British control within an idealistic framework, and liberation as a holy cause.[13] They initiated the process of recalling the native language and culture with attendant myths and legends that were as vital to Irish nationalism as similar concepts were to other national movements in nineteenth century Europe. Poets made Gaelic an important tool in the revival of nationalism. In so doing, the literary phase of the Irish struggle took on a romantic aspect similar to European struggles. The rich legacy enhanced western literary tradition as did the emerging Irish theater.

The Theater's Effects on Irish Nationalism

As part of the literary movement the theater not only reinforced the message of nationalism spread by the poets, but did so with even greater impact. The most influential playwrights were W. B. Yeats, George Russell, Lady Augusta Gregory, J. M. Synge, Padraic

---

12 *Ibid.,* p. 161.
13 *Ibid.,* p. 37.

Colum and Sean O'Casey. They were abetted by Gaelic advocates Douglas Hyde and Padraic Pearse.[14]

In 1902, Yeats, Lady Gregory, George Moore and J. M. Synge established the world-renowned Abbey Theater. Yeats felt that the Irish consciousness should be expressed in the English language as well as in Gaelic.[15] Few of the natives understood Gaelic, thus limiting the scope of Ireland's cultural revival. A further limitation was that the poets were affected by and appealed to the Anglo-Irish upper class, thus denying their appeal to much of Catholic Ireland.[16] The theater could do much to remedy that situation.

Yeats initially did not intend for his plays to promote political change[17] as did the National Literary Society. This body, which was founded in the mid-ninetheenth century to preserve the Gaelic language, used literature as a political tool. It expressed what was wrong with the British establishment and ignored the more positive aspects of Irish culture. Yeats believed the intellectual was an artist who remained true to his convictions.[18] He also harbored reservations about making literature subservient to politics. Even so, his research brought new life to a cultural legacy of folk heroes, legends and myths that stirred the imagination.[19] His writings had no direct political aim but did draw the populace's attention to their rich cultural background which offered them a sense of pride. Whether or not Yeats intended it, his plays contributed immeasurably to a sense of nationalism and desire for national liberation.

It was significant that the Irish theater addressed itself to all social classes.[20] Through this medium the *literati* made audiences aware of Ireland's ancient mythology and the realities of the more

---

14 For a review of Irish plays see Curtis Canfield, *Plays of the Irish Renaissance, 1880 - 1930* (Plainview, New York: Books for Libraries Press, 1974).

15 Kenny, p. 181.

16 Mansergh, p. 280.

17 *Ibid.,* p. 267.

18 W. B. Yeats, *Essays* (London: 1921), pp. 254 - 255.

19 Mansergh, pp. 284 - 285.

20 David Marcus, "The Irish Mode," *Poetry of Ireland* (1970; RPT, Nendeln/ Liechtenstein: P. J. Madden, 1970); p. 13.

recent Great Famine and the Fenian revolts that led to national demoralization.[21] The poets and playwrights focused primarily on either the ancient or the immediate past in terms that were romantic and sentimental in nature. They drew clear dichotomies between good and evil or the weak and strong.[22] Yeats was noted for endowing characters with superhuman powers that dramatized his heroes and appealed to the reader's mind and heart. These traits of power and superhumanism were most apparent in plays based on ancient Gaelic legends and tragedies. Plays had enormous appeal to the general audience.[23] The Irish historian Robert Kee noted these elements had great appeal to the natives who were relegated to an inferior economic and social position. The ideas of power and superhumanism provided a " . . . natural myth for intoxication."[24]

It would seem that, like Yeats, other playwrights were unaware of the long-term impact their plays would have on Ireland's political consciousness. It should be re-emphasized, however, that plays were not directly intended to inspire revolutionary zeal as they were primarily idealistic and spiritual. It was the growing spirituality of nationalism, interwoven with a traditional Christian faith, and the land that were considered to have been the three most powerful value structures in Irish society. Irish intellectuals spoke to and used these qualities in their literature.[25]

Yeat's most powerful and significant plays were *Countess Kathleen,* first published in 1892, and *Cathleen ni Houlihan,* written about 1902.[26] The plays were performed in the Abbey Theater

21 Mansergh, p. 272.
22 Robert O'Driscoll, "Introduction," in *Theatre and Nationalism in Twentieth-Century Ireland* (Toronto: University of Toronto Press, 1971), p. 13. (Hereafter cited as O'Driscoll, *Theatre*).
23 Canfield, pp. 15 - 26.
24 Robert Kee, *The Green Flag: The Turbulent History of the Irish National Movement* (New York: Delecorte Press, 1972), p. 434.
25 Marcus, p. 13.
26 A. N. Jeffares and A. S. Knowland, *A Commentary on the Collected Plays of W. B. Yeats* (Stanford, California: Stanford University Press, 1975), p. 27.

and published in many periodicals. *Cathleen ni Houlihan* was a classic in promoting deep feelings of nationhood. According to the story, Cathleen was an old woman who stopped at a peasant's cottage and asked a young man if he would fight for the cause of Ireland's freedom. After she departed, the man's brother asked if he had seen a tragic old woman hobbling away. He responded: "I did not, but I saw a young girl and she had the walk of a queen." This single line ending the play received the most credit for sparking an open conflict with England. Kee felt the play served as " . . . a model for an entire renewal of patriotic Irish thought."[27] Another author and critic, Stephen Gwynn, described his reaction as:

> I went home asking myself if such plays should be produced unless one was prepared for people to go out and shoot and be shot. Yeats was not alone responsible; no doubt Lady Gregory had helped him to get the peasant speech so perfect; but above all Miss Gonn's impersonation had stirred the audience as I have never seen another audience stirred.[28]

Yeats in his later years reflected on "Cathleen":

> Did that play of mine
> Send out certain men the English
> shot?[29]

The play demonstrated just how effectively Ireland's intellectuals could inspire an audience during the 1900-1920 period.[30] The *literati* created a national consciousness built upon native folklore and legend. By so doing Yeats and others presented an image of a nation state.

Cathleen ni Houlihan became the symbol of the whole of Ireland before Eire became independent. "She was Ireland, herself . . . "[31] As such, she became the model for resurgent Irish nationalism. The

---

27 Kee, p. 434.
28 A. N. Jeffares, p. 22.
29 Jeffares and Knowland, Quoting Yeat's "The Man and the Echo," p. 31.
30 See: A.N. Jeffares, *The Poetry of W. B. Yeats* (London: Edward Arnold Publishers, 1963).
31 Jeffares and Knowland, p. 30.

Irish historian Mansergh cites the play as being " . . . the spark that brought men and women to the rebellion in 1916."[32] It was Yeat's most nationalistic play, appealing more to the consciousness of the general audience than strictly to the middle class.[33]

The Countess Kathleen was performed in 1899, 1902 and in the Abbey Theater in 1904. This drama of a woman willing to sell her soul in order to feed Ireland's hungry people conveyed the message of sacrifice. This spirit was expressed in Yeat's commentaries in 1902 when he wrote of " . . . the perpetual struggle of the cause against private hopes and dreams, against all that we mean when we say the world."[34]

Language and the Theater

The revival of Gaelic and a revitalized theater accomplished two things: (1) it provided a way for the Irish to better understand themselves in relation to their historical roots; and (2) it drew attention to the contemporary political and economic realities. Irish values expressed in poetry and plays stressed principles of good and evil aspects of Ireland at the turn of the century. This dichotomy was an essential prerequisite to mobilizing the population for revolutionary action.

Many of Ireland's intellectuals alluded to their struggle as a revolution, but this term was misleading. They did not mean the complete overturning of the social and economic order. As many writers came from the land-owning class, one can appreciate their position. Rather the degree of transformation sought was political more than economic. Revolution would break the political ties with Britain and establish an independent state. The historian Crane Brinton does not believe that any cause for complete upheaval was present.

32 Mansergh, p. 267.
33 Kenny, p. 208.
34 *Ibid.*, pp. 27 - 28.

"Ireland by 1916 was not experiencing extreme problems of economic deprivation that had to be overturned."[35] Kee supports this contention, noting that Ireland's economy changed drastically from the nineteenth century:

> The poverty-stricken insecurity of the population of the land, with its menace of starvation, eviction, and enforced emigration had disappeared forever. Landlords had actually disappeared and the great majority of Irish holdings were actually owned by Irish peasants, sons and grandsons of men who had often been treated with less respect than cattle.[36]

This being true, then why the tensions? The major reason was that the Irish gave a reality to the national self-consciousness developed by the intellectual community. Along with this, it became clearer that a contrast existed between what Ireland was under British rule and what she might become as an independent state. So long as the country's internal economic and political affairs remained subordinate to British law and to the Crown, achieving complete emancipation was seen as requiring a revolution.[37] Brinton cites this subordination as inhibiting political and economic growth under British rule. The intellectuals served the role of providing the essential spiritual qualities or, what Brinton calls, " . . . a moral transformation" before men would take up arms.[38] This had to come before armed conflict which, in any case, would go beyond the world of poetry and theater.[39]

Writers, Alienation and National Fervor

The foregoing authors disagreed not only philosophically but also in their interpretations of Irish society and what kind of country

---

35 Crane Brinton, *The Anatomy of Revolution* (New York: Random House, 1965), p. 30.
36 Kee, p. 353.
37 *Ibid.*, p. 352.
38 Brinton, p. 35.
39 *Ibid.*, p. 36.

Ireland should become. Many expressed deep-seated and long-standing antipathies toward the society in which they lived. They came from the middle and upper class and looked upon Ireland as being generally Philistine in taste, without cultural depth, and as one succumbing to Victorian morality which they considered hypocritical and narrow.[40] The intellectuals attacked those who saw evil where it didn't exist or ignored it where it did. They called for a new spirit of reform and renewal of social morality in which self-criticism was encouraged as a healthy and necessary process toward political maturity. But the populace did not welcome or understand such criticism. When John M. Synge's *Playboy of the Western World* criticized Irish bigotry, it was taken as an attack on the people. A similar event occurred when Yeat's *Countess Kathleen* raised the moral issue of selling one's soul for material gain and was received with " . . . hisses and boos."[41] Ignored was Yeat's attempt to show how people without money to buy food were symbols of Ireland's spiritual poverty.[42] Even O'Casey's *Juno and the Paycock* was thought by most viewers to be discrediting Irish heroes. Plays such as these angered audiences to the point of rioting at the Abbey Theater.[43]

Plays are known to elicit both positive and negative reactions. But the negative audience reaction likely reflected a "love it or leave it" mentality. These feelings usually resulted from a misinterpretation of symbols or misunderstanding societal criticisms. Nevertheless, the negative behaviors exhibited did not weaken the quality of the artistic achievement which flourished during the 1890-1920 period. But nationalist reactions to the works of many playwrights resulted in the latter feeling alienated. In spite of the love they professed for Ireland, they became expatriates and wrote of their native land from afar.

Perhaps the intellectuals indulged in the technique of shocking audiences for their own sake or even to instill a spirit of self-criti-

---

40   O'Driscoll, p. 17.
41   Loftus, pp. 9-10.
42   Jeffares, p. 7.
43   Loftus, p. 13.

cism. But it is difficult to say to what extent ego gratification motivated Yeats, O'Casey, Synge or Moore. All of them indulged in
shocking and riling their audiences.[44] Such tactics were bound
to receive negative reaction. The social and cultural *avant-gardism*
which contained satires against Catholicism were fashionable but
insensitive. It was the mark of the intellectual and was in keeping
with European anti-clericalism of the period. It seemed, however,
that the Irish writers attempted to out-do each other in this technique.[45] The spirit of iconoclasm, unorthodoxy and anti-clericalism
was expected in some writers who were at odds with society's
traditional values, including Irish Catholicism.

The writer George Moore viewed Irish society as narrow in political
as well as religious outlook. He saw the nation's problems as primarily
internal and lacking in the cosmopolitan spirit of the French he
so admired. In his view, political violence was not a solution to the
problem of British rule. Moore's disdain for Irish narrowness and
the use of violence led to his alienation. He left Ireland in 1911
to live in England.[46]

Sean O'Casey was equally criticized for his Marxism and anti-
Catholicism.[47] James Joyce broke with Catholicism, left the country
and became an expatriate.[48] Joyce was a typical example of noted
writers who wrote scathing criticism of their homeland. In his work,
Portrait of an Artist as a Young Man, he described Ireland as " . . .
primitive, blind, and groping," lacking in a sense of purpose.[49] These
criticisms were the antithesis of Yeat's idealization of Ireland and

---

44 Herbert Howarth, *The Irish Writers: 1880 - 1940* (New York: Hill and Wang,
    1958), p. 69.
45 Jan Hajda, "Sociology of Intellectuals," Portland State University, October
    1978.
46 Malcolm Brown, *George Moore: A Reconsideration* (Seattle: University
    of Washington Press, 1955).
47 Kenny, p. 245.
48 *Ibid.*
49 Howarth, p. 255.

were aimed at " . . . the desecration of household gods," the " . . . mockery of national ideals," and the absurdity of materialsm.[50]

Criticism of native society became fashionable among the Irish *literati.* This was important as it served to challenge the populace. Whether or not this was the intent of these writers is unclear, but the fact remains that they did prompt their audiences to act in defense of traditional values[51] In this respect the stage promoted the habit of rebellion. Regardless of the negative responses of the audiences, Mansergh stated that the literary movement produced an attitude that " . . . was also revolutionary in its impact."[52]

The Apoliticals

There existed a group of writers less separated from Irish institutions and more apolitical in outlook. These included Douglas Hyde, a product of Trinity College from a middle class background, and George Bernard Shaw, who was a member of the gentry. Neither acted as an apologist for any political system. Rather their literature expressed a love for Irish culture and admonished readers not to allow their patriotism to become a blind and impassioned chauvinism that would foster a hatred of anything non-Irish.[53]

They did not hate England nor did they concern themselves with destruction of British ties to Ireland. In fact, Shaw had little faith or confidence that Ireland would ever achieve full national independence. He saw Irish nationalism as both divisive and regressive. He believed Ireland's future lay in an organic connection such as a federal relationship to Britain. The writer Robert O'Driscoll credits Shaw's "guardian complex" as the result of his aristocratic background.[54] Shaw's political philosophy was more in the direction

50 David Krause, "Sean O'Casey and the Higher Nationalism: The Desecration of Household Gods," in *Theater and Nationalism in Twentieth-Century Ireland,* Ed. Robert O'Driscoll (Toronto: University of Toronto Press, 1971), pp. 114 - 133.
51 O'Driscoll, p. 15.
52 Mansergh, p. 270.
53 O'Driscoll, p. 11.
54 *Ibid.,* p. 17.

of universalism and away from a proliferation of tiny nation states, each with its separate loyalties.[55] This could only lead to each blindly following nationalistic values which, in turn, would lead to extremist views by creating revolutionary societies that would make such values a matter of dogma.[56] This was the direction in which Ireland was moving.

Action Intellectuals

So far this chapter has treated those intellectuals who were, for the most part, Anglo-Irish in attitude and background. Generally their works focused on the mystical and spiritual aspects of Ireland. Their literature was introspective and treated of the nation's soul, or spiritual and idealistic side during this period.[57]

But there existed another group of people who were equally significant and were involved in removing the social, economic and political inequities confronting the Irish industrial and agrarian classes. Like the poets and playwrights already discussed, this group was individualistic, idealistic, and highly motivated. However, in contrast to the others, they sought action. Theirs was a call to revolution more direct than those involved in the Gaelic League or Abbey Theater. The historian Francis Jones describes them as having " . . . combined the pen with the sword."[58] Theirs was a call to open conflict. They were convinced of the righteousness of their cause and said so in newspapers and books. They left no doubt as to who was the enemy.

Yeats, Shaw, Hyde and others saw the world in terms of good and evil. These characteristics were ill-defined, nebulous, or tied to symbols relating to honor and dishonor, strength and weakness, pride and degradation. The action intellectuals defined the terms concretely. The evil was Britain; the good was Ireland and its people;

---

55 Mansergh, p. 274.
56 O'Driscoll, p. 12.
57 Mansergh, p. 280.
58 Jones, pp. 103 - 164.

the issue was freedom and the means to success was armed rebellion.

But there were differences in approach. Jones described them as " . . . all quiet men, little given to talk or display. All of them were workers, whether in college, the office, or the store."[59] They called attention to the conditions of urban workers and farmers and promoted land reform. George Russell edited the *Homestead* which spoke of the importance landownership had for the people. Russell was acutely sensitive about this and pushed for land reform.[60]

Others used newspapers to inform their readers about the economic and political issues. These publications, rather than being critical of Irish culture and attitudes, focused on self-reliance, sacrifice, patriotism, and promoted the idea that violence was necessary to change the *status quo.*[61] Men such as Eamond Ceannt, Thomas Clarke, Sean MacDiarmada, Robert Childers, Arthur Griffith, Thomas MacDonagh, Joseph Plunkett, John MacNeill, James Connolly and others addressed the evils of social, economic and political inequities that must be eliminated from Irish national life.[62] They did little introspection and concentrated their criticisms on institutions in need of change. The evils were viewed as externally caused and the solutions lay not in Ireland changing her culture and spiritual values, but in the simple answer of eliminating the British presence. Their writing described Ireland as fertile yet susceptible to famine; possessing good harbors and other economic assets, but only serving as a source of raw materials for Britain's industry.[63]

Their writing possessed a religious intensity equating patriotism with a sacred sense of mission.[64] Padraic Pearse expressed this feeling just three weeks before the 1916 Easter rebellion. This attitude was also emphasized in Irish newspapers such as *The Spark, Honesty, The Gael* and *The Gaelic Athlete.* In the latter Pearse wrote the following:

59 *Ibid.,* p. 169.
60 Kenny, p. 188.
61 Mansergh, p. 264.
62 Strauss, pp. 250 - 251.
63 *Ibid.,* p. 222.
64 Lieberson, p. 18.

Comrades, everything favors us. Now or never for the final onslaught. The shades of our immortal dead, the graves of the unavenged, the harrowing cries of our murdered priests, of our violated women, of the coffinless dead who were whitening the Atlantic's broad floor — all rise up and command us to do the noble deed.[65]

Rise to Action

The effect of poetry, books, newspapers and plays on public opinion cannot be measured. Whether the intellectuals' writings provoked the 1916 outbreak or whether the participants were simply responding to the existing situation is an open question. Brinton pondered this in his works on historical revolutionary movements. This may account for the sense of political powerlessness, referred to by O'Driscoll, that prevailed at the turn of the century. The idea of national independence became like a star, something to be seen but not to be touched. Thus Ireland's political expressions prior to the Easter Rising were manifested in literature and theater, as O'Driscoll pointed out:

Great moments of theatrical achievement have often coincided with moments of national excitement and tension. In times of acute national consciousness the theater is the form of literature which makes the most direct impact on the people, becoming at times a means of propaganda, ultimately the means by which the deeper life of the people is expressed.[66]

The British did recognize the power of the revolutionary ideology being expressed by these intellectuals. In a report to the war office the military authorities described the article "The Work Before Us" which appeared in *The Gael* as being " . . . highly seditious and prejudiced to the public safety and defense of the realm."[67] Between

---

65 Jones, p. 156.
66 O'Driscoll, p. 12.
67 Breandan MacGiolla Choille, *Intelligence Notes: 1913 - 1916* (Dublin: Government Publication Office, 1966), p. 163.

1913 and 1916 all weeklies of more than 20,000 circulation were suppressed.[68] An additional thirty-four American newspapers were proscribed because of their anti-British tone.[69] Certainly this is evidence of how those against whom the action intellectuals wrote felt about the proverbial power of the press.

The intellectuals played many roles. They combined their writing with active participation in organizations that sought radical transformation of institutions. They not only were involved in writing polemics and organizing resistance but they were quite willing to man barricades.

The socialist James Connolly not only expounded Marxism through his paper *The Irish Worker,* but also led the Irish Transport Union and was later given a revolutionary military command during the Easter Rising. Arthur Griffith contributed his ideas to several newspapers and edited the radical *United Irishman.* [70] He also founded the *Sinn Fein* party.[71] Writers who took part in the resistance expressed the need for some kind of blood sacrifice, and all were actively involved in such action groups as the secret Irish Republican Brotherhood, the Citizen Army, the Irish Volunteers and *Sinn Fein.* [72]

It was their deaths that aided in forming the Irish revolutionary consciousness. While those who fought the British were only a fraction of the populace, their deaths for a cause gave the revolution an aura of respectability. Because they sowed the seeds of self-awareness and sacrifice, the revolution flourished.[73] Their deaths became the catalyst in the final struggle for independence which came in 1924. As Yeats wrote, "All changed, changed utterly; a terrible beauty is born."[74]

68 *Ibid.,* p. 164.
69 *Ibid.,* p. 165.
70 Jones, p. 179.
71 *Ibid.*
72 Martin Gilbert, *Winston S. Churchill: The Stricken World, 1916 - 1922,* 4 vols. (Boston: Houghton Mifflin Co., 1975), p. 669.
73 "The Easter Rising," BBC Home Service Production, No. 5328, narrated by Robin Holmes.
74 Holt, p. 123.

By taking an active role these intellectuals seem to realize that their words were not enough in themselves to cause revolution. Rather their deaths were the final step to Ireland's moral transformation. The historian Michael Laffan reported that most of the Irish initially felt the uprising was an " . . . irresponsible and potentially disastrous escapade."[75] But British reprisals shifted the populace's attitude of anger toward the rebels to one of sympathy with them. As Laffan states, "Resentment of the rebel's conduct was overshadowed by resentment at their fate."[76] Seen in this light, the British policy of firing squads and imprisoning hundreds not only failed to quell the revolt but also provided the Irish nation and its revolutionaries a number of martyrs. Those responsible for the Easter uprising became heroes, and their writings the revolutionary *credo*. Their deaths appeared as the culmination of their literary endeavor, which seemingly entertained a premonition of death:

> The days of our doom and our dread
> Ye were cruel and callous
> Grim death with our fighters ye fed
> Through the jaws of the gallows.[77]

Professor Walter Starkie, a friend of Yeats and director of the Abbey Theater in 1928, explains how that martyrdom became a weapon. While the British executed leaders of the Easter revolt one by one over a ten day period, " . . . a strong nationalist feeling was generated and the country rose up."[78]

It appeared that intellectuals sought to lose the first military action in the 1916 Easter uprising so as to win a greater political victory. Their battle plan called for the occupation of militarily-untenable sites such as the General Post Office, North Kings's Street, the College of Surgeons, Four Courts, and one or two other places within the city of Dublin. According to Starkie, there was no opportu-

75 Michael Laffan, "The Unification of Sinn Fein in 1917," in *Irish Historical Studies*, Ed. T. W. Woody and T. D. Williams, XVII (March, 1971), p. 353.
76 *Ibid.*, p. 354.
77 Jones, p. 165.
78 "Irish Culture During Rebellion," Center for Cassette Studies, No. 27278.

nity for maneuvering or effective action. The idea was to hold their positions until they were overrun. Their force of 400 men possessed 250 different types of weapons, with about five rounds of ammunition per weapon.[79]

Using any criteria, historians tend to interpret the 1916 revolt as abortive and suicidal. Militarily it was a disaster. Yet by their writings such men as Connolly, Plunkett, Pearse, MacDonagh, Clarke, Mac Diarmada, and Ceannt, caught the tenor of the political climate,[80] and by their deaths drew attention to their cause. It appeared they were pursuing a collective death wish so as to provide greater validity to the purity of their objectives and their willingness to die for Ireland.There was the example of Terence MacSwiney, poet and author of the play *The Revolutionist,* who starved to death in a British prison. His martyrdom and funeral inspired anti-British protest.[81]

Sean MacDiarmada, one of the signers of the Provisional Government Proclamation, reflected on his own death just moments before his execution when he responded to a concerned elderly lady by saying. "Oh, don't worry about me my friend. I'm going to be shot! And if I'm not shot, all this is worthless."[82]

Summary. The literary movement seemed to ignore the nationalism of Ulster's Protestant majority. Efforts to revive Gaelic were considered an important beginning of the Celtic Renaissance toward renewing Ireland's cultural heritage as well as historical events attendant to Ireland's history of struggles for national independence. Playwrights dramatized Ireland's cultural background, calling to mind Ireland's romantic past and Ireland's condition under British rule. National feeling was symbolized poignantly in Yeats' plays, *Cathleen ni Houlihan* and *The Countess Kathleen.*

Patriotism was further generated by "Action Intellectuals" whose belief in the rightness of Ireland's struggle inspired a call for self-reliance, sacrifice and violent revolution. These were essential in order to achieve political freedom from Britain and a change in the economic order.

79 *Ibid.*
80 Jones, p. 169.
81 Kenny, p. 213.
82 Easter Rising, BBC.

Attitudes prevalent in 1916, enable one to assess where the Irish people stand today, whether Protestant or Catholic, whenever they identify with political objectives. The following chapter discusses how today's Protestant of Northern Ireland views the Roman Catholic Church as an obstacle to unity with the Republic.

CHAPTER V

Protestants, Catholics and Political Unity

> Catholics in Ireland are no more able to recognize all the things that in-
> furiate Protestants than Protestants are to recognize what infuriates Cath-
> olics.
>
> A. E. Spencer, Catholic Sociologist

In Northern Ireland the political climate is influenced by a spirit
of romantic nationalism exemplified by the Irish Republican Army.[1]
Acting on behalf of the Catholic minority, the IRA in 1969 launched
a campaign of violence to expel the British and unite Ulster with
the rest of Ireland. On the other hand, Protestant Unionists (also
called loyalists) saw the IRA's activity as " . . . deliberately aimed
at destroying Ulster. They were part of a great conspiracy for ex-
acerbating the secular feeling between the Roman Catholics and
Protestants."[2] Unionists were determined to resist a unity with the
south and to remain united with Britain. Thus Protestant nationalism
saw its interests best served by maintaining political and economic
power. Convinced that the combination of IRA nationalism and the·
Catholic south were dangerous to their way of life, any change in
the *status quo* was looked on as an attack on them.

Irish Catholicism has consistently supported the idea of Irish
independence from Britain while condemning the violence used
by some to achieve it. The hierarchy has also supported civil rights
and condemned violence.[3] It is ironic that the Catholic Church in
its role as defender of human dignity is described by some as authoritarian, reactionary, motivated by power and self-interest, at times
conspiratorial, spreading heresy and undermining human liberty.[4]

---

1 Bowden.
2 Buckland, p. 172.
3 Liam Ryan, "Church and Politics: The Last Twenty Years," *Furrow* (January,
  1979), p. 17. (Hereafter cited as Ryan, "Church and Politics").
4 "Will Protestant Truth Conquer?" *Orange Standard* (May, 1980), p. 3. Also see
  "Vatican in Secret Moves to Fix Pope's Visit to Britain," *Protestant Telegraph*
  (January, 1980), p. 9, and Jill and Leon Uris, p. 180.

These are the perceptions of the Roman Church by Ulster Protestants. They view the power and influence of the Church in the Republic as a major argument against any north-south union. Both sides identify the Roman Catholic hierarchy as a fourth power along with the *Fianna Fáil,* the Orange Order, and the Unionist Party.[5] The southern government is viewed as one " . . . dictated to by its own Catholic Church," with the clergy exercising undue influence on the constitution. Catholic moral theology is reflected in the civil law on matters of abortion, euthanasia, contraception, education and divorce.[6]

The Catholic Church sees its social and economic values safeguarded in Ireland's legal code. The Irish constitution is viewed as important to the nation's political evolution. The original document, known as the Free State Constitution, was adopted after independence from Britain. It, along with the Treaty of 1921, provided for sovereignty but kept a special relationship with Britain. Basil Chubb, Professor of Political Science at the University of Dublin, states:

> The Constitution of the Irish Free State made Ireland a sovereign state within the British Commonwealth with safeguards for defense, and the well-being of Ireland's Protestant minority.[7]

In 1948 Ireland declared itself a republic. Its present Constitution recognizes Roman Catholic principles. As Chubb notes, "Mixed with the liberal and democratic elements derived from the British tradition are principles and precepts drawn from Catholic social

---

5 "Pro Mundi Vita Document," *Furrow* (September, 1973), p. 570.
6 Statement by Sam Duddy, personal interview. Duddy is Public Relations Officer for the Ulster Defense Association, Belfast, Northern Ireland, May, 1979. Hereafter cited as Sam Duddy interview.
7 Basil Chubb, *The Government and Politics of Ireland* (London: Oxford University Press, 1970), pp. 62 - 63. For an account of the civil war between the IRA and Irish Free State forces following the Treaty of 1921, see Nicholas Mansergh, *The Irish Question, 1916 - 1922* (New York: MacMillan Co., 1960) and Gary MacEoin, *Northern Ireland: Captive of History* (New York: Holt, Rinehart & Winston, 1974).

theory and in particular, the papal encyclicals."[8] The Constitution also emphasizes the family as having primary rights in a child's educational training. Article 41 of the Constitution states:

> The State recognizes the Family as the natural primary and fundamental unit group of Society, and as a moral institution possessing inalienable and imprescriptible rights, antecedent and superior to all positive law.
>
> The State, therefore, guarantees to protect the Family in its constitution and authority, as the necessary basis of social order and as indispensable to the welfare of the Nation and the State.[9]

The 1937 version of the Constitution granted a pre-eminent position to the Catholic Church while also recognizing other religious denominations. This was changed by constitutional amendment in 1972 when the section which recognized the Church's favored position was deleted.[10] Regardless of the change, northern Protestants see the Republic as " . . . a Catholic country determined to uphold the public moral order of the Catholic faith, whatever the wishes of its non-Catholic minority."[11] Protestants have no problem with the principles set forth in Article 40, which guarantees the right to form associations and to assemble freely without political, religious or class discrimination. They argue, however, that the Church's influence has placed a legalistic code of morality on the Constitution that could deny such individual rights as free expression and free choice. They cite Article 40's treatment of "indecent literature" as permitting infringement on a free press should it publicly express anti-Catholic views.[12] They also object to Sections 2 and 3 of Article

---

8 *Ibid.*, p. 67.
9 Republic of Ireland. *Bunreacht Na Heiremann, Constitution of Ireland,* Art. 41, Section I, (Dublin: Government Publications, 1942), p. 136. (Hereafter cited as Constitution of Ireland).
10 MacEoin, p. 291.
11 Norbert Paul Engel, "European Court Slams Irish Law on Divorce Ban," *Orange Standard* (June, 1970), p. 2. (Hereafter cited as Engel).
12 "Andy Tyrie Speaks to Guardian," .*Ulster* 2,(n.d.), p.14.(Hereafter cited as Andy Tyrie Speaks).

41 making divorce illegal and not recognizing marriages dissolved outside the Republic. This latter denies divorced parties the right of re-marriage in Ireland " . . . so long as the other party is still living."[13]

The matter of constitutional law relating to marriage is viewed as a special problem to non-Catholics living throughout the island and is cited by northern Protestants as a reason for not seeking unification. The interpretation and application of canon law regulating Catholic marriages has been liberalized as a result of Vatican Council II, but Protestants feel the changes have had little effect in the Republic.[14]

Canon 1061 that concerns mixed marriages was liberalized by the Vatican, but the application was left to the local hierarchy[15] since it was in the form of a recommendation rather than a command.[16] Under the changes only the Catholic partner declares and promises to have offspring baptized and reared in the Catholic faith while the non-Catholic partner is to be informed.[17]

Protestants living in both north and south have criticized the Catholic clergy for their reluctance to implement the more flexible 1970 Vatican changes. They indicate that non-Catholic partners are still obligated to promise to rear the children as Roman Catholics. Their criticism is most valid as it applies to the Diocese of Cork where Catholics still cannot obtain dispensations to enter a mixed marriage.[18] Some critics do concede there is no problem in marriage where only one partner is an active church member. The real stress occurs when both are active practitioners of their respective creeds.[19]

13 Constitution of Ireland, p. 138.
14 S. E. Long, "Mixed Marriages: Rome Maintains Strict Rigidity," *Orange Standard* (May, 1980), 2. (Hereafter cited as S. E. Long, "Mixed Marriages").
15 National Conference of Catholic Bishops, *Matrimonia Mixta,* Canon 1061, Sec. 7, p. 716.
16 *Ibid.,* Annex "A": "Procedure for the Celebration of a Mixed Marriage with a Dispensation from the Canonical Form," Sec. 1 - 4, pp. 721 - 722.
17 *Ibid.,* "Declaration Concerning the Preparation of the Parties to a Mixed Marriage," Annex B, Sec. 1 - 2.
18 Statement by Samuel Points, Church of Ireland Bishop of County Cork, Cork City, Ireland, June, 1979. (Hereafter cited as Points interview).
19 S. E. Long, Mixed Marriages.

Even if the Roman Church implemented the canon as written, Protestants consider it too rigid, as it favors Roman Catholicism.[20] Northern Orangemen also complain that the authority of local Roman Catholic bishops is inviolable. As Bishop Points of the Church of Ireland has stated, "No matter what the *Directive on Mixed Marriages* permits, the Roman Catholic bishop can enforce the rules of pre-Vatican II."[21] Irish interpretation of canon law is said to be so conservative as to be intolerable. "It's out-Poping the Pope:"[22] The policy is described as " . . . Roman intransigence on all matters which concern it deeply."[23] It decimates the minorities with a resulting decline in numbers. Nowhere is this more apparent than in the Republic's Jewish population which has been absorbed through mixed marriages so that currently they comprise only 0.1 percent, a decrease from approximately 0.9 percent following the Second World War.[24]

Andy Tyrie, Chairman of the Ulster Defense Association, (UDA), outlined the Protestant status in the Republic:

> The one-time 13 percent Protestant population in the Republic was cruelly reduced to the present figure of 2 percent and Ulster loyalists see this as an example of what would happen to Protestant people if a united Ireland situation was created.[25]

This decline is viewed as a deliberate effort to reduce the Protestant presence to a minimum. It is also cited as evidence that Catholic influence in the Republic is oppressive whenever canon laws regulating marriage and divorce affects non-Catholics.[26]

Tyrie's statement leads one to assume that Ireland's Protestant minority is subject to harassment and discrimination similar to Ulster's Catholic minority. Some say that such an attitude is an

20 Points Interview.
21 S. E. Long, Mixed Marriages.
22 Points interview.
23 S. E. Long, Mixed Marriages.
24 Points interview.
25 Andy Tyrie Speaks.
26 *Ibid.*

exaggeration. Samuel Points, the Church of Ireland's prelate at Cork, stated, "We are not a harassed people, but there are pressures in regards to marriage."[27] The Church of Ireland is separate from the Church of England, but is united in matters of doctrine. It is an autonomous national Church of Ireland.

Fear of union with the Republic goes beyond that of simple harassment. Northern Protestants of Scotch and English descent see themselves as culturally different. Unification could allow a dilution of the Ulster identity. They cite as an example the fact that Gaelic is the official language of the land and English remains secondary. This would deny them access to civil service positions in the Republic since they do not speak Gaelic and English is the language of Ulster.[28]

Northern Protestants also argue that the Constitution of Ireland emphasizes the rule of the majoritiy to the detriment of minority rights. Mary Redmond, who is considered an authority on the Constitution, warns that Article 41 prohibiting the dissolution of marriage is an example where law is applied to the " . . . unanimous ethos," or majority, rather than the dignity of the person. The public moral order as expressed in the Constitution could pose an unwarranted infringement upon individual freedom of choice.[29]

27 Points interview.
28 Andy Tyrie, Mixed Marriages.
29 Mary Redmond, "Constitutional Aspects of Pluralism," *Studies: An Irish Quarterly Review* 57, (Spring-Summer, 1978), p. 44.

A Destroyed Roman Catholic Church

Republican Catholic attitudes were shaped by Ireland's history of being subject to British rule. Reaction to this produced a vigorous religious nationalism which the Irish historian Lawrence McCaffrey explains: "Catholicism was the symbol of an independent Irish identity. It was the only thing that commanded the loyalty of the Irish masses."[30] Being a colony produced a sense of national inferiority resulting from having been a victim of religious and social bigotry. McCaffrey cites the attitudes of the English bureaucracy as representing a closed mind toward the natives and their problems. Nowhere was this more evident than during the Great Famine of 1845 to 1851 when over one million people died of starvation. While the potato crop failure was due to a fungus, the British generally explained it as a result of "Irish stupidity," "Irish laziness," and corruption bred by "popery." Charles E. Trevalyan, Under-Secretary of the Treasury and in charge of famine relief, explained the tragedy as " . . . a divine judgment on a wicked and perverse people."[31]

Ireland's political attitudes reflect a defensive mentality that was shaped by its historical experience. Irish spiritual and cultural institutions were attacked and pilloried. The Penal Laws of 1795 were aimed at destroying native religion and forcing Irish Catholics into economic submission. As it turned out, these Penal Laws had the opposite effect of creating a militant and uncompromising Catholic national spirit which is still very much alive.[32]

Linking Catholicism with a national identity during the period of oppression accounts for the present close relationship and gives credence to McCaffrey's statement quoted previously. It also explains why the public moral order is distinctly Catholic rather than secular and pluralistic.

Lately a more pluralistic attitude has emerged. Described as " . . . a tremendous opening up to wider issues," this change is

---

30 McCaffrey, p. 43.
31 *Ibid.*, p. 72. (See Penal Laws in Definition of Terms).
32 *Ibid.*, p. 15.

believed due in large part to Ireland's membership in the European Economic Community.[33] Ireland joined the EEC when 83 percent of the voting populace supported entry in 1973.[34]

Closer ties with other predominantly Catholic countries may also have a liberalizing effect on the Republic. Such influence was seen in a recent ruling by the European Court of Human Rights which condemned the Irish constitutional ban on divorce as a violation of the European Human Rights Convention.[35]

This growing pluralism may be giving rise to more intellectual diversity in the Catholic Church, thus impacting society at large, including the nations's legal, political, administrative and informational structures. A special report entitled *Pluralism in Ireland* by the Irish Presbyterian Church made the following statement:

> It should be noted that in RTE (Government-controlled Radio-Television in Eire) a considerable place is given to non-Catholic religious programs and on secular programs great freedom is given to the expression of views contrary to traditional moral and religious belief.[36]

The Irish Church is viewed as moving toward a position more in harmony with Vatican II in respect to Church-State relations. One of the statements that came out of Vatican II was:

> Christians should recognize that various legitimate though conflicting views can be held concerning the regulation of temporal affairs. They should respect their fellow citizens when they promote such views honorably even by group action.[37]

This has very important implications for the development of a more tolerant Irish society.

33 *Facts,* p. 230. See European Economic Community in Definition of terms.
34 Engel, p. 2.
35 *Ibid.*
36 *Pluralism in Ireland: How People of Different Communities May Live Together in Toleration and Cooperation. A Report Prepared by the Committee on National and International Problems of the Presbyterian Church of Ireland* (Belfast: Church Publications, 1977), p. 7.
37 "Politics and the Church," *The Document of Vatican II* (Western Printing and Lithographing Co., 1966), p. 287.

The development of a more democratic spirit leading to a suitable climate allows open discussion for possible union. The Irish Jesuit John Brady suggests, "Pluralism in the south should be expressed in such a way that Catholic politicians can feel free to differ with the clergy as how society ought to be run."[38]

The above statements concerning tolerance are especially applicable to any society aspiring to pluralism and are comparable to the rights of freedom of expression in the political, social, and religious spheres found in the First Amendment of the United States Constitution. In Ireland the view that Catholic moral teaching and civil law do not have to agree is indeed a pluralistic concept now accepted by the Irish hierarchy. The Irish Bishops stated in 1973:

> Those who insist on seeing the issue purely in terms of the state enforcing or not enforcing Catholic moral teaching are missing the point. As far as the state is concerned the question is the impact on society which a change in the law would be likely to have. Would it tend to change the character of society for the worse, to weaken the family, to make decent living more difficult for the young? These are questions open to public debate. Would divorce damage children's upbringing when they come from broken homes? This social dimension is usually ignored. Instead, the question is discussed in the false context as to whether the state should impose Catholic moral teaching on all, irrespective of their beliefs - - something which the bishops have never suggested.[39]

In June 1976 that group, meeting at Maynooth, re-affirmed this attitude in respect to the law:

> It is not the view of the Catholic hierarchy that, in the law of the state, the principles peculiar to *our* faith should be made binding on people who do not adhere to that faith.[40]

Fr. Liam Ryan, Professor of Sociology at St. Patrick's College in Maynooth, explains that the influence of the Roman Catholic Church derives from its historic claim to speak out on matters

---

38 John Brady, S. J., "Pluralism in Northern Ireland," *Studies: An Irish Quarterly Review* 57 (Spring-Summer, 1978), p. 89.
39 *Ibid.*, p. 90. (Quoted from *Furrow,* July, 1978, pp. 444 - 445).
40 *Ibid.*

of faith and morals. In fulfilling its traditional missions, however, it does not claim to formulate Ireland's civil laws treating of divorce, contraception, education, abortion, violence, injustice, poverty and inequality. "Its role is not that of legislating to the legislators," asserts Ryan, "but in making its position known on matters of faith and morals, the Church acts as a conscience of society."[41]

Denying Orange claims that Roman Catholicism dictates government policy, Ireland's Catholic bishops have expressed a position they believe reasonable and fair. They claim the Church has no intention of imposing its beliefs on anyone not a Catholic. Some clergymen have insisted that in a secular-pluralist state, Protestant beliefs are just as inviolable as Catholic beliefs. In respect to intermarriage, the state cannot legislate which partner should give up the basic right to raise children in his or her own faith. Traditionally the Catholic answer to this dilemma has been to discourage interreligious unions. It has been shown that when this did transpire, the children frequently became "diplomatic fodder" between the parents and placed a serious strain on family unity.[42]

Though these problems are social in nature they do form an important part of the whole political issue of division for Protestants. On the other hand, several of the Catholic clergy have criticized their own Irish Church for its almost obsessive attention to matters of sexual morality and marriage. They indicate that the Irish hierarchy tends to emphasize the Papal Encyclical *Humanae Vita* that treats sexuality rather than *Mater et Magistra, Pacem in Terris,* and *Populorum Progressio* which focus on critical problems of world population, hunger, racism, the inequitable distribution of natural resources, the brutality of war and the denial of human rights. As applied to the Northern Ireland situation encyclicals are important in that they treat of economic, political and social issues.[43] But, the Irish Church

---

41 Ryan, Church and Politics, p. 17.
42 Statement by Fr. Michael Crowley, a sociologist and chaplain at the University College at Cork, Ireland, June 1979. (Crowley spent 10 years in Peru where, as a member of the Saint James Society, he worked for social change. Hereafter cited as Crowley interview).
43 *Ibid.*

appears to treat issues relating to sexual morality as having more importance.

In both north and south a more fundamental concern is Protestant and Catholic willingness to compromise so as to heal divisions. The basic challenge is seen as the willingness to find other than comfortable answers. As Michael Crowley, an Irish Catholic priest and sociologist declares, "The problem is really an issue about Ecumenism. Until the leadership finds answers to this very practical problem Ulster will never achieve a truly viable society."[44]

Ulster's Protestants are not likely to accept a unity in which the south assimilates Northern Ireland's institutions and structures so as to make them conform to its needs. Jack Lynch, former Taoiseach (Prime Minister) of the Republic, has stated Ireland's position:

> There should be negotiation, but it should be about a New Ireland. The Constitution of this New Ireland must reflect the values and meet the legitimate interests of all sections of the population. In the United Kingdom the Ulsterman counts for little. In a new union of Irishmen he would command considerable authority.[45]

Such vague assurances do not lessen Protestant fears. The old loyalist slogan "Home Rule is Rome Rule" is reflected in the present attitude towards the power of the Catholic Church. Because this power is seen as all pervasive in Irish life, it is also considered as an interference in the democratic process. Former Peace People Chairman Alan Senior has amplified this point:

> This is a form of clericalized society that is in fact quite frightening to Catholics from most other places . . . And although the clause in the Republic's constitution giving pre-eminence to the Roman Catholic Church was repealed some years ago, there is little doubt that the threads of clericalism have been so closely interwoven into the fabric of that society as to be now inextricable.[46]

Donal Barrington, a Dublin constitutional lawyer, argues that politicians and churchmen must discuss statute changes and institutional re-

44 *Ibid.*
45 Robb, p. 13.
46 Alan Senior, "A House Divided," *Peace by Peace,* (May 8, 1981), p. 7.

organization within the Republic in an attempt to ease Protestant fears of the Catholic majority. The secularization of Ireland's constitution must become fact before Protestants can seriously consider living in a united Ireland or sharing political power in Ulster. This demands responsible leadership on both sides. Barrington warns that it is quite unrealistic for the Republic to envision political unity while at the same time holding fast to an ideal of a "Catholic State." Until this contradiction is resolved any hope of a united Ireland is not possible.[47]

Summary. Ireland's colonial past and adherence to Catholicism are viewed as having shaped that nation's political and religious consciousness. But those aspects should not be considered as a Popish plot designed to suppress a non-Catholic minority.

Ulster Protestant fears concerning unification, however, appear justified, especially when one reviews laws applicable to intermarriage. Responsible individuals have attempted to clarify the official position of the Irish Church and its relations with the Republic. They also cite the Catholic leadership as recognizing the need for pluralism and for a formulation of an attitude concerning separation of church and state. The hierarchy accepts the fact that the Church should not dictate to the State the laws of the land. Thus one can purchase contraceptives legally despite the opposition of Church doctrine. But the present reality is that the Irish Constitution reflects Catholic moral doctrine in issues pertaining to marriage and sexuality and the matter of abortion.

In a nation whose population is 95 percent Roman Catholic, one should expect some interaction and cooperation between the secular and religious spheres. What further steps the Republic may take toward pluralism, however, is an open question. But Ireland's growing exposure to the international community and her response to it should greatly influence that development.

Nevertheless, Protestant images of Roman Catholic power and influence on Ireland's public moral order remain crucial factors.

---

47 Donal Barrington, "Violence in Ireland," *Furrow* (February,1970), p.70. Barrington is a leading constitutional lawyer and President of the Irish Association in Dublin.

As was noted earlier, Protestants do have grounds for concern. Whatever is being done within the Irish Church to clarify its position and change its image has had only minor success. Community attitudes change slowly. Negative images about the Catholic Church which Ulster Protestants continue to hold have over the years influenced their behavior toward their own Catholic minority. Especially when Unionists perceived the IRA as an extension of Catholic nationalism, they resorted to violence against Ulster Catholics. For both sides, political and economic discrimination were seen as weapons for keeping the Catholic minority from ever becoming strong enough to challenge them successfully.

As was pointed out in the chapters on Ireland's history and literary renaissance at the turn of the century, the Irish people experienced political grievances against Britain which, by 1916, Catholic nationalists had openly confronted. On the other hand, Protestant loyalists in Ulster were also committed to defending their supremacy over the northern six counties. Since the Government of Ireland Act of 1921, Protestants have stood on the British Guarantee which gave assurances that Ulster would remain part of Britain so long as the majority of the population in the north desired it. But, for many Unionists, the Guarantee meant an exclusively "Protestant parliament for a Protestant people."[48]

Chapter Six discusses the practice of exploiting religious differences in order to favor one group over another in employment and housing in Ulster. This is important in order to show that economic discrimination is practiced by both sections of the population. Even more important, it shows how Unionists have defended their monopoly of power.

48 Tony Gray, *The Orange Order* (London: Bodley Head, 1972), p. 224. Sir James Craig, one of the founders of Ulster and first Prime Minister of Northern Ireland, 1921 - 1940, made this statement to an Orange gathering. In 1974, Craig declared before the British House of Common, "All I boast is that we are a Protestant Parliament and a Protestant State." (*Ibid*).

CHAPTER VI

Economic Barriers to Resolution in Ulster

Capital in Ulster is dominated by the Protestant majority who retain a monopoly over land-holdings, commerce, industry and government. This monopoly was strengthened when thousands of Catholic rural laborers sought employment in the urban centers during and after the Great Famine. Sectarian differences were further exacerbated by the Protestant practice of giving the better jobs to non-Catholic laborers. Loyalists then and now resort to economic discrimination whenever Catholic nationalism and population growth threaten the Protestant majority.[1]

Loyalists believe they must retain their political advantages by every means possible.[2] They believe their worst fears about Catholics and, therefore, are reluctant to initiate reforms. Indeed, rather than present reforms, the Unionists have used the ballot box as a means to maintain control over the Ulster Parliament at Stormont. The political theorist Richard Rose sees the northern Irish civil rights movement as analogous to the southern White exclusion of Blacks prior to the American civil rights movement.[3] This was further amplified by the Catholic socialist Bernadette Devlin's comment: "Something is wrong with a structure which represents so few of us." This former Member of Parliament points to the lack of representation as containing the source of the conflict.[4]

Because of the persistent discrimination, Catholics began in 1966 a series of civil rights demonstrations in Belfast aimed at obtaining electoral rights and administrative changes.[5] The result was the

---

1 MacEoin, pp. 129-132.
2 Great Britain, Her Majesty's Stationary Office, *Report of the Commission Appointed by the Governor of Northern Ireland,* Cnd., 532, "Disturbances in Northern Ireland," 1969, p. 65. (Hereafter cited as "Disturbances").
3 Richard Rose, "On Priorities," p. 260.
4 Bernadette Devlin, *The Price of My Soul* (London: Andre Deutsch, 1969), pp. 189-206.
5 Rose, p. 291.

Downing Street Declaration of 1969. This initiated reforms in the electoral system, local government, police forces, public housing authority, the Northern Irish Parliament, as well as several other measures to end discrimination.[6]

Nevertheless, the Declaration implemented by the British in 1969 did not pacify the IRA. Between 1969 and 1972 the IRA conducted a campaign of violence in Londonderry (called Derry by the Catholics) and Belfast. Violence was counteracted by the actions of the Royal Ulster Constabulary (RUC) and the Ulster Special Constabulary known as the "B Specials."[7]

The IRA saw the reforms as being insufficient to handle the massive unemployment in Belfast's ghettos.[8] That group believes the only true solution is that of 1916: British withdrawal and union with the South.[9]

The "Protestant Paradigm", described earlier by William Kingston, has created " . . . a very low minority tolerance factor," which has been little changed from the past.[10] Ulster has become a society in which local level discrimination is a traditional way of life for both sides. A pattern of treatment based on Catholic councilors who favored Catholics, and Protestant councilors who favored Protestants prevailed.[11]

With the passage of the Northern Ireland Act in 1974, Britain appointed a Secretary of State to be responsible for all aspects of constitutional government. This also included security in social and economic matters. Business matters pertaining to agriculture, commerce, unemployment, education, finance, and health services were handled by government committees responsible to a Central Secretariat who acts as coordinator and then, in turn, reports to the Secretary of State. Local services of employment, education and

6 British Information, *Northern Ireland*, p. 6.
7 *Ibid.*, p. 5.
8 Great Britain, National Council of Civil Liberties of Great Britain, *Bulletin of Peace Proposals*, 29 September, 1971, p. 3. (Hereafter cited as *Peace Proposals*).
9 "Ireland", *Political Quarterly* 43 (April - June, 1972), p. 141.
10 Kingston, "Elements," p. 202.
11 "Disturbances," pp. 56, 64.

housing are administered by twenty-six district councils. The Northern Ireland Housing Executive, one of seven departments close to the central government, handles the building and management of all public housing including the power to determine the liveability of private as well as public housing.[12]

While Unionists are not a majority everywhere in Ulster, they have made effective use of the gerrymander to dominate political life from the parliament to the local district councils.[13] It is in this way that Catholics receive the brunt of discrimination, especially in employment and housing.[14]

Government tables show the Catholic disadvantage even in districts where they are the majority. The voting pattern of 1967 in Londonderry is a prime example of the effectiveness of Unionists gerrymandering.[15] (See Table 1:)

TABLE 1

Voting Patterns in Londonderry

		Catholic Voters	Other Voters	Seats
North Ward:		2,530	3,946	8 Unionists
Waterside Ward:		1,852	3,687	4 Unionists
South Ward:		10,047	1,138	8 Non-Unionists
	Total:	14,429	8,781	20 (12 Unionists & 8 Non-Unionists)
		23,210		

SOURCE: Government of Northern Ireland, *Disturbances*, p. 59

12 *Facts*, pp. 76-79.
13 *Ibid.*, p. 57.
14 D.P. Barritt and C.F. Carter, *The Northern Ireland Problem: A Study in Group Relations* (London: Oxford University Press, 1962), p. 98. (Hereafter cited as Barritt and Carter, *Northern Ireland Problem*).
15 "Disturbances," p. 59.

Table 1 shows the voting pattern and seats held in Londonderry County Borough in 1967, where 60 percent of the adult population was Catholic but where 60 percent of the council seats were held by Unionists.

The report of the Commission investigating the discrimination stated:

> In each of the areas with Unionist majorities on their council, the majority was far greater than the adult population would justify. In Londonderry County Borough, Armagh Urban District, Omagh Urban District and County Fermanagh, a Catholic majority was converted into a large Unionist majority on the Councils. In the two Dungannon Councils a very small Protestant majority held two-thirds or over of the seats on the Councils. The most glaring case was Londonderry County Borough, where 60 percent of the seats on the Corporation were held by Unionists.[16]

Some Unionists were reluctant to supply any information to the Commission investigating the situation.[17]

It should be pointed out that Catholic Councils implemented similar policies whenever that group had control. A prime example is the Newry district controlled by Catholics. Protestants suffered employment discrimination in Newry because of Catholics in local government.[18] Thus discrimination is practiced by both sides.

The Fair Employment Agency (FEA) for Northern Ireland, sponsored by the British, reports that statistics alone are not sufficient to prove discrimination. The Agency does admit, however, that political circumstances gave rise to demonstrations and violence because there was a lack of " . . . equality of opportunity within Ulster's economic and political system. This placed Catholics at a disadvantage."[19]

16 *Ibid.*
17 *Ibid.*, p. 63.
18 *Ibid.*, p. 64.
19 Great Britain, Fair Employment Agency for Northern Ireland, "An Industrial and Occupational Profile of the Two Sections of the Population in Northern Ireland: An Analysis of the 1971 Population Census," p.15. (Hereafter cited as FEA).

The FEA study, based on the 1971 census, was not analyzed until 1977. Despite the time gap, the employment profile presented facts indicating that lack of equality of opportunity is a serious problem in Ulster. It outlined the economic activity rate as " . . . the ratio of those who are employed and those who are not employed, but are seeking employment."[20] The FEA study (also outlines activity rates to Ulster's total population by sex, main religious groups and other very small non-Catholic groups. Such groups are, however, so small as to be inconsequential. Percentages are given in Table 2.[21] Their significance can be appreciated when compared to the major religious groups in Table 3, showing growth patterns between 1951 and 1961.[22]

TABLE 2

Small Non-Catholic Groups in Ulster

Religious Group	Number	Proportion of Total Population
Jehovah's Witnesses	1, 041	0. 07 %
Mormon	975	0. 06 %
Jewish	959	0. 06 %
Hindu	651	0. 04 %
Buddhist	67	- - - - - -
Muslim	275	0. 02 %

Source: 1971 Northern Ireland population census: Religion tables included in *Fair Employment Agency for Northern Ireland, An Industrial and Occupational Profile of the Two Sections of the Population in Northern Ireland: An Analysis of the 1971 Population Census,* p. 15. (Hereafter cited FEA).

20 *Ibid.,* p. 3.
21 *Ibid.,* p. 2.
22 Barritt and Carter, *Northern Ireland Problem,* p. 19.

TABLE 3

Large Religious Groups in Ulster

	1951	1961
Catholic	471,460	498,031
Protestant		
Presbyterian	410,215	413,006
Church of Ireland	353,245	344,584
Methodist	66,639	79,912
Baptist	17,845	NA
	827,944	837,502

Source: Barritt and Carter, *Northern Ireland Problem,* p. 19.

Table 3 shows a slightly greater growth rate of the Catholic population in comparison to other religious groups and it would appear that Protestant fears of being "outbred" are exaggerated.

TABLE 4

Activity Rates by Sex

	Total Economically Active (a)	Total Population 15+ (b)	Total Population (c)	Activity Rates (1966) (% a/b)		(% a/c)
Men	403,317	505,819	741,436	79.6	(83.5)	54.5
Women	200,415	556,852	778,204	35.8	(35.7)	27.8

Source: FEA, p.3.

Table 4 shows activity rates by sex, i. e., " . . . the ratio of the total population of an age to be economically active." This refers to the total number of men and women in Ulster who are employed and unemployed. Letter (b) under total population 15+ indicates the number of employed and unemployed who are age 15 and over. Numbers under Activity Rates show the percentages of males and females who are 15 and over in relation to the total economically active population. Letters under (% a/b), i. e., numbers of total economic activity and total population of age 15 and over, show percentages of males and females age 15 and over who were unemployed in 1966. Category (% a/c), i. e., total economic activity and total population, shows the percentage of males and females in relation to the whole population who were unemployed in 1966.[23]

By 1971 the activity rate for Roman Catholics was 36 percent whereas for the Protestants it was 42 percent.[24]

TABLE 5

Activity Rates (in Relation to Total Population 15 and over) by the Main Denominations and Sex

Religious group	% Male	% Female	% all persons 15+
Roman Catholic	78. 4	35. 2	55. 8
Church of Ireland	80. 3	37. 1	57. 7
Presbyterian	79. 9	35. 6	57. 7
Methodist	79. 9	38. 1	57. 2
Other Protestant	79. 8	36. 4	56. 9

Source: FEA, p. 3.

23 FEA, p. 3.
24 *Ibid.*

In Table 5, the economic Activity Rates for the total population are shown, including males and females from ages 15 and over. Here Catholics scored 55.8 percent as against 56.9 percent for Protestants.[25]

The FEA also gives a "not-stated" category which denotes individuals who did not list their religious affiliation. The level of "non-stated" was 9.4 percent of Ulster's total population. The agency breaks this group down into 60 percent Catholic and 40 percent Protestant. Thus the activity rate for Catholics, including the non-stated group, is 36.8 percent.[26]

According to the FEA Report, the unemployment rate for the same period for all groups was 8.5 percent. In that category Catholic males were 47.4 percent and females were 41.5 percent.[27]

Table 6 further delineates the working population by industrial skills areas which are classified as primary, secondary and tertiary. Catholics, who comprise better than one-third of the population, constitute only one-fifth of the work force, one-third agrarian and over one-fourth in service positions.[28] Protestant males have a significantly higher employment rate in manufacturing and services, and Protestant women also enjoy a disproportionate employment in the primary sector.[29]

Tables 6 and 7 of Industrial Order show where the disparity of employment exists. Noteworthy are differences in shipbuilding, metals, coal and petroleum.[30]

The Irish sociologist, Edmund Aunger, indicates further differences. Using the Hall-Jones system of classifying occupations from professions to unskilled and unemployed, he presents a hierarchy of occupation in Table 8. Aunger explains:

25 *Ibid.*
26 *Ibid.*, p. 2.
27 *Ibid.*, p. 5.
28 *Ibid.*
29 *Ibid.*
30 *Ibid.*, pp. 6 - 7, 9.

78

TABLE 6

Distributions of Religious Groups by Industrial Order

Industrial Order	% Roman Catholic	% Protestant	% Not Stated
Agriculture, Forestry, Fishing	31. 0	60. 7	8. 3
Mining, Quarrying	32. 0	58. 8	9. 2
Food, Drink & Tobacco	21. 4	60. 9	7. 7
Coal & Petroleum Products	10. 6	78. 8	10. 6
Chemicals & Allied Industry	24. 3	66. 6	9. 1
Metal Manufacture	18. 2	72. 0	9. 8
Mechanical Engineering	16. 0	77. 0	7. 0
Instrument Engineering	19. 8	73. 8	6. 4
Electrical Engineering	19. 3	72. 6	8. 1
Shipbuilding & Marine Engineering	4. 8	89. 5	5. 7
Vehicles	11. 7	79. 5	8. 8
Metal goods not elsewhere specified	21. 7	69. 7	8. 6
Textiles	23. 6	69. 1	7. 3
Leather, Leather Goods & Fur	39. 8	50. 7	9. 5
Clothing & Footwear	40. 1	50. 7	9. 2
Bricks, Pottery, Glass, Cement	27. 2	64. 1	8. 7
Timber, Furniture etc.	24. 9	66. 6	8. 5
Paper, Printing & Publishing	19. 6	71. 3	9. 1
Other manufacturing Industries	29. 1	60. 8	10. 1
Construction	37. 0	52. 9	10. 1
Gas. Electricity & Water	15. 4	78. 2	6. 4
Transport & Communication	26. 2	64. 4	9. 4
Distributive Trades	23. 5	68. 0	8. 5
Insurance, Banking, Finance & Business services	16. 2	75. 2	8. 6
Professional & Scientific services	28. 1	62. 0	9. 9
Miscellaneous services	31. 8	58. 5	9. 7
Public Administration & Defence	19. 6	71. 7	8. 7

Source: 1971 Northern Ireland population census: religion tables.

TABLE 7a

Distributions of Religious Groups by Sex in Industrial Order

Industrial Order	– Males –	% Roman Catholic	% Protestant	% Not Stated
Agriculture, Forestry, Fishing		31.6	59.9	8.5
Mining, Quarrying		32.6	58.1	9.3
Food, Drink and Tobacco		22.3	69.6	8.1
Coal and Petroleum Products		12.0	76.8	11.2
Chemicals and Allied Industries		25.9	64.4	9.7
Metal Manufacture		18.7	71.5	9.8
Mechanical Engineering		16.8	75.9	7.3
Instrument Engineering		19.4	74.1	6.5
Electrical Engineering		18.4	72.9	8.7
Shipbuilding & Marine Engineering		4.8	89.9	5.7
Vehicles		11.9	79.3	8.8
Metal goods not elsewhere specified		22.1	68.7	9.2
Textiles		22.9	69.0	8.1
Leather, Leather Goods and Fur		38.8	52.2	9.5
Clothing and Footwear		29.5	62.1	8.4
Bricks, Pottery, Glass, Cement		27.6	63.5	8.9
Timber, Furniture etc.		25.9	65.4	8.7
Paper, Printing and Publishing		15.3	75.8	8.8
Other Manufacturing Industries		30.3	59.1	10.6
Construction		37.6	52.2	10.2
Gas, Electricity and Water		15.6	78.1	6.3
Transport and Communication		26.7	63.7	9.6
Distributive Trades		24.5	66.2	9.3
Insurance, Banking, Finance and Business Services		15.7	75.1	9.2
Professional & Scientific Services		23.3	64.5	12.2

Source: 1971 census, Northern Ireland

TABLE 7b

Distributions of Religious Groups by Sex in Industrial Order

Industrial Order	— Females —	% Roman Catholic	% Protestant	% Not Stated
Agriculture, Forestry, Fishing		20. 4	76. 1	5. 5
Mining, Quarrying		18. 1	75. 9	6. 0
Food, Drink and Tobacco		19. 7	73. 2	7. 1
Coal and Petroleum Products		. . . .	. . . .	. . . .
Chemicals and Allied Industries		16. 2	77. 9	5. 9
Metal Manufacture		13. 5	76. 9	9. 6
Mechanical Engineering		10. 5	84. 4	5. 1
Instrument Engineering		20. 3	73. 5	6. 2
Electrical Engineering		20. 5	72. 4	7. 1
Shipbuilding & Marine Engineering		4. 9	88. 3	6. 8
Vehicles		9. 1	82. 8	8. 1
Metal goods not elsewhere specified		19. 7	74. 2	6. 1
Textiles		24. 4	69. 4	6. 2
Leather, Leather Goods and Fur		43. 6	46. 8	9. 6
Clothing and Footwear		41. 9	48. 8	9. 3
Bricks, Pottery, Glass, Cement		23. 7	70. 4	5. 9
Timber, Furniture etc.		17. 2	76. 1	6. 7
Paper, Printing and Publishing		19. 5	72. 6	7. 9
Other Manufacturing Industries		24. 4	67. 8	7. 8
Construction		20. 6	71. 6	7. 8
Gas, Electricity and Water		13. 8	79. 1	7. 1
Transport and Communication		23. 0	68. 9	8. 1
Distributive Trades		22. 2	70. 4	7. 4
Insurance, Banking, Finance and Business Services		16. 7	75. 6	7. 7
Professional & Scientific Services		30. 7	61. 6	8. 6

Source: 1971 census, Northern Ireland

TABLE 8

Religion and Occupational Class 1971, Economically Active Men and Women

Occupational class	Hall-Jones Classification	Catholic	Protestant	Total
1. Professional and managerial	I, II, III	12 %	15 %	14 %
2. Lower grade non-manual	IV, V (a)	19 %	26 %	24 %
3. Skilled manual	V (b)	17 %	19 %	18 %
4. Semi-skilled, manual	VI	27 %	25 %	26 %
5. Unskilled, unemployed	VII	25 %	15 %	18 %
Total		100 %	100 %	100 %

N equals 564, 682

Source: Barritt and Carter, *Northern Ireland Problem* included in Edmund A. Aunger, "Religion and Occupational Class in Northern Ireland," *Economic and Social Review,* VII, (1975 - 1976), p. 4.

The results of the classification (Table 8) show that Protestants are disproportionately represented by high numbers in non-manual and skilled manual occupations, while Catholics are disproportionately represented by high numbers only in the semi-skilled, unskilled and unemployed classes.[31]

In spite of religious segregation, a Catholic middle class of limited influence has taken root. This has also occurred in Northern Ireland's highly segregated parochial and public educational system where

31 Edmund A. Aunger, "Religion and Occupational Class in Northern Ireland," *Economic and Social Review* 7 (1975 - 1976), p. 4.

Catholics comprise 39 percent of the employed teachers.[32] In areas of public employment, however, there˙ is a noticeable imbalance according to religious affiliation. In the universities Catholics are only 17 percent of the faculty, 15 percent in school administration, and generally fewer in other positions of authority.[33] Aunger summarized this imbalance as follows:

> While a clerk may be a Catholic, it is more likely that the office manager will be a Protestant. While a skilled craftsman may be a Catholic, it is more likely that the supervisor will be a Protestant; and while a nurse may be a Catholic, it is more likely that the doctor will be a Protestant.[34]

TABLE 9
Religion and Non-Manual Occupations, 1971, Employed Men and Women

Occupational group	Hall-Jones Classification	Total Employed	% Women	% Catholic
A. "Catholic" occupations				
1. Publicans, innkeepers	IV	2,026	21 %	73 %
2. Waiters, waitresses	V	2,145	84 %	50 %
3. Hairdressers, manicurists		2,828	76 %	49 %
4. Domestic housekeepers	V	1,582	100 %	48 %
5. Nurses	III	12,249	90 %	43 %
6. Primary, secondary teachers	II - III	15,726	63 %	39 %
B. "Protestant" occupations				
1. Company secretaries	I	347	15 %	7 %
2. Police officers & men	V	4,046	3 %	10 %
3. Chemists, biologists (i)	I	711	11 %	11 %
4. Engineers (ii)	I	3,282	. . . . .	11 %
5. Managers (iii)	II	10,312	6 %	12 %
6. Senior government officials (iv)	I	1,383	10 %	13 %

Source: Aunger, p. 7.

32 *Ibid.*, p. 6.
33 *Ibid.*
34 *Ibid.*, p. 8.

Table 9 also provides a series of non-manual "Catholic" and "Protestant" occupations reflecting class consciousness and the degree to which religion and social position have become institutionalized.[35]

A 1978 FEA report also points out that Northern Ireland's unemployment rate in the 14-24 age groups is the third highest in Europe.[36] Even with educational standards being equal, the FEA has documented that Protestant young men from less privileged backgrounds have more opportunities to seek professional and skilled positions than their Catholic counterparts.

Peter Arnlis, writing in the IRA's newspaper, *An Phoblacht*, notes the following as an example of an entrenched patronage system based on religion:

> The importance of the network of family and friends in finding work suggests a major mechanism whereby existing patterns of employment are being reproduced . . . Personal recommendations rather than formal examinations or references appear to be the most significant factors relied on by employers in recruiting workers.[37]

Relations between Catholic unions and the government have also given rise to work stoppages and are a contributory cause to societal divisions. In September 1980, the 340-member Irish Transport and General Workers Union (ITGWU) charged the British government with allocating large sums to "loyalist" industries, thus insuring employment for Protestants and ignoring Catholic industries. A cited example was the Protestant Harland and Wolff Shipyard receiving £42 million.[38]

35   *Ibid.*, p. 7.
36   Peter Arnlis, "Job Bias Against Catholic School Leavers," *An Phoblacht/ Republican News*, September 13, 1980, p. 3. Also see: Great Britain, Fair Employment Agency for Northern Ireland, "Ireland into Work? Young School Leavers and the Structure of Opportunity in Belfast, 1978." (Reportedly, the Republic of Ireland has the highest unemployment rate of 16.4 percent, followed by Italy).
37   *Ibid.*
38   Aunger, p. 12. (Author's research shows that approximately 600 to 700 Catholics out of a total of 7,000 non-clericals were employed at the Harland and Wolff Shipyard, about 10 percent of the work force.

84

Disputes involving Catholic dock worker's grievances in 1980 have also exacerbated tensions. The strikers complain that the government threatened to re-introduce the "casual labour system," abolished in 1972. It required that men line up while stevedores select who work each day.[39] Catholic workers refer to this practice of selecting labour as a "slave market" and an insult to them. Since the majority of the dock workers are Catholic, they claim they are being victimized by a sectarian, bigoted government.[40]

Other studies show male unemployment during the 1946 to 1959 period to be four times higher in Ulster than in any region in England. By 1966 the average worker income for Northern Ireland was still 25 percent below the English average.[41]

The policy of discrimination is not only applied towards hiring practices but also to housing allocations. Its original purpose was to alleviate societal differences but has instead been even more divisive. Where Unionists controlled the councils, the Catholic housing allocation was not commensurate with that group's numbers. This discriminatory behavior was practiced by the British even prior to the establishment of the Stormont Parliament. "What Westminister built and later permitted the Unionists merely repeated and refined.[42]

The shortage of new housing has been a continuous problem since before World War II. Between 1921 and 1939, 28,450 housing units were authorized by the Northern Ireland housing authority. The political analyst Geoffrey Bell outlines the housing problem in relation to the Belfast population density pattern for the 1926-1937 census. Table 10 compares living space per person in the Catholic Falls district and the Protestant Shankill section. It would appear that the depressed Protestant working class fares a little better.

39 Peter Hayes, "Deep Sea Docks Dispute: Low Pay and Casual Labour Keeps Workers Out," *An Phoblacht/Republican News*, September 6, 1980, p. 8. (Hereafter cited as Hayes, "Dock Dispute").
40 *Ibid.*
41 Geoffrey Bell, *The Protestants of Ulster*. (London: Pluto Press Ltd., 1976), p. 25. (Hereafter cited as Bell, *Protestants*).
42 Hayes, "Dock Dispute."

TABLE 10

Housing Density in Belfast: 1927, 1937

Ward	Catholic population, 1937 (percent)	No. of rooms per person, 1926	No. of rooms per person, 1937
Falls	91	.81	.89
St. Anne's	37	.88	.99
St. George's	4	.84	.99
Shankill	5	.90	1.05
Smithfield	91	.71	.81
Woodvale	4	.85	.89

Source: Geoffrey Bell, *The Protestants of Ulster* (London: Pluto Press, Ltd., 1976), p. 32.

In 1969, when the massive demonstrations and riots erupted in Londonderry, Armagh, Newry and Dungannon, 22 percent of the nation's houses were classified as unfit for habitation.[43] This meant 100,000 had no baths, hot water or inside toilets or lacked all three. This was further compounded by the fact that half of housing was at least fifty years old.[44] Even as early as 1914 only 5,412 units were built in the public sector, far too few to meet the demand. Public pressure for housing legislation continued as a source of tension, especially between Catholics and the government. According to Bell, "Wards in Belfast which had the worst housing were also the wards with the most Catholics."[45] This fact is a major reason for the feeling of alienation Catholics have toward the government.

43 *Ibid.,* p. 25.
44 "Disturbances," p. 59.
45 Bell, *Protestants,* p. 25.

There is a marked correlation between unemployment rates and poor housing. Tables 11 and 12 illustrate the patterns of employment and varying qualities of living standards. In Table 11 we observe housing with fixed baths and hot water and those without them. Table 12 shows the differences in the number of households with cars.[46]

A 1975 survey reflected the correlation between substandard housing and unemployment for both Protestant and Catholic. The study, conducted by the Housing Executive of the Corporate Planning Department (CPD) points to a combination of low income, inadequate resources, and lack of purchasing power as ongoing con-

TABLE 11

Living Standards of Catholics

	Catholics as percentage of males of working age	no fixed bath	no hot water	no wc	inside wc	householders in shared dwellings
	Per Cent					
Dock	62.86	57.8	38.1	1.2	44.0	0.80
Falls	79.02	50.6	32.9	0.6	46.6	0.96
Pottinger	11.64	37.8	24.4	0.1	59.4	0.58
Shankill	7.84	48.0	28.0	0.4	51.6	0.68
Victoria	3.78	29.9	18.6	0.1	66.5	0.57
	Owner-occupied houses					
	Total Owner-Occupied					
Falls	7,849	1,463				
Shankill	10,633	4,095				

Source: 1971 census, Northern Ireland

46 *Ibid.*, pp. 29-30.

TABLE 12

Patterns of Employment of Catholics

	Total	Catholics	unem-ployed	self-employed with staff	managers	foremen super-visors	pro-fessions	house-holds with cars
		Percent						
Clifton	15,632	34.93	9.32	2.74	3.56	3.16	0.29	43.47
Court	1,618	34.15	20.27	0.5	0.37	1.17	0.06	13.13
Cromac	6,631	27.33	7.64	2.78	5.30	2.47	4.99	48.26
Dock	2,961	62.86	17.56	0.87	1.04	1.65	0.16	14.98
Duncairn	10,396	17.37	7.29	2.73	4.04	3.57	1.56	44.26
Falls	10,138	79.02	19.64	0.86	0.94	1.67	0.17	17.44
Ormeau	12,703	14.17	5.51	2.29	3.99	3.63	1.54	46.53
Pottinger	13,392	11.64	6.98	2.49	5.16	3.60	2.23	50.75
Shankill	11,123	7.84	9.43	1.38	2.36	3.32	0.74	34.76
Smithfield	1,182	74.67	16.20	0.53	0.37	0.91	0.05	8.73
St. Anne's	6,580	34.65	11.01	1.32	1.65	3.14	0.85	28.33
St. George's	2,996	2.16	10.14	0.67	0.80	1.63	0.86	18.70
Victoria	10,682	3.78	5.96	2.67	5.86	3.84	3.02	53.38
Windsor	6,820	16.16	5.57	4.74	5.26	2.72	6.57	59.91
Woodvale	8,521	15.80	12.55	1.10	1.61	2.94	0.63	30.16

Source: 1971 census, Northern Ireland

ditions that are likely to continue to dominate the housing situation even should the economic picture change for the better:[47]

> Even with the revival of the economy and the trend towards smaller households, large sections of the population will remain in housing need. The extent to which these needs are met and the groups who will or will not benefit depend on levels of public provision and the nature of public intervention in the housing market. Only substantial changes in the real income and major economic changes will reduce the need for public intervention. In present circumstances of scarcity it is important that policies are developed and assessed in terms of social objectives and priorities.[48]

The CPD recommended changing housing policy so as to benefit the citizens most often overlooked. These include the unemployed, large family units and the elderly. It was further suggested that funds be made available for the upgrading of dilapidated housing, privately rented, overcrowded and unfurnished sectors in areas of decline in both urban and rural sections.[49]

The extent of the housing problem appears out of proportion for a modern, industrialized state of one-and-a-half-million people. The following government figures enumerate the extent of poor housing conditions.

A. 52 percent of the 73,490 families living in houses that require renewal do not have the necessary resources for that purpose.

B. 25,000 families who live in improved and renewed housing are overcrowded.

C. Six percent of the remaining 317,660 families live in overcrowded conditions and below their adequate needs.

D. 39,000 urban and rural families live in privately rented houses that require renewal or improvement.

E. 48,000 owner-occupied houses in urban and rural areas require renewal or improvement. In this owner-occupied category, an additional 25,000 houses require substantial repair. Of these, 18,860 are located in rural areas and 9,570 are in urban areas. They are large families and large adult households.

47 *Ibid.*
48 Great Britain, Her Majesty's Stationary Office, *Report of the Housing Executive Corporate Planning Department,* "Northern Ireland Housing Survey, 1975," p. 63. (Hereafter cited as CPD).
49 *Ibid.*

F.   There are 13,480 families renting government housing under the CPD, that requires renewal or improvement. The majority of these families have been living there several years and are older people on low incomes.

G.   An additional 27,400 tenant families live in government housing that is overcrowded. Families are large, with wage-earners who are engaged in low skill manual work with a low income, or they lack employment altogether.[50]

According to the Housing Executive Report, a total of 153,840 families in Ulster live in houses that require renewal or improvement, or are overcrowded. Furthermore, 17 percent of all families, or 25,540 households, are reported to live in overcrowded conditions, while 35 percent live below their adequate needs and 25 percent live in houses that require improvement or renewal.[51]

Bernadette Devlin questions whether the Ulster conflict is really along religious lines. Though religious differences have been used to differentiate the "ins" and the "outs" of Northern Ireland, Devlin argues that the most basic reason for it is because there aren't enough jobs. Chronically high joblessness, asserts Devlin, is because corporate investment into the economy is based on profit rather than the needs of the population. The popular view that the issue is one of Catholic versus Protestant ignores this important economic problem.[52]

Protestant spokesmen, too, have expressed very similar views that serious unemployment in Ulster is being experienced on both sides of the religious divide, and is described as " . . . a soul-destroying experience for anyone who wants to work."[53] While not mentioning capitalism   by   name, an Orange spokesman blames the competitive economics as practised by the international community, the imbalances in British trade, the loss of revenues, and the high government spending on Middle Eastern oil, as among several reasons for the cut-backs in housing, health and welfare services. Furthermore, the effects on the nation's economy and the social dangers

50   *Ibid.*, p. 56.
51   *Ibid.*
52   Devlin, p. 59.
53   S. E. Long, "The Economics of Common Sense," *Orange Standard* (October, 1980): 3. (Hereafter cited as: Long, "Economics").

accompanying high unemployment are believed to be self-evident. As the Unionist writer S. E. Long explains:

> The extent of the trouble is such that a large cross-section of the population is affected by lack of work, from unskilled labourers through skilled craftsmen, to managers and owners of businesses.[54]

In its editorial on economic inequities in Northern Ireland, an Orange publication has stated that the government has failed because its economic policies were not formulated in the interests of all citizens:

> Government acts responsible when it creates jobs. The view that work must bring profits to justify itself is nonsense. Profit from work is to be found in people who are enjoying a useful, meaningful life. Waste is not in over-production, but in under-distribution of our wealth in labour materials.[55]

In contrast to Ulster is the Republic's economy, which sustained rapid economic growth during the 60s and 70s, when over 500 new plants began production there and increased Ireland's industrial output by over 70 percent.[56] This has accounted for nearly one-third of the Gross National Product and 30 percent of the work force.[57]

In recent years, Ireland discovered lead and zinc deposits which are believed to be the largest of their kind in the world. The export value of these minerals increased from barely £ 20,000 in the 1950s to over £ 10 million in 1978.[58] In 1973, a gasfield was discovered off Ireland's south coast containing approximately one

---

54 *Ibid.*
55 *Ibid.*
56 "Comment: Employment and the Want of It," *Orange Standard* (May, 1980): 4.
57 Kevin M. Cahill, "America and Ulster: Healing Hands," *Foreign Policy* 4 (Winter, 1979-80): 92.
58 Industrial Development Authority, *Ireland: The Most Profitable Industrial Location in the EEC*, Dublin: Colorman Ltd., 1978, p. 2. (Hereafter cited as "Ireland: The Most Profitable"). The Republic's industrial development authority is an autonomous state body responsible for promoting industrialization and encouraging foreign manufacturers to set up new industries in Ireland.

91

million-million cubic feet of high quality natural gas. Other sources are being developed in the southwest, west, northwest and east. Currently, a comprehensive drilling program is underway off Ireland's continental shelf. Government analysts speculate that even one relatively small well would make Ireland an energy-sufficient nation.[59]

Because of these discoveries in natural resources, Ireland is moderately optimistic about the future. In 1979, its annual growth rate was 9 percent in industrial output and 15 percent in exports of manufactured goods. The trend has included an encouraging projection of new industries increasing employment by over 10,000 more jobs per year.[60] Industry from the United States accounts for about 48 percent of the total foreign investors. This includes 206 manufacturing projects employing over 33,000 people, with a total investment of $ 466 million in 1978.[61] At that time, industry from the United Kingdom (UK) amounted to 17 percent of the total foreign investment, followed by 12 percent from Japan, 9 percent from Germany and 14 percent from the rest of the world.[62]

Meanwhile, economic conditions in Northern Ireland appear to encourage discrimination in jobs and public housing in both Catholic and in Protestant-controlled district councils. Such bodies are motivated to respond to their own kind so as to assure political support from their constituents. The resultant effect has been to further divide Ulster society by intensifying sectarian consciousness and feelings of mistrust.

A recent study on pluralism by the Presbyterian Church in Ireland reports that since the late sixties there has been an exodus of over 15,000 families out of "mixed" neighborhoods so as to feel more secure in and among people of their own religious faith. This has produced trauma and alienation. The study noted that sectarian politics has made any hope of healing societal divisions very remote:

---

59 *Ibid.*, p. 7.
60 *Ibid.*, p. 25
61 Industrial Development Authority, *IDA Industrial Plan: 1977-1980*, Richview: Brown and Nolan Ltd., p. 15.
62 "Ireland: The most Profitable," p. 7.

This has led to a concentration in and expansion of "Catholic" areas and a matching retreat and scattering of "Protestants" into their more widely spread majority situation. It is unlikely that these people will be induced to resume "integrated" living in the foreseeable future.[63]

The studies have also shown that in Ulster discrimination in employment and in housing are so serious as to perpetuate social division and disharmony in which the working class continues to be the most seriously affected. The social inequities in employment are also exacerbated by Northern Ireland's depressed economy and third highest unemployment rate in Europe. This has created a condition in which it is quite normal for employers who happen to be Protestant or Catholic to take care of their own. Bell explains that although the working class generally has suffered from economic and social conditions, the Protestant workers have not suffered as much as their Catholic counter-parts. Ulster's politics of favoritism have served to maintain different degrees of suffering.[64]

Favoritism appears to be inevitable whenever there is strong competition for employment. Where jobs are scarce, Protestant and Catholic workers are caught in a situation which requires them to choose employment even though the choice involves over-stepping another person who doesn't qualify because of religion. As has been pointed out:

> The Protestant worker may be called bigoted, but when he is standing in a dole queue beside a Catholic worker and it is he who gets the job and not the Catholic, to blame him for taking the job or for developing a view that he has a prior right to the job, is to ignore the size of the dole queue.[65]

Summary. The glaring inequities in jobs and housing indicate that the long history of sectarian politics influences political decision-making. And the employment line means that too few jobs serve to intensify the sectarian issues. As Long sees it, "What is needed is work for all. Work opportunities are the answer to discrimination in employment."[66]

63 John Hume, "The Irish Question: a British problem," p. 305.
64 Bell, p. 33.
65 *Ibid.*
66 Long, "Economics," p. 3.

The practice of discrimination deprives the ordinary working men and women, Catholic and Protestant alike. Their economic grievances have created a scapegoat mentality in which each group has been disposed to blame the other for the condition of their lives. Societal frustration expressed by Celtic Renaissance writers of the past, has today become deeply entrenched in Northern Ireland's urban ghettos.

A marked change toward an improved economy with full employment should be viewed as a prerequisite toward lessening but not altogether eliminating sectarian politics. This researcher believes that improved Protestant-Catholic relations can result from an improved economic climate. However, as was discussed earlier, reforms relating to the allocation of jobs and housing are inhibited by a sectarian state of mind which can color objectivity in decision-making. This must be considered when any attempt is made to implement political, social or economic reforms that might lead to a united Ireland.

The political, economic, cultural and historical forces discussed in this and earlier chapters point to the depth of the problem. Political manipulation, too, exploits suspicions and fears long established in the public consciousness. Because sectarian propagandists have not been effectively challenged, people continue to hate one another. Chapter VII discusses the problem of manipulation which serves to maintain a divided Ulster and prevents effective dialogue among the working class.

March through Newry

Newry, Northern Ireland — Thousands of Roman Catholics march silently through the streets of Newry, Northern Ireland, in a civil rights march. The two-hour demonstration, which openly defied a ban on marches in Northern Ireland, avoided the center of the city and any confrontation with hundreds of British soldiers. An estimated 15,000 to 20,000 persons from the Irish Republic and Northern Ireland took part in the march, which grew into a major protest after the killing of 13 Catholic civilians in Londonderry.

(Religious News Service Photo)

The Two Irelands . . .

Belfast, Northern Ireland: British soldiers move past homes wrecked by violence in the Catholic Clonard area of Belfast. There are two Irelands. There is Northern Ireland, its six counties associated with Britain and now ruled direct from London. The headlines and television news programs tell of its troubles. (This picture was made during filming of "A Tale of Two Irelands," a CBS News Special to be telecast on the CBS-TV network Thursday, March 20, from 10:00 to 11:00 p.m., EDT.)

(UPI)

Territory between Protestant Shankill and Catholic Falls Road called "No man's land"

Writing on wall — on Falls Road.

CHAPTER VII

Power Politics and Divisiveness in Northern Ireland

Divide et impera — divide your slaves and so rule them. At one time sixty million slaves of the Roman Empire were held in subjugation chiefly through this device. The skilled slaves were encouraged to look with contempt on the unskilled.

Eric Hass[1]

The modern practice of dividing the workers has remained an unspoken stratagem stimulating negative feelings long after any justification for such attitudes has ceased to exist. Political leaders use the same device to fan the fires of narrow, vindictive nationalism so as to further promote their own political ambitions.[2]

On the eve of World War I, the socialist Daniel De Leon cited the underlying cause for societal conflict as the manipulation of socio-economic differences. In his pamphlet, *The Socialist Reconstruction of Society,* De Leon noted that community interests cause politicians to put aside differences and make accommodations or compromises. De Leon argued that modern industrialism portrays unionism as radical and revolutionary when it seeks to overcome social inequities. When unionism became successful, it "sold out" and defended the *status quo.* De Leon asserted that organized labor became an accomplice in capitalist crimes.[3] He believed that certain

---

1 Eric Hass, *Socialism: World Without Race Prejudices* (New York: New York Labor News Co., 1945), p. 18. (Publication is that of the American Socialist Labor Party. The author insists that unity of all workers is required for the establishment of a world without exploitation, and without class rule).

2 Arnold Peterson, *Capitalism is Doomed: Socialism Is The Hope Of Humanity* (New York: New York Labor News Co., 1952), p. 25. (This pamphlet is a report to the 1952 Socialist Labor Party National Convention. It includes a section entitled, "Debauching the Labor Class").

3 Daniel De Leon, *The Socialist Reconstruction of Society* (New York: New York Labor News Co., 1968), pp. 26-27. (De Leon became a socialist in 1900 and Secretary of the Socialist Labor Party of America until his death in 1914).

elements of the working class remained apart and divided, unable to affect any real change in the economic order.[4]

James Gilhooley, a Catholic priest, similarly assesses the Northern Ireland conflict in terms of economic and political interest. He identifies the "haves" as the upper and middle income groups that comprise a 70 percent majority which happens to be largely Protestant.[5] Gilhooley expressed views almost identical to De Leon's. With specific reference to Northern Ireland Gilhooley alludes to the 'sops and paliatives' that are handed to the workers by the the ruling classes in order to pacify them. Such views are important if one is to understand the complicated Ulster problem. Gilhooley writes:

> Whenever the Catholic have-nots make unpleasant noises about such expensive goals as election reforms, decent housing, and better jobs, as say, in Derry in 1969, the haves tell the Protestant have-nots about the unruly Papists now threatening the little they have. Result: the trench coats are shook out, the Smith and Wessons oiled, and the fighting begins.[6]

While Protestants have grounds for concern about the Republic's Catholic influence, the average Protestant workers have been conditioned to believe that a united Ireland would surely eliminate their privileged, albeit limited economic position. Moreover, the majority believe they would be " . . . trampled underfoot by hordes of IRA, egged on by Catholic clergy."[7]

In this atmosphere conflict has become the norm, thus making political compromise difficult. Northern Ireland's political leaders are seen as unable or unwilling to take a middle ground of promoting reforms affecting the allocation of jobs and housing. Nowhere is this more evident than in those areas. Thus workers are manipulated against each other by politicians concerned only with their own

---

4   De Leon, pp. 36-37.
5   James Gilhooley, "On the Road To Drogheda," *Commonweal* 104 (March 18, 1977): 78.
6   *Ibid.*, p. 78.
7   Coogan, IRA, p. 261.

gain. Politicians on both sides have exploited sectarian tensions by citing half-truths or imputing evils to each other.[8]

Devlin explains the manipulation factor as coming from Protestant Unionist politicians and Catholic nationalists alike. Each side denies it discriminates, yet both Unionist and nationalist leaders are to blame for much of the social polarization and violence:

> Both use religion to divide and rule the working class. It is only less serious on the Catholic side because there are fewer Catholic bosses and fewer Catholic local authorities in a position to discriminate. It is a tactic that has made the ruling minority look like a majority and has kept the Unionist Party in power since Northern Ireland's inception.[9]

It is apparent that economic and political interests are often exploited by calling attention to sectarian differences. The problem is largely a Protestant and Catholic one in which the two groups have been educated to accept views about each other that are often half-truths and falsehoods. This researcher argues that were high employment and economic prosperity to come to Northern Ireland, this could contribute to an environment in which people of different faiths would be more likely to communicate with one another without feeling that their security was threatened. Such interaction could lead to better understanding of one another's situation. On the other hand, better economic conditions alone cannot be expected to eliminate sectarianism altogether as this is in the hands of leadership on all levels of society. Meanwhile, in an economically depressed situation, religious symbols are continually manipulated to maintain the economically powerful over the powerless.

Anders Boserup of the Institute for Peace and Conflict Research discerns the conflict as being stimulated and prolonged by organizations that encourage a spirit of no political compromise and no

8 Statement by Fr. Patrick Gallinagh, Ecclesiastical Inspector at St. Malachy's College and Assistant Pastor of St. Patrick's Church, Belfast, Northern Ireland, May 12, 1979. (Hereafter cited as Gallinagh interview).
9 Devlin, pp. 34-35.

cooperation among the religious factions. This destroys any hope for reconciliaton, much less a sense of community.[10]

Social tensions are not stirred up by the mainstream religious establishment but by what is described as a privileged Irish patrimony that has held economic and political ascendancy for 400 years and now vigorously reacts to change. According to Trevor Beeson:

> The religious labels of the two groups serve as useful identity tags because no others are readily available and because tribal antagonism has in the past been nurtured by religious bitterness of a notoriously unChristian character.[11]

Ulster's political leadership is frequently seen as believing more in Orange versus Green than in better conditions. It insists that sectarian issues are really more important than solving the complex socio-economic issues. Their loyalties are given to flying different flags and manipulating people by sloganizing and " . . . beating the drums."[12] It is felt that if all labor unions united on non-sectarian grounds and tried to resolve the issues of housing, unemployment, wages and the like, politicians would seek to ruin those efforts by exploiting Protestant fears about living in a predominantly Catholic united Ireland. Thus, the use of sectarian diatribes. The old labels such as, "You're British, You're Irish, You're Catholic, You're Protestant," tend to inspire the predictable conditioned responses.[13] The ruling class sees nationalism as negative if it means uniting to solve social problems. Ignored is the fact that when intersectarian cooperation is undermined, the whole community suffers. This creates an uncompromising political atmosphere wherein the electorate votes along narrow religious lines rather than the common good.

10 Anders Boserup, "Power In A Post-Colonial Setting: The Why and Whither of Religious Confrontation in Ulster," *Bulletin For Peace Proposals*, (August, 1969): 62.
11 Trevor Beeson, "The Impotence of the Churches," *Christian Century* 89 (September 13, 1972): 888. (Hereafter cited as: "Impotence").
12 Statement by William Graham, of the political staff of the Belfast Telegraph, principal newspaper in Northern Ireland, Belfast, May 13, 1979. (Hereafter cited as: Graham interview).
13 *Ibid.*

Thus, " . . . sectarianism serves to push nationalism to an extreme form which turns to fascism."[14]

The Unionist majority, loyal to Britian, manipulates the instruments of democracy to maintain permanent control. Potentially the working groups have the power to defy manipulation, but they lack the political acumen to unite for this purpose. Therefore, the manipulative technique cited by De Leon and Gilhooley has served the elite interest and prevented the growth of a pluralistic spirit. As Brady explains:

> Political life remains abnormal and sterile . . . Northern Ireland continues to be a politically neurotic society, one in which the principal and perennial object of discussion is how political life is to be organized and constitutionally channeled. This is an enormous waste of energy and a diversion from the normal tasks of politics in achieving economic and social progress.[15]

The democratic concept of government appears limited in Ulster. The Democratic Unionist Party (DUP) focuses only on the inherent right of the majority to rule at the expense of the minority.[16] Their social alienation is the result when the control of political structures and interpretation of justice and loyalty are claimed as being exclusive to one side.[17] Over half of the Catholics, in turn, see Protestant concessions on elections and housing as never enough and too late, and cherish the dream of unity with the Republic.[18]

Most Protestants have replaced their own denominational schools with public schools, while Catholics have retained a strongly conservative parochial system. In both systems the student's intellectual views about society and politics are formed along religious lines.[19] They are said to create the myths by which people would be willing to live and die.[20] Catholic schools are cited as being nationalistic

---

14 *Ibid.*
15 Brady, p. 89.
16 R. S. P. Elliot and John Hickie, *Ulster: A Case Study in Conflict Theory* (London: Longman Group Ltd., 1971), p. 35.
17 John D. A. Robb, p. 14.
18 Elliott and Hickie, p. 35.
19 Barritt and Carter, p. 47.
20 MacEoin, p. 46.

rather than ecumenical, emphasizing the Gaelic language, culture, history and Ireland's struggle against England. In Ulster today England's continued political and military presence is turned into classroom condemnation where there is a tendency " . . . to think the worst of the other side."[21] Protestantism has frequently been misconstrued to mean a quasi-Christianity and shallow materialism that threatens the true faith.[22] Catholic bias is further shaped by the belief that their inferior status resulted from Masonic conspiracies. The Irish sociologist Eamon McCann comments, "Catholic schools, including those in the north, have pumped children full of history and a history distorted so as to idealize the gun."[23]

Similarly public schools tend to emphasize an English version of Irish history, extolling English culture and occasionally alluding to papal conspiracies to justify their colonial policies. Simple conspiracy explanations for complex problems add to the siege mentality of both communities. The principal differences according to the Irish historian Owen Dudley Edwards is that the Protestants exercise a greater social influence than that of the Catholic minority.[24] Sectarian attitudes are further compounded by the denominational schools not rejecting inherited stereotypes of each side. The schools, as well as the churches, have been too slow in reaching out to their fellow citizens of whatever religion.[25]

Referring to Devlin's comments about her 'militantly Republican school', the Irish journalist Gary MacEoin makes the following statement:

> She suggests that not all Catholic schools were as extreme as hers, but many are. And today, extracurricularly, the students learn while still in grade school how to conduct hit-and-run attacks on British soldiers.[26]

21 Barritt and Carter, p. 155.
22 McCaffrey, p. 159.
23 Eamon McCann, *War In An Irish Town* (Middlesex, England: Penguin Books, Inc., 1974), p. 117.
24 Owen Dudley Edwards, *The Sins Of Our Fathers: Roots Of The Conflict in Northern Ireland* (Dublin: Gill and MacMillan, Ltd., 1970), p. 181.
25 Barrington, p. 68.
26 MacEoin, p. 46.

MacEoin also blames school segregation for perpetuating social division and raises the question concerning the value of parochial education in light of the fact that 69 percent of the Catholic population would prefer an integrated school system. MacEoin questions whether parochial schools prefer integrated schools. He doubts whether Catholic schools really have any socially redeeming value in Northern Ireland, where a religiously pluralistic spirit is so lacking. He further suggests that segregated education is advantageous to vested interests of both sides rather than to the whole community.[27] Even so, Catholic clergy continue to defend the parochial school system.[28]

At the college level the clergy's resistance to integration appears openly controversial because this position is in opposition to student's wishes. Christine Donaghy, Deputy President of the Union of Students in Ireland (USI), reports that students at their 1979 Congress voted unanimously in favor of integrated education. That Congress not only included the USI and the National Union of Students of the United Kingdom and Northern Ireland, but also unions from the Roman Catholic colleges of St. Joseph's and St. Mary's which sought integrated teacher education.[29]

Donaghy, who is also President of St. Mary's student union, reported that it was the administration that was vehemently opposed to integration and threatened students with negative references if they continued to seek integration:

> The threat of bad references has been used to scare students into silence on the issue where they disagree with the authorities. Fear has risen so much because of the heavy-handed action by the authorities that it has led to a loss of courage on the part of students so that they cannot make independent decisions.[30]

Donaghy further claims that St. Joseph College President Michael Dallatt composed a resolution opposing integration and instructed

---

27 *Ibid.,* p. 306.
28 Coogan, IRA, pp. 254 - 255.
29 Paul McGill, "R. C. Church 'No' To Education Integration," *Orange Standard* (July, 1980): 7.
30 *Ibid.*

a delegate to present it at the USI Congress.[31] Sister Cornelia, Principal of St. Mary's, denied the school had ever raised the threat of negative references, but admitted that the students were lectured to shortly after the USI Congress on the subject of integration and the dangers that might pose to their faith. The Church's position was described as " . . . absolutely against integrated education."[32]

Parochial school authorities refused to accept the resolutions of their own student representatives favoring integration. Threatened or not, it was likely that the strong opposition which students received from authority figures created a climate of intimidation and stifled open discussion considered vital to academic freedom.

Because the Catholic hierarchy remains unwilling to relinquish its control over parochial education, it must accept responsibility for delaying the social assimilation of Catholic youth. Ecclesiastical unwillingness to secularize the system precludes the development of a more liberal learning environment. Such recalcitrance is also exhibited by public school authorities who permit classroom teaching to re-enforce old bigotries and promote narrow cultural biases. Both systems are forums for indoctrination rather than vehicles promoting respect for Catholic and Protestant values.

Paisleyism

In Northern Ireland, "Protestant" and "Catholic" have been described as tribal terms, not Christian terms. Rather than connoting love and a sense of community, they have become scare words and taboo symbols that people dare not discuss with strangers. Because political leaders have perceived the taking of a middle ground as selling out to the enemy, the Protestant and Catholic populations have been manipulated against each other.[33]

Disturbing to Northern Ireland's Catholic is Rev. Ian Paisley, a Presbyterian cleric who, several years ago, was disowned by the

31 *Ibid.*
32 *Ibid.*
33 Hurwitz interview.

Elders of the Presbyterian Church. Thereafter, Paisley founded the Free Presbyterian Church outside the official body.[34]

Paisley is an outspoken Unionist and defender of the Protestant community. IRA terrorism has given Paisley and the Unionist party opportunities to speak convincingly and with a greater degree of authority concerning the aggressive and dangerous tactics of Irish Republicanism. Even though the IRA numbers are estimated to be less than one percent of the total population of the north, Unionist spokesmen have implied that the Catholic community *per se* is a carrier of Republican subversion, that IRA violence has the quiet consent of the clergy, and that Protestants would be the victims of every form of repression by the Catholic majority within a united Ireland.[35]

Catholic nationalists describe Paisley as having been the backbone of the troubles in 1968 - 1969, when the heavily Catholic civil rights movement for political reforms gained momentum in several Northern Ireland cities. Paisley used his gift of oratory to convince large numbers of Ulster's Protestants that their real enemies were the Papacy, the Communists and the Jews, all of which constitute a triangle of power against Christ's second coming. More specifically, Paisley says Ulster is confronting a monolithic Catholicism that threatens to subvert the sacred creed of Unionism to unite Ulster with the Republic.[36]

Many Protestants have called attention to the Catholic hierarchy's reluctance to openly confront the issue of terrorism. With reference to their own repeated condemnations of violence, an *Orange Standard* editorial asks:

> What comparable action has been shown by the Roman Catholic hierarchy in making representations to the Provisional IRA to cease their campaign of murder, plunder, bank raiding and destruction? Cardinal O'Fee is the bishop of an area which includes the by now notorious South Armagh 'bandit country' where the assassination rate resembles that of the worst ghettos of Chicago or New York.[37]

---

34 R. Scott Kennedy and Peter Klotz-Chamberlin, "Northern Ireland's Guerrillas of Peace," *Christian Century* 304 (August 31, 1977), p. 746.

35 Beeson, "Can Order Come?" pp. 720 - 724.

36 G. Bell, p. 42.

37 "In Civilian Raiment," *Orange Standard* (November, 1980), p. 4.

109

Shortly after becoming the new Catholic Primate of the Republic and Northern Ireland in 1978, Archbishop Tomas O'Fiaich (Gaelic spelling) infuriated Unionists by calling upon England to make a declaration of intent to withdraw from Northern Ireland. For this, Ian Paisley claimed the Roman Catholic Church is " . . . deeply involved in the IRA terrorist campaign," and that Catholic clergy are " . . . deep in active service with the IRA both with bullets and bombs."[38]

Protestants have called upon the Catholic Church to suspend and excommunicate two priests who were involved in terrorist activities, Fathers Vincent Forde and Bartholomew Burns. Thomas Passmore, the Orange Grand master of County Belfast Grand Lodge, strongly condemned such activity and the Roman Catholic hierarchy when he said, "It is remarkable that the Roman Church still excommunicates members of the Masonic Order, yet refuses to take similar action against members of the IRA."[39]

Tim Pat Coogan, noted authority on Irish Republicanism and editor of the Irish Press, could give no reason why the Catholic Church in Northern Ireland did not formally excommunicate Catholics who engaged in paramilitary activity.[40] On the other hand, in two recent declarations the Irish Church reiterated its long-standing condemnation of extremism as a violation of God's law, just as it did in 1916 and in ensuing conflicts. With reference to the killing of British and Unionists officials and members of the security forces, Cardinal O'Fiaich has said:

> Most of the murders have been claimed by the IRA. Let me therefore state in simple language, with all the authority at my command, that participation in the evil deeds of this or any other paramilitary organization, which indulges in murder, wounding, intimidation, kidnapping, destruction of property and other forms of violence is a mortal sin which will one day have to be accounted for before God in judgment . . . To cooperate in any way with such organization is sinful and if the cooperation is substantial

38 "Priests in IRA Service," *Ulster* (July 19, 1979), p. 3.
39 "Priests and Terrorism," *Orange Standard* (April, 1981), p. 1.
40 Coogan talk.

the sin is mortal . . . Revenge is prohibited by God's law and can only lead to a further spiral of hatred and murder.[41]

Roman Catholic Bishop Edward Daly of Derry has also condemned IRA activities in a pastoral letter which was read at all the masses in his diocese in November, 1981:

> No member of our Church can remain a member of our Church and at the same time, remain a member of any organization that decides of its own accord to perpetrate cold-blooded murder as a central part of its strategy, whatever the motive, whatever the ideal.[42]

Even with the Church's historic position on violence clearly stated the DUP leadership continues to say that the Roman Catholic hierarchy has not openly confronted the nationalists but instead encourages violence as a legitimate weapon for achieving its objectives of control and power.[43] The majority's fears concerning "Rome Rule" have been exploited whenever the Democratic Unionist Party (DUP) denounces efforts toward understanding. This is evident in its newspaper, *Protestant Telegraph,* which describes Anglican-Roman Catholic dialogue and ecumenical meetings as a capitulation to Rome and " . . . a malicious web of their conspiracy."[44]

Many loyalists accuse Roman Catholicism of having penetrated and gained some control over the communications systems. This includes national television, namely, the British Broadcasting Corporation (BBC) as well as newpapers and magazines, and holding key positions in trade unions, universities, the government and in the Protestant churches themselves.[45]

41 "Murder Is a Mortal Sin Say Irish Bishops," *London Tablet* (November, 1981): n.p.
42 *Ibid.*
43 "Roman Catholic Hypocrisy," *Protestant Telegraph* (October 3, 1981), p. 9.
44 William Beattie, "The Visit of the Pope to the U. K. in 1982 Must Be Resisted," *Protestant Telegraph* (May 2, 1981), p. 8.
45 "McKee Hits Trades Council," *Protestant Telegraph* (May 2, 1981), p. 11; "A Surfeit of R. C. Talk," *Orange Standard* (November, 1981), p. 5, 8; "31,278 Fermanagh and South Tyrone RCs Vote for the Murder of Protestants," *Protestant Telegraph* (September 5, 1981), pp. 1-2.

Protestants are prone to believe in the conspiracy theory professed by the DUP and to think of Republican extremism as linked to Catholic power and papal domination. The loyalist press says:

> . . . As far as the Church of Rome is concerned in this island, murder and violence are permissible in order to achieve their ends. The Jesuit motto sums up only too well the attitude of Rome as 'The end justifies the means.'[46]

The *Protestant Telegraph* has not provided evidence to support these charges. But in Northern Ireland if such charges are made forcefully and repeated often, they can be so convincing as to provoke popular emotions. Meanwhile, IRA-INLA extremism serves to provoke fear and animosity and to harden Protestant support for Paisley's anti-Catholic campaign.[47] The media is most often used to amplify the Catholic threat to Protestants. The following quotation from the *Protestant Telegraph,* published in April, 1962, was circulated to Orange lodges throughout Northern Ireland. Purporting to be the official oath of the *Sinn Fein,* it illustrates the kind of rhetoric used by Paisleyites to exploit popular suspicions and fears of the Catholic Church:

> These Protestant robbers and brutes, these unbelievers of our faith, will be driven like the swine they are to the sea by fire, the knife, or by poison cup until we of the Catholic Faith and avowed supporters of all Sinn Fein action and principles, clear these heretics from our land . . . At any cost we must work and seek, using any method of deception to gain our ends toward the destruction of all Protestants and the advancement of the priesthood and the Catholic Faith until the Pope is complete ruler of the whole world . . . we must strike at every opportunity, using all methods of causing ill-feeling within the Protestant ranks and in their business. The employment of any means will be blessed by His Holiness, the Pope.[48]

46 "Rome – The Dragon on Our Streets," *Protestant Telegraph* (August 8, 1981), p. 1.
47 Letter from Jim Watson to Donald Doumitt, March 17, 1981. (Watson is an Ulster Protestant who has worked for several years with victims of terrorism).
48 Coogan, IRA, pp. 261 - 262.

Acting on such propaganda, the Unionists countered with organized massive demonstrations and strikes, and intimidated workers to oppose the "Romeward trend" of Protestant Christianity in Ulster. Paisley's efforts were to discredit Ulster's Catholic nationalists, accusing them of disloyalty to the British Crown and openly defying law and order. So volatile was this effort that it prompted the former Ulster Prime Minister and Unionist Terence O'Neill to denounce Paisley as a neo-fascist, resorting to racism and sectarian hate propaganda.[49] As a propagandist, Paisley's techniques are reminiscent of Adolf Hitler's method of beginning his speeches on a low key, then gradually increasing in force and loudness to a climactic attack on his enemy. Paisley implies that the alleged international conspiracy alluded to earlier has been phenomenally successful in undermining the faith of Northern Ireland Protestants.[50] He uses the technique of the Big Lie when alluding to the "Papal Trojan Horse" conspiracy. Irish Historian O. D. Edwards has noted:

> His distinctive talent, which he shares with Hitler, lies in capturing the mental framework of his audience, and specifically in arousing anti-Catholic sentiments from the hitherto subconscious to the conscious mind.[51]

O'Neill's opposition to Paisley seems aimed at stifling his influence with the DUP rather than trying to satisfy the objections of the Catholic minority. The Unionists are in no way disposed to eliminate the practice of sectarian manipulation from their own arsenal of weaponry. As Edwards further explains:

> Captain Terence O'Neill opposed Paisleyism, not because he disliked its intolerance — it was much more that he disliked the vulgarity of its intolerance — because he himself had a thoroughly rational policy of weakening the economic power of Catholic-dominated areas.[52]

The "vulgarity of its intolerance" to which O'Neill referred has contributed to social polarization. But it has also strengthened

49 Richard Rose, *Governing Without Consensus: An Irish Perspective* (London: Faber and Faber Ltd., 1971), p. 100. (Hereafter cited as Rose — *Governing*).
50 Owen Dudley Edwards, p. 40.
51 *Ibid.*, p. 41.
52 *Ibid.*, p. 337.

Paisley's support from the Protestant working class as well as among large numbers of Unionist ultras in Northern Ireland where he continues to win elections. Paisley won a seat in the European Parliament (EEC) by a heavy margin in May, 1979. He is reputed to be the most influential clergyman in Ulster because he tells people what they wish to hear.[53] Paisley's thinking reflects that of the Protestant lower classes whence he came, a mentality which is " . . . burdened with sectarianism, violence and self-righteousness."[54]

Paisley's popularity receives impetus from the presence of a war mentality and fears engendered by IRA bombs and violence. Relatives and friends of every person who is killed fall in behind Paisley and the Unionists, convinced that " . . . That man speaks for us."[55] Paisley has been able to identify Unionism with Protestantism and united Ireland nationalism with Catholicism. He has reinforced clear-cut political divisions along religious lines. He perceives any signs of clerical ecumenism or British negotiations with the Republic as a threat and possible sell-out to the Catholic south.[56] The sociologist Robert Moore has commented, "The Protestants are, in Ian Paisley's words, 'engaged in a great battle of biblical Protestantism against popery.' "[57]

Whenever there are any high-level communications between the British Government and the Republic, Unionists in the north begin to suspect a possible compromise agreement that could lead to an "enforced settlement" in favor of a united Ireland.[58] Unionist politicians and loyalist newspapers condemned a Dublin meeting in April, 1980, between Northern Ireland's Secretary of State Humphrey Atkins and the Republic's Taoiseach (Prime Minister) Charles Haughey and cabinet ministers. Atkin's purpose was to present his analysis of the Ulster situation and to seek the Republic's

53   Beeson, "Impotence," p. 888.
54   G. Bell, p. 47.
55   Points interview.
56   Coogan, IRA, p. 216.
57   Robert Moore, "Race Relations in the Six Counties: Colonialism, Industrialism, and Stratification in Ireland," *Race* 14 (n.d., 1972), p. 36. (Moore is a Senior Lecturer in sociology at The University of Aberdeen).
58   "Blood, Sweat, Tears and Talk," *Orange Standard* (June, 1980), p. 4.

cooperation concerning security along the border.[59] It is common knowledge that the IRA crosses the border to hide in the Republic after attacking targets in the north.[60]

As Britain's security problems and financial burdens increase in Ulster, Protestants are more convinced that the Conservative Government is now more disposed to compromise loyalist interests in exchange for more cooperation in apprehending IRA terrorists. The Provisional *Sinn Fein* alludes to this in citing a British Government report released in September, 1980. The report states that Britain has lost £ 350 million in property damage and paid out an additional £46 million in claims. The *Sinn Fein* also reports:

> A large proportion of this total of £ 400 million damages has, of course, been caused by the IRA through its commercial bombing campaign, one aim of which is precisely, to raise the Brits' cost of occupation.[61]

When Ulster leaders meet with Dublin officials to discuss matters of border security, misleading signals are transmitted:

> The best help the government can give the security forces is to desist from behaving in a way which conveys to the IRA the message that a radical change in the status of Northern Ireland may be imminent.[62]

This situation is further intensified by those fearing a possible British pull-out. One official of the UDA stated in June, 1980:

> On the question of British withdrawal, we feel sure that 1985 (or before) will see the troops being removed from Ulster. I would like to be able to say that this will come about because people have forgotten their tribal differences, but that will hardly be the case.[63]

Paisley Unionists were particulary alarmed at meetings with the former Taoiseach Haughey because of his suspected secret contacts

59 "Ulster After a Year of Thatcher Rule," *Orange Standard* (June, 1980), p. 1.
60 "Fears For the Future in Border Areas: Provos Have Death List — DUP Claim," *Orange Standard* (May, 1980), p. 1; "Death on the Border," *Ulster* (November, 1980), p. 6. (Hereafter cited as, "Provos Have Death List").
61 "£ 400 Million Damage," *An Phoblacht/Republican News* (September 20, 1980), p. 3. (Hereafter cited as: "400 Million Damage").
62 "Ulster After a Year," *Orange Standard* (June, 1980), p. 1.
63 Letter from Sam Duddy to Donald Doumitt, June 21, 1980.

with the IRA and his dreams for a united Ireland. Haughey was believed to have been involved with the IRA and gunrunning while holding a cabinet post in the Republic. It seems that Haughey's alleged secret meeting with IRA Chief of Staff, Cathal Goulding, resulted in an agreement whereby the IRA would end its operations in the Republic in exchange for a free hand to carry on its war in Northern Ireland and to cross the southern border at will.[64]

Any communication with the Republic is cause for Unionists to believe that another subversion is at work. The covert side of Haughey's past activities also provides grounds for believing that the Republican leadership is supportive of IRA goals and activities. Such possible behavior increases loyalist fears of subversion by the Catholic minority: "When the Catholic community looks to the south for help, the Protestant ascendancy treats this as one more proof of their seeking to overthrow the constitution."[65]

Paisley's own declaration of faith is indicative of his relating Protestantism to political ideology:

> I am loyal to the Principles of the great Protestant Reformation and refuse to barter my heritage for a mess of ecumenical pottage. I am loyal to the Queen and throne of Britain, being Protestant in terms of the Revolution settlement. I am loyal to Ulster, the Ulster of our founding fathers.[66]

This is not original with Paisley but reflects the view long expressed by members of Northern Ireland's ascendancy elites such as James Craig (Lord Craigavon), former Prime Minister, and Sir Basil Brooks (Lord Brookeborough). The latter, when Minister of Agriculture, specifically stated:

> Many in this audience employ Catholics, but I have not one about my place. Catholics are out to destroy Ulster with all their might . . . I would appeal to Loyalists therefore, whenever possible, to employ good Protestant lads and lasses.[67]

---

64 Cameron, "Arms and the South," *Combat: Journal Of The Ulster Volunteers* 4 (December, 1980), p. 3.
65 Elliott and Hickie, p. 34.
66 Rose, Governing, p. 227.
67 Robert Moore, p. 28.

His compatriot Craig reinforced such an attitude publically: "I have always said I am an Orangeman first and a politician and a member of the parliament second . . . I recommend people not to employ Roman Catholics, 99 percent of whom are disloyal."[68]

Despite such statements of the 1930's, sectarian differences at that time were frequently ignored by the 30 percent unemployed, and Protestants from Shankill joined Catholics from Falls Road in protest. Frequently there was violence and bloodshed, but none of the sectarian enmity common to the current situation. Rather, one observed non-sectarian clashes between the working class and authorities over jobs and housing.[69] Thus, in one of the rare moments in Ulster's history, Protestants and Catholics crossed denominational lines. Such collaboration prompted Unionist politicians to "play the Orange Card." This phrase, coined by Lord Randolph Churchill in 1885, was a response to the fears of working class solidarity and its alleged threats to capitalism in Northern Ireland. Churchill used the Orange Order to inflame old religious fears and hatreds to undermine the labor movement. As Edwards explains:

> Above all, Belfast capitalism found it advantageous to exploit any working class divisions that might exist in the interest of weakening labour organization and increasing its leverage power to increase job competitiveness.[70]

Such manipulation of sectarian fears remains the principal *modus operandi* for separating Northern Ireland's Protestants from their Catholic neighbors.

Brian Faulkner, elected Prime Minister in 1971, consistently fought reforms. He discredited the Northern Ireland Civil Rights Association (NICRA) in 1968 by branding it as Communist and Catholic Republican as well as being a covert movement out to destroy the state of Ulster. Though large numbers of its members were Catholic and Republican, the organization contained some liberal Protestants in its rank and file and on its executive board. NICRA did not advocate a united Ireland as one of its goals.[71]

68 De Paor, p. 115.
69 O. D. Edwards, p. 123.
70 *Ibid.,* p. 132.
71 Feeney, p. 305.

Each time the NICRA demonstrated they were countered by organized loyalists whose pamphlet handouts charged the movement as spearheading illegitimate Catholic-Republican interests behind the facade of civil rights. The historian E. V. Feeney explains:

> The triumvirate of Craig, Faulkner and Paisley were instrumental in preventing the NICRA from attracting a mass Protestant following, a deliberate attempt to sectarianize what was intended to be a non-sectarian civil rights movement.[72]

The sociologist Robert Moore argues that such appeals are attempts to convince northern Protestants, particularly the working class, that they stand to gain more by maintaining their sectarian ties with the Unionists than by uniting with the Catholic workers.[73]

Ulster's Protestants have historically highly valued personal and political liberties for themselves. Since the sixteenth century, Scottish Presbyterians have been conscious of the class division between themselves and the Established Church of England. Because of their dissenting position vis-a-vis Anglicanism, Presbyterians were placed on a lower priority within the English landholding system. Their feelings of discrimination were evident from the early seventeenth century.[74]

There were alliances of Protestants and Catholics in common cause against economic and social discriminations. This was evidenced in the Presbyterian-Catholic uprisings in 1778. The alliances were tenuous because Catholics were not as influenced as were the Presbyterians by the concepts of liberty, equality and fraternity associated with the American and French Revolutions. As MacEoin explains:

> All the members of each faith had in common was the desire to end the hegemony of the Established Church and cut for themselves a part of the action. The emotional identification of Irish Catholics with "the land of the free" would not start for another 50 years, and they shared the pope's

72 *Ibid.*, p. 104.
73 *Ibid.*
74 De Paor, pp. 166 - 167.

118

horror of the French Revolution with its rejection of the divine and the distortion of human values. Presbyterians, for their part, did not share, indeed scarcely suspected, the Catholic dream of equal access to and influence in the new political institutions they would build together. They assumed a Protestant Parliament in which they would be the spokesmen and decision-makers for the Catholics as well as themselves.[75]

Today Northern Ireland's Protestant community becomes fearful when authorities whom they respect and trust portray the Catholic Church as an insidious power structure intent on destroying their freedoms. The Irish historian Liam De Paor quotes an official statement by the General Assembly of the Presbyterian Church in 1950 as further illustrating the kind of material which elicits deep suspicions in the minds of Protestants:

> One root of the Catholic-Protestant conflict, especially here where numbers are sometimes nearly equal is the fact that the Roman Catholic Church is a world-wide religious organization that seeks to gain control of the institutions of mankind and of public life generally; it is not merely a Church, it is a political organization.[76]

Similar Orange statements accuse Catholics of practising a double allegiance, one to the state of Ulster, the other to the papacy. Feeney cites the *Belfast Telegraph* on a July 12th commemoration of the Protestant victory of the Battle of the Boyne River. Specifically referring to the Catholic Church, it reads:

> As we all know, its members are bound to submit to another power under certain circumstances and they are, therefore, unable to fulfill the basic obligations which are required before the privilege of democracy can be enjoyed.[77]

This notion is held with deep conviction by most northern Protestants. It receives reinforcement from the Orange-loyalist press and Unionist Party. Well-disciplined parades and colorful marching bands have become traditional expressions of resistance to "monolithic Catholicism" and Republican nationalism.[78]

75 MacEoin, pp. 42 - 43.
76 De Paor, p. 126.
77 Feeney, p. 104.
78 *Ibid.*, p. 305.

119

The British political sociologist David A. Roberts explains Orange-men's contempt for Catholicism as resting on both theological and political grounds:

> Orangemen have felt that the key to understanding the majority of Roman Catholic political activity is disloyalty, since the devotees of an international Church can never be sincere citizens. Orangeism perceives the lack of civil and religious liberty associated with Roman Catholicism, and exemplified in countries with Roman Catholic political domination.[79]

Ulster's Protestant fundamentalists fear the "Catholic theocratic tyranny." They cite the situation of Catholic theologian Hans Kung as the kind of tyranny they could expect to suffer in a Catholic Republic and which they are determined to resist. The Orange press condemned the Vatican's disciplining of Kung in 1980. They see the loss of his title of "Catholic Theologian" because of his dissenting statement on papal infallability, the teaching authority of the bishops, transubstantiation, and the role of Mary in Catholic theology as a blow to intellectual freedom inside Roman Catholicism. Moreover, Protestants allude to a statement by Catholic thelogian Gabriel Daly as expressing a concern for the lack of freedom that is needed for a healthy exchange of ideas: "The tragedy of authoritarian intervention stifles professional criticism which can be so effective in correcting errors and promoting truth."[80]

The Protestant media ignore the fact the Roman Catholic Church expects its members to believe the articles of faith yet respect the rights and beliefs of those outside the faith. The Church has insisted that Catholics follow its teachings on faith and morals. Moreover, modern Popes have maintained that political freedom and economic justice are moral imperatives for the avoidance of social conflict. That is, social peace can only be achieved within

---

79 David A. Roberts, "The Orange Order in Ireland: A Religious Institution?" *British Journal Of Sociology* 22 (September, 1971), p. 275.
80 "Roman Catholic Dissent and the Dangers," *Orange Standard* (April, 1980), p. 7; Michael Novak, "Behind the Kung Case," *New York Times Magazine*, (March 23, 1980), p. 34.

the context of freedom and justice.[81] On the issue concerning "Politics and the Church," Vatican II has emphasized the importance in pluralistic societies of maintaining a clear distinction between the role of the Church and that of the State, describing this relationship as "mutually independent and self-governing." Admittedly, the Irish Catholic Church has not adhered to the reforms of Vatican II, regardless of statements to the contrary by Catholic spokesmen. (See Chapter V on Protestant, Catholic, and political unity). Catholicism's role is independent from and must in no way be confused with the political community, nor bound to any political system. However, it does insist that:

> She (the Church) also has the right to pass moral judgements, even on matters touching the political order, whenever basic personal rights or the salvation of souls make such judgements necessary.[82]

Such claims to moral authority in political and personal matters are seen by Protestants as dangerous to individual freedom. This attitude is further compounded by the Protestant view that Catholicism's perception of Church-State relations is strictly medieval. Ignoring the need for understanding in a pluralistic society, the loyalist press strives to preserve sectarian barriers. Therefore, it too must share responsibility for preserving Ulster as a society where one's being a Catholic or Protestant means separation and war with one another. Thus, Ulster's citizens remain victims of a volatile situation over which they have no control. As MacEoin explains:

> Each lives by a set of claims and myths which make his position reasonable for him, that of the other absurd and obscene. Social institutions also serve to protect both individual and community from exposure to and contamination by the other myths . . . Northern Ireland is where friends and enemies are identified by religious affiliation.[83]

81 Edward Reed, Ed., *Pacem in Terris/Peace on Earth. Proceedings of an International Convocation on the Requirements of Peace*, sponsored by the Center for Democratic Institutions. (New York: Pocket Books, Inc., 1965).
82 Official texts promulgated by the Ecumenical Council, *Documents of Vatican II: 1963 - 1965* (New York: The Guild Press, 1966), p. 288.
83 MacEoin, p. 361.

Sectarian policies are, therefore, viewed as a means to save Ulster from Catholic subversion toward a united Ireland and allow Unionist leaders like Ian Paisley to convince his constituents they are defending from popery the last citadel of Protestantism.[84]

Such attitudes have scarred the people of Northern Ireland. Those scars could have been avoided if both religious establishments had worked on resolving or accommodating long-standing differences relative to political reform and unification. As Devlin explains:

> In the north the churches, Catholic and Protestant, should have been campaigning for the dignity of the people years and years ago. They never did. They should have been making some effort to break down religious sectarianism in the country. They did nothing. Very few sermons have I heard preached on tolerance of people who have different views from you.[85]

Some militants are realizing that the political leadership has used its power to employ the working class as a buffer to defend its present position against any possible reform such as power sharing. The Provisional IRA (Provisionals or "Provos") blames the ruling ascendancy class for deliberately using sectarianism to keep the Catholic and Protestant workers divided and weak. It also claims the workers of Northern Ireland are influenced by deliberate engineering by this one class whose allegiance is to the Unionist Party. The result of a weak labor movement is that the Northern Ireland's business sector pays lower wages than can be earned in England:[86]

> The over 100,000 Catholics in West Belfast are the most seriously deprived minority group in Western Europe. This minority suffers from an unemployment rate of between 40 and 50 percent, according to British Government figures, which is twice to three times higher than Protestant areas. The overall unemployment rate in the six counties is 13 percent, while wages in Northern Ireland are 80 percent that of Western Europe.[87]

84 Robert Moore, p. 36.
85 Devlin, p. 72.
86 McAuley interview.
87 *Ibid.*

The IRA has noted the social commonality it shares with the rank and file of the Protestant paramilitaries. One IRA objective is then to achieve a state of Ulster, in which " . . . Catholics and Protestants will share political power and work together in a nine-county system within a 32 county Ireland".[88]

Protestant paramilitaries share the same concerns about working class membership, noting that Protestant-Catholic extemists " . . . have been influenced by the *Fianna Fáil* (Republican Party) in the south and the Unionist Party in the north. According to a Protestant source, both have a vested interest in a divided people"[89] but this is denied by the *Fianna Fáil*.

The Provisional's counterpart, the UDA, also believes they are victims of social engineering. Their spokesman Glenn Barr, Chairman of the UDA's New Ulster Political Research Group and independence advocate, has blamed Ulster's strikes and turmoil in 1974 on Unionist politicians. "It was clear to us that with the UWC strike we were being used by politicians for their own narrow sectarian end."[90]

The UDA periodical *Ulster* outlines the problem as one of manipulation of the poor by the wealthy by means of sectarianizing:

> They sowed the seeds by shepherding us from childhood into Orange and Green ghettos . . . We have realized that we the ordinary people, if we come together instead of continuing to be apart as the Mick and Prod factions, we can overcome even these differences in doctrine and get a change where change really matters. Sectarianism can be beaten. It had nearly beaten us - - it had nearly put its death grip upon us, upon our very survival. The big money, big time brainwashers kept us apart, blinding us with their propaganda which they told us was indeed the truth. Now we know the real truth. We know that our fellow sufferers cannot really be our enemies, nor can we be theirs. We know that the men of wealth who kept us in our ghettos and put the wall of fear between us, must be, and is, our natural, true and only enemy.[91]

88 *Ibid.*
89 "The Failure of the Provisional IRA," *Ulster* (April, 1979), p. 1.
90 "UDA Plans for Ulster Independence," *Ulster* (April, 1979), p. 2.
91 "Sectarianism: The Enemy Within the Gates," *Ulster* (April, 1979), p. 3.

How widespread this attitude is among Protestants is impossible to measure. But to have appeared in the *Ulster* is important, as that is the major organ of the UDA, the largest paramilitary group. Its editor notes, however, that articles submitted for publication may or may not reflect the views held by the Ulster Defense Associaton.[92]

As with the Provisionals, the UDA does not favor the British connection, as do the Orange Order and other loyalist groups. In 1979, a UDA spokesman expressed a strong mistrust and negative attitude toward the British presence and intentions in Northern Ireland:

> The UDA is now telling both Britain and the Republic, hands off Ulster! We feel that if Britain had her way she would turn Ulster over to the Republic. Britain wants out with some honor. She hopes that a majority of the Northern Irish people will vote for a united Ireland. That would solve her problem. On the other hand, a million Protestants will resist union with the Republic. We are growing more disillusioned toward both the British Labour Party and Conservative Governments because neither have shown the will to root out the Provisional IRA.[93]

Summary. This chapter on "Power Politics and Divisiveness in Northern Ireland" alludes to theories which apply to the Ulster problem. Politicians and media disseminate sectarian prejudice to defend or attack the *status quo.* They are viewed as propagandists who capitalize on loyalist-Republican fears. Because they remain vulnerable to manipulators, Northern Ireland's Protestants and Catholics remain divided, weak and unable to effectively challenge the power structure.

At this writing (1982), there has been no strong surge among the working class on either side toward more communication with one another on non-sectarian grounds. Few have risen above sectarian barriers to risk a viable unity under a secular, pluralistic banner. Nothing yet has created any lasting momentum to lift Northern Ireland's siege mentality. Nevertheless, there is a discernible awareness among some militants on both sides that they have been used.

---

92 *Ibid.*, p. 2.
93 Duddy interview.

Even Protestant and Catholic paramilitaries indicate that they are disposed to respect the common ground which they see in each other. They both come from the ranks of the working class and from poverty, but are fundamentally divided on the issue of a united Ireland.

Divisiveness inherent in Ulster's politics leads to bloody conflict. Chapter VIII examines several societal differences and analyzes Northern Ireland's violence as an acculturated condition.

Rubber Bullets Turn Back Parade

Dungiven, Northern Ireland — British soldiers aim rubber-bullet guns at an advancing parade of militant Protestants in the Catholic village of Dungiven, near Londonderry, Northern Ireland. Troops also used tear gas to disrupt the parade by members of the Orange Order, who were defying a government ban. Four persons, including a clergyman, were arrested after violence erupted between the marchers and the police and soldiers. *(Religious News Service Photo)*

Unrest in Northern Ireland

Belfast, Northern Ireland — Club-wielding policemen beating a civil rights demonstrator (right) exemplify the continuing and growing unrest in Northern Ireland as Catholics continue to agitate for voting reforms which will give them a more representative voice in local elections. Key men in the controversy are the Rev. Ian Paisley, head of the small but highly active and vocal Free Presbyterian Church of Ireland. Mr. Paisley, presently in prison, is violently anti-Catholic and has accused the present government of Northern Ireland of discriminating against Protestants. Northern Ireland's Prime Minister, Capt. Terence O'Neill, (lower left) placed his political career at stake in an effort to secure a "one man — one vote" reform.   *(Religious News Service Photo)*

Ulster Protestants March

Belfast — As police stand alongside the parade route, Northern Ireland Protestants march in the annual parade of the fraternal Orange Order in Belfast. The parade commemorates a Protestant victory in the Battle of Boyne in 1690. The Orange Order takes its name from the victor, King William III, formerly William of Orange, who defeated the Catholic forces of the deposed James II.

Eleven thousand British troops stood guard throughout Ulster as over 75,000 marched in 19 different parades. While the parades themselves were uneventful, violence broke out in a Roman Catholic neighborhood and a British soldier was killed by a sniper. *(Religious News Service Photo)*

CHAPTER VIII

Sociology of Violence

Before attempting to analyze the polarities in Northern Ireland, the concept of violence itself needs to be examined. Violent conflict is not rational behavior for dealing with social problems. Sociologist Judson Landis analyzes it as particularly evident in societies that place a high value on individualism and competition.[1] Differences engendered by such attitudes give rise to group conflicts in the social and economic sectors as between management and labor, ingroups and outgroups, the majority and the minority. Landis' study also shows that competition frequently leads to social and economic inequality which, when reflected in people, results in some being consciously viewed as superior and some as inferior. This allows for discrimination on all levels.[2] He defines prejudice as:

> . . . an unfavorable attitude toward a person or thing prior to or not based on actual experience. A prejudiced person ignores the individual and his particular qualities or characteristics, and groups the person with others who happen to have the same type of skin color or speak with the same accent or have the same type of name or come from the same part of the country.[3]

This concept is further clarified as " . . . the actual behavior un-favorable to a specific individual in-group. When people desire equality of treatment and are denied it, they are being discriminated against."[4]

Prejudice leads to discrimination which may be based on economic differences, social position, ethnic background, religion and other factors. Long-standing discrimination engenders a sense of inferiority

---

1 Judson R. Landis, *Sociology: Concepts and Characteristics* (California State University, Belmont: Wadsworth Publishing Co., 1977), p. 421. (Unless otherwise noted, all individuals quoted in this chapter are research specialists on societal conflict and the social ramifications of violence).
2 *Ibid.*
3 *Ibid.,* p. 178.
4 *Ibid.*

causing some to identify with the dominant group and adopt its prejudices towards themselves. In time the oppressed minority becomes willing to adopt the mentality of the oppressor as a form of self-hatred.[5] As described by Herbert Gans:

> Inequality gives rise to feelings of inferiority and self-hate, or anger. Feelings of inadequacy or self-hate, more than poverty, account for the high rates of pathology — anger results in crime, delinquency, senseless violence and, of course, political protest as well.[6]

Sociologist Jan Hajda observed in his study of social alienation in America that a sense of powerlessness and meaningless is expressed by discriminated minorities. These feelings stem from the " . . . relative inability to influence or control one's social destiny and an accompanying feeling that this powerlessness is wrong and unjust.[7]

Lewis Coser contends that hostility is difficult to control in a closed and unequal environment. When the objectives of rebellion are blunted, the hostility and frustrations continue and are frequently aimed at substitute objects.[8]

David Rapoport, a political scientist, has observed that when urban guerrillas inflict atrocities on one another and innocent parties, a war-zone environment is produced. Non-combatants who endure it become less disposed to accept compromise. Instead they become eager to support one side and prolong if not expand the conflict.[9] Citing the Algerian war as an example, he writes:

---

5 *Ibid.*
6 Herbert Gans, "The New Egalitarianism," *Saturday Review* (May 6, 1972), pp. 43-46.
7 Jan Hajda and Robert Travis, "Causes and Consequences of Powerlessness." Paper presented in a sociology seminar at Portland State University, Portland, Oregon, October, 1978. (Mimeographed).
8 Lewis Coser, *The Function of Social Conflict* (New York: The Free Press, 1956), p. 33. (Author is a conflict sociologist).
9 David Rapoport, "Politics of Atrocity," in *Terrorism: Inter-Disciplinary Perspectives,* Ed. Yonah Alexander and S. M. Finger (New York: John Jay Press, 1977), p. 54. (Rapoport is a Professor of Political Science at the University of California at Los Angeles. Hereafter cited as: Rapoport, "Politics of Atrocity," in Terrorism).

A similar National Liberation Front terror (FLN) produced 'Arab Hunts' when French colonials killed every Moslem they saw and thereby unintentionally strengthened support for the terrorists.[10]

Sociologists Lee Sigelman and Miles Simpson see that a linear relationship exists between economic inequality and violence. The level of the violence is often in proportion to the level of economic inequality.[11] This relationship is amplified by Pitirim Sorokin's discussion of hunger. Referring to conditions in Russia after World War I, this former member of Prime Minister Kerensky's Provisional Government emphasized the scarcity of food, energy, jobs and housing as creating the conditions for violent insurrections. As scarcity and hunger are forms of violence, the victims resort to extreme acts to strike back at their oppressors:

> Hunger, or the threat of it, gives rise to war when there are no other means of satisfying it, and war, in turn, gives rise to more hunger. These twins almost always are inseparable and they travel together all over the world.[12]

Michael Parenti, an American political scientist, accuses modern capitalism of being responsible for the unequal distribution of social needs that are determined by the unequal resources of power. In this way, the inequities of capitalism contribute to the conditions of powerlessness and want which reinforce each other. "Those most in need are most likely to have their claims neglected or suppressed."[13]

10 *Ibid.,* p. 50.
11 Lee Sigelman and Miles Simpson. "A Cross-National Test of the Linkage Between Inequality and Political Violence," *Journal of Conflict Resolution: Research on Peace and War Between and Within Nations* 21 (March, 1977), p. 106.
12 Pitirim A. Sorokin, *Hunger As A Factor In Human Affairs* (Gainsville, Florida: University of Florida, 1975), p. 201. (Author, a conflict sociologist, was former Cabinet Member of Prime Minister Kerensky's Provisional Government in Russia prior to the Bolshevik takeover in 1918. Sorokin founded and headed the Department of Sociology at Harvard University in 1930 until his retirement).
13 Michael Parenti, *Power and the Powerless* (New York: St. Martin's Press, 1978), p. 75.

Meanwhile the ingroup sees any social antagonism as an attack on their wealth. Parenti explains:

> If it is assumed that there is not enough to go around, then one tries to keep a tight hold on what there is. In the minds of the haves, the equalization of life conditions means not only the end of the enjoyment of class privileges but a loss of the good things, the special things, that make life worth living. The owning class is committed, with all its ferocity of self-interest, to the principle of socio-economic inequality. This commitment is not merely a matter of greed or malice but a manifestation of a class defending its privileges, that is, a class defending its life.[14]

Gans cites the United States as an example of serious inequality creating the tensions that lead to violence. He describes social violence as a way in which one group gets even with the system that keeps them economically deprived. Violence becomes a primitive kind of income distribution allowing the community to be aware of economic disparities between the rich and the poor.[15]

Conflict sociologist Robert Lauer refers to a society whose political structure allows the economically strong to exploit others as a "sick society." He sees institutionalized injustices as a result of modern industrial capitalism creating the conditions of poverty and alienation. This aggravates societal differences by concentrating wealth in the hands of a few.[16] Other observers, e.g., sociologist Bruce Brown, explain economic inequality as stimulating more than just social tensions. It also creates a psychological aggression which victims of oppression internalize. Therefore, such an individual is inclined to react neurotically or psychotically towards people or institutions which he feels are the cause of his condition.[17] In some way that individual participates in " . . . the violence of a

---

14 *Ibid.,* p. 92
15 Gans, pp. 43 - 46.
16 Robert H. Lauer, *Perspectives on Social Change* (Boston: Allyn and Bacon, Inc., 1973), p. 58.
17 Bruce Brown, *Marx, Freud, and the Critique of Everyday Life: Toward a Permanent Cultural Revolution* (New York: Monthly Review Press, 1973), p. 84.

world estranged by the evolution of an all-consuming capitalism," which magnifies societal differences.[18]

Open conflict between the haves and have-nots becomes likely whenever the less privileged become aware they are victims of exploitation or are denied basic rights to which they feel entitled.[19]

Whenever the have-nots are struggling with war or unemployment, they are inclined to overreact to their sense of powerlessness by lashing out in " . . . irrational, destructive and authoritarian ways. Ironically, they are also responding to the irrationality of the social order."[20] Such behavior naturally follows from the individual's feeling of being powerless and alone and " . . . threatened by gigantic forces."[21] The Orange writer, Derek McMeekin graphically describes:

> Here the furnace of pain and sorrow is at its height, and the forgotten heroes are the weeping widows and crying children whose homes have been plunged into needless sorrow and whose dreams have been shattered.[22]

Loyalties Versus Social Order

Prejudice and discrimination weaken Northern Ireland's social cohesion and reinforce the concept of " . . . the end justifies the means." Survival at any cost is a priority that permits acceptance of violent retaliation. Such attitudes are "revengeful violence of self-preservation" in which alienation and anxiety become the promoters for mass behavior and collective action.[23]

Social anger over transportation costs is a case in point:

18 John D. A. Robb, *New Ireland: Sell Out Or Opportunity?* (Dublin? s.n., 1972), p. 8. (Author is a widely traveled Ulster Presbyterian. He became a Fellow of the Royal College of Surgeons in 1961).
19 Coser, p. 33.
20 Bruce Brown, p. 119.
21 Erich Fromm, *Escape From Freedom* (New York: Farra and Rinehard, Inc., 1941), pp. 32, 144.
22 Derek G. McMeekin, "In God's Name Call Off This Fast," *Orange Standard* (May, 1981), p. 7.
23 Robb, p. 8.

In Belfast, people on the Falls Road became so fed up with the high cost of bus fares from their area to city center, they burned up one bus and proceeded to create their own cheaper transportation system. They collected a fleet of black taxis and today one can observe the Peoples' Taxis moving back and forth from the ghetto to the city center. They are well-used, very accessible, and cheap.[24]

There are other forms of violence of which Northern Ireland also is a victim. As mentioned earlier, the scarcity of jobs and housing encourages politicians and owners of businesses to practice discrimination in employment and in the allocation of housing wherever they can. Moreover, discrimination itself is a form of violence because it deprives one group while favoring another group.[25]

Anger over pervasive unemployment and related poverty creates a momentum leading to a violent behavior that is *sui generis.* This is most apparent in the rural and urban ghettos where unemployment is the norm. A case-in-point is the Bally-Murphy section of Belfast where joblessness is said to reach 73 percent.[26] In other areas of West Belfast such as Falls Road - Shankill Road and Markets areas, which have borne the brunt of the violence, one finds housing without sanitary plumbing, segregated schools based on sectarian differences, and an overall unemployment rate of 41 percent.[27]

In stark contrast to those regions, the South Belfast area is a relatively affluent suburb with beautiful homes in a tranquil setting. The inhabitants are predominantly from the Protestant ascendancy business class.[28]

---

24 Interview with William Graham, Belfast Telegraph, Belfast, May 12, 1979. (Graham is on the Political Staff of the Belfast Telegraph. Hereafter cited as: Graham Interview).
25 Interview with Cecil Hurwitz, Cork Peace Council, Cork, April 26, 1979. (Hurwitz is a member of a peace group which calls itself "Prayer, Enterprise and Christian Effort." He is a principal organizer of National Peace Week in Ireland. Hereafter cited as: Hurwitz Interview).
26 Tim Pat Coogan, "Troubles in Northern Ireland," A talk given to the Irish National Caucus, Portland, Oregon, March 23, 1981. (Coogan is Editor-in-Chief of the Irish Press. Hereafter cited as: Coogan Talk).
27 Graham Interview.
28 *Ibid.*

Violence in Belfast

Belfast, Northern Ireland – Masked youth holds brick aloft in front of a stolen truck which was set on fire 5/4 in the Unity Flats district of West Belfast, a predominantly Catholic area. Tensions in the city continued to rise as it was reported that Maze Prison hunger striker Bobby Sands was in a coma in the 65th day of his fast.   *(UPI gk/Gary Kemper)*

Bullet-Riddled Window

Belfast, Northern Ireland — Mrs. Anne-Marie Young, of Belfast's Meyard Park district, comforts her 18-month-old daughter, *Anne-Marie*, as she stands before the bullet-riddled window of her home August 10. The Young home was one of many hit by small weapons fire as British troops battled snipers in the violence-torn capital of Northern Ireland.
(UPI cablephoto)

In Memory: Crosses for the dead in Belfast.

(NC Photo, 2/4/72)

Security Sign

SUPPORT LAW & ORDER

THE SECURITY FORCES REGRET THE
INCONVENIENCE CAUSED BY THESE BARRIERS

UNFORTUNATELY THEY ARE ESSENTIAL
FOR PUBLIC SAFETY AND TO ASSIST
IN THE DEFEAT OF TERRORISM

Security Sign

Battle in the Streets

Belfast — British paratroopers return sniper fire during a gun battle with members of the Irish Republican Army in the streets of Belfast. Two IRA gunmen were killed in the battle, which was fought from noon to dusk about a half-mile from the center of town. *(Religious News Service Photo)*

Show of Strength

Carrying the Union Jack, masked Ulster loyalists march through the streets of Enniskillen, Northern Ireland. Ulster Unionist leaders have threatened to make Northern Ireland ungovernable unless Britain cracks down on terrorism. In Maguiresbridge, Northern Ireland, (below) the widow of a slain Ulster Defense Regiment member, Albert Beacon, weeps at her husband's funeral as a relative tries to comfort her. The Provisional Irish Republican Army claimed responsibility for the murder as well as the recent killing of three other UDR members.

(NC Photos from Wide World and UPI)

England Takes Over

Belfast — A British paratrooper stands guard at Stormont Castle as more than 50,000 Protestants gather outside the site of Northern Ireland's parliament to protest the British government's take-over of the autonomous province. The parliament went into suspension March 28 for a one-year period and London began direct rule of troubled Ulster. *(Religious News Service Photo)*

As has been noted, the presence of serious social inequality is important to the study of violence. Persons perennially unemployed seek radical solutions and, in turn, become victims of a violence which feeds on itself.[29] Yet, open political explosions from either side are counterproductive. Protestant extremism cannot force Catholics to remain quiet; nor can the IRA bomb a million Protestants into a united Ireland.[30] While this may seem obvious to many, it is apparently not clear to the IRA, the UDA, the Unionists, and to many Republicans in the north and south. Each group views force as a legitimate option to achieve its ends.

Catholic extremists argue that the government's only purpose for initiating reforms in response to class tensions is to separate revolutionaries from moderates " . . . to silence middle class nationalists on socio-economic issues."[31] When this fails, the struggle becomes more open and bloody, permitting the government to adopt a more conservative law and order stance, and its position toward the opposition becomes intractable.

Meanwhile, Republican nationalists condemn the British for defending an unjust *status quo*. They point to Britain's use of the media to publicize IRA killings and bombings. In so doing, the government is accused of heaping discredit upon the Republican movement by its blatant disregard for everything civilized. The media is said to constantly associate Republicanism with cruelty and with a radical communist ideology that is supported by Marxist liberation fronts in Europe and elsewhere.[32] The Provisional *Sinn Fein* further asserts that British authorities try to develop the concept that "IRA revolutionaries are really communists . . .", thereby " . . . separating the Provisionals from the Catholic people and isolating it."[33]

29 Coogan Talk.
30 Hurwitz Interview.
31 Richard McAuley, "Insight Into Imperialism," *An Phoblacht/Republican News* (September 13, 1980), p. 10. (Hereafter cited as: McAuley, "Imperialism").
32 *Ibid.*
33 *Ibid.*

142

The Provisional wing of the IRA is Republican-socialist as distinct from the "Officials", who are Marxist. Richard McAuley, press officer for the Provisionals, has asserted:

> The Provisionals are more closely associated with European socialism and are strongly influenced by the political philosophy of James Connolly, a labour movement organizer prior to the 1916 Rising. The British Government does not recognize the political nature of the IRA and they say Republicanism is a criminal conspiracy made up of psychopaths and opportunistic criminals.[34]

Terrorism

Whatever the positions of the IRA and the government, the situation has created an atmosphere of terror. It is this phenomenon that governs the habits of everyday life and has given rise to paramilitary organizations.

Paramilitarism clearly violates the civil liberties of a society at large by inflicting harm to persons and property while ignoring the due process of law.[35] It is more than a political weapon. In Ulster it is another way of conducting the business of politics.[36]

In 1976 the Irish political scientist Richard Rose, reporting on the results of terrorism, said:

> Since August, 1969, more than 1500 persons have died in political disturbances in Northern Ireland, the equivalent in population terms of 52, 000 deaths from political violence in Great Britain or 207, 000 deaths in America.[37]

Since this report, casualties have increased to 2, 000 (1980) and are continuing to rise. Table 13 shows the increase in deaths resulting.

34 McAuley Interview.
35 Irving Louis Horowitz, "Transnational Terrorism, Civil Liberties, and Social Science," in *Terrorism,* p. 285. (The author is a Professor of Sociology and Political Science at Rutgers University.)
36 Bowden, *IRA,* p. 425.
37 Richard Rose, "On Priorities," p. 260.

TABLE 13

Number of Shooting Incidents in Northern Ireland, 1970 - 1976 (Raw Data)

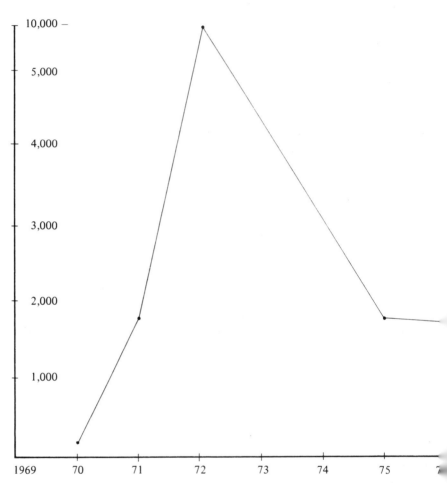

Source: P. Crowther, Central Statistical Office, Northern Ireland Office, London.

[a] Estimated from first three months of 1976.

144

from terrorism between 1969 and 1976.[38] The number of casualties in no way approaches those of the Vietnam or the Lebanon conflicts, but Northern Ireland contains the potential for escalation into a holocaust involving large-scale human suffering. Like the Middle East and South East Asia, Ulster's conflict appears to be incomprehensible, 'irrational and pointless to casual observers. With specific reference to Vietnam, Senator Edward Kennedy in 1971 called upon the British Government to recognize the similarity, to withdraw its forces and to dissolve Britain's colonial-type Direct Rule.[39]

Table 14 shows a marked deterioration in the social order by 1972, with Britain substantially increasing its military presence. At the time, security forces and Protestant-owned businesses had become particularly vulnerable to a wave of IRA bombings. Protestant paramilitaries such as the Ulster Defense Association (UDA) and the Ulster Volunteer Force (UVF) retaliated with indiscriminate sectarian murders. As Rapoport explains, "IRA random bombings stimulated Protestant 'Paddy-bopping' reprisals, the local term for random assassinations of Roman Catholics."[40] By September of that year a total of 343 Protestants and Catholics were killed by the violence, including 81 Catholics and 40 Protestants by direct assassination.[41]

The Catholic writer Michael McKeown's study of violence presents the following statistics. Two out of every ten were security forces killed by the IRA bombing or assassination. Four of the ten were people who happened to be in the immediate vicinity of explosions and in the path of rifle fire, or " . . . were killed for being Catholic or Protestant," and for being a member of the enemy faith.[42]

38 Downey, p. 55.
39 Edward Kennedy, "Senator Kennedy Calls for Talks by All Parties to Promote Unification of Ireland," *The Times of London* (October 21, 1971), p. 4.
40 Rapoport, "Atrocity," in *Terrorism*, p. 50.
41 J. Bowyer Bell, *The Secret Army: The IRA, 1916 - 1974* (Cambridge, Mass: The M. I. T. Press, 1974), pp. 394, 398. (Hereafter cited as: J. Bowyer Bell, *Secret Army*).
42 Michael McKeown, "The Christian Conscience," *Furrow*, (September, 1973), p. 588. (Article is based on a report of *Pro Mundi Vita*, an international research and information center to all decision makers in the Catholic Church around the world).

TABLE 14

Total Deaths in Northern Ireland Resulting from Terrorism, 1969 - 1976, (Raw Data)

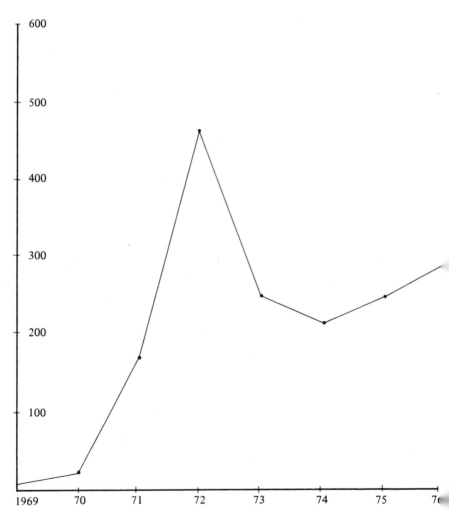

Source: Fortnight 125 (April 23):9.

146

Sectarian deaths and casualties are disproportionately higher than those suffered by the security forces. Murders of Protestants and Catholics between January, 1969, and March, 1975, totaled 857 civilians. Casualties include members of the British Army, the Royal Ulster Constabulary (RUC) and the Ulster Defense Regiment (UDR). Civilian injuries during the same period amounted to 9, 477.[43] These figures represent a significant loss for a tiny country with a population of only one-and-a-half million. The extent of violent activity for the period was 4, 456 explosions, 978 attacks on police stations and 83 tarrings and featherings.[44]

In addition to the human loss, Britain expends approximately £ 2 billion annually on internal forces.[45] The Republic spends £ 100 million in cooperating with Britain on border security.[46]

Because Ulster's Protestants and Catholics remain diametrically opposed in their political objectives, extremists view compromise as a betrayal of their ideological positions. Catholic nationalists do not hesitate to use extremism for achieving their goals. The IRA is inspired by the spirit of romantic nationalism of the Irish writers whose influence inspired the events of 1916.[47] The IRA is inflexible in its goal to achieve a new, socialist, united and free Ireland.[48]

The Provisional *Sinn Fein* is the legal spokesman of the outlawed Provisional IRA (PIRA). This group, also known as the Provos, describes the struggle as one not directed against people because of their Protestant affiliation. It is not a war against Protestantism in Ulster. Its struggle is against British rule as symbolized in the security forces and the British Army in which some Catholics also serve. The PIRA is said to be very Catholic, but " . . . there are some Protestants in its ranks who feel strongly about structural inequities."[49]

43 Utley, p. 152.
44 *Ibid.*
45 Coogan Talk.
46 *Ibid.*
47 "Connolly's Words and the Morality of the Freedom Fight," *An Phoblacht/ Republican News* (May 12, 1979), p. 5.
48 "Struggle on All Fronts," *An Phoblacht/Republican News* (May 12, 1979), p. 5.
49 McAuley Interview.

The Provos see the struggle as an extension of the early IRA leader's goal of political unity and autonomy of the island's 32 counties. Nationalists are motivated by the 1916 phase of their revolutionary history that recalls a long list of martyrs such as James Connolly, Padraic Pearse, Joseph Plunkett, Thomas MacDonagh, John MacBride, Sean MacDiarmada, and others who died leading the Easter Rebellion.[50] The IRA claims roots with the early Republican martyrs. Inside the Provisional *Sinn Fein* Headquarters in Belfast hangs a plaque containing photographs of the leaders of the Easter Revolt. Above it is a statement which says, "They called these men terrorists."[51] This is viewed as a contradiction by today's IRA who are hunted as criminals. The terrorists of 1916 are today regarded in the Republic as national heroes ". . . Fathers of Eire" and the " . . . noblest of Ireland and of the world."[52]

The Provos see extremism as their only realistic hope of winning objectives. In an interview in 1979 a spokesman explained:

> Violence is bad, but it becomes necessary when faced with an oppressive state which kills. Northern Ireland is a state which is totally oppressive. So, violence has become the only effective method of change where no other method has worked. How else do you fight oppression and deprivation where this has been so deeply rooted?[53]

As a result, PIRA uses harassment and murder against the British Army and the RUC. The government, therefore, faces a protracted struggle as conventional forces appear ineffective in coping with the unconventional Provos who can strike whenever and wherever they choose. British security forces are caught in the precarious and demoralizing position of not knowing when or where the next blow will fall, as every week the death toll rises. Paramilitary activities affect the farmers living close to the border of the Republic because of the IRA intimidation. Loyalists claim nationalist strategy is to pressure Protestant farmers to abandon their businesses and farms.

50 MacManus, pp. 704 - 705.
51 Personal Observation.
52 MacManus, pp. 704 - 705.
53 McAuley Interview.

Fear is so pervasive among Protestant farmers in County Fermanagh that wives also defend the homestead with weapons. Fear and intimidation are heightened by the belief that PIRA has a death list of key personalities living along the border who are marked for extermination.[54]

The strength of the IRA was outlined by the disclosure of a British Ministry of Defense Secret Report, "Copy No. 37", leaked to and published by Ulster's leading newspaper the *Belfast Telegraph* in May, 1979. The report entitled "Northern Ireland's Future Terrorist Trends" outlined the structure, manpower and funding of the IRA.[55] The most striking aspect of the report shows the IRA growing in strength rather than weakening. The IRA's technical sophistication has been improving and, by the early 1980s, it will have acquired heavy weapons such as SAM-7 missiles.[56] Copy No. 37 also revealed that British officials had conceded that the Provo's efficiency had grown so that Britain's forces in Northern Ireland were unable to defeat them:

> They inflict high cost damage and they expose the inadequacy of the security forces. The Provisional's campaign of violence is likely to continue while the British remain in Northern Ireland . . . We see little prospect of political developments of a kind which would seriously undermine the Provisional's position.[57]

In spite of IRA strength the bombings of Protestant pubs and selective assassinations have done nothing to improve the position of the Catholic minority. Organized terrorism serves only to increase fears and alienation between Protestants and Catholics. Rapoport argues that each group is inclined to support the growth of its own system of protection via paramilitarism. IRA Provisionals do not recognize that by being dogmatically committed to their objectives of national unity, they are destroying any possibility for reason to prevail.

54 "Provos Have Death List," p. 1.
55 "Secret File Was Lost in the Post," *Belfast Telegraph* (May 11, 1979), pp. 1, 4. (Hereafter cited as "Secret File").
56 *Ibid.*, p. 4.
57 *Ibid.*, p. 1.

Rapoport again emphasizes that the PIRA " . . . cannot understand that they are making Protestants believe that no compromise is conceivable and that Republican inflexibility would characterize politics in a united Ireland."[58]

IRA offensives have not weakened the resolve of Protestants to defend themselves. This is illustrated by the formation of the Ulster Defense Association (UDA) in 1972 that has become the largest Protestant paramilitary force in Ulster.[59] The UDA insists that if its concept of an independent Ulster is not given a chance, " . . . The only solution will be a bloody one and civil war will be inevitable. We will wait and see and keep our powder dry."[60]

The Irish educator Cecil Hurwitz views this period as especially frightening as the ranks of each party's paramilitaries grew and those small groups " . . . could hold the whole nation as hostage."[61] The historian John Robb clarified it as a development of "reactive violence", or the ". . . violence of self-protection" in response to "revengeful violence" which was motivated by destruction for its own sake.[62]

The random murder of Catholics by Protestant extremists during this time did not diminish IRA violence. Rather it had the effect of driving Catholics to seek IRA protection and condone their methods. The Irish historian J. Bowyer Bell states:

> The Provo's great strength has been the flowering of the Northern IRA, a spontaneous reaction to the threat of programs and the actions of the British Army. This supplied GHQ with closely knit units tied into neighborhoods, defenders of their own people.[63]

By 1976, however, Protestant paramilitaries acknowledged that violence was counter-productive. "Find your enemy (namely Catho-

---

58 Rapoport, "Politics of Atrocity," in *Terrorism,* p. 54.
59 Interview with Sam Duddy, UDA Headquarters, Belfast, May 14, 1979. (Duddy is the Information Officer for the Ulster Defense Association).
60 *Ibid.*
61 Hurwitz Interview.
62 Robb, p. 8.
63 J. Bowyer Bell, *Secret Army,* p. 405.

lics) and shoot to kill," was no longer the UDA's methodology. Sam Duddy, Press Officer for the UDA, stated:

> The UDA admits the atrocities were futile as they were headed in the wrong direction and losing much support. Compared to the period before 1976, we have had relative peace. Yet, we do continue to shoot people who are definitely known to be with the Provisional IRA.[64]

In 1976 a truce developed between the UDA and the Provos calling for an end to indiscriminate sectarian killings. The Provos then focused on banks and corporate establishments, and increased their attacks on British Army patrols and police, and continued selective assassinations of prominent British citizens, of whom Lord Louis Mountbatten and Sir Norman Stronge are classic examples. This increased the need for high level security, particularly in urban areas.[65]

It must be noted that Northern Ireland's working class ghettos are and have long been spawning grounds for paramilitarism and terrorism in the same way as the Palestinian refugee camps have been for the Palestine Liberation Organization (PLO). Britain's traditional view of the rioting and violence is that such problems should be discussed and resolved by the government of Northern Ireland rather than at Westminister. As long as the violence and disturbances were localized phenomena, the British Parliament treated them with relative indifference. Geoffrey Bell noted, however, that when the bloodshed increased, as it did during the 1969 - 72 period, Britain did not hesitate to intervene directly. This necessitated a high level of security in the cities and countryside. Until this time, ". . . a Northern Ireland in which a divided working class was a quiescent working class was allowed to go its own way."[66]

---

64 Duddy Interview.
65 Airey Neave, former Secretary of State for Northern Ireland was assassinated reportedly by the Irish National Liberation Army (INLA), a splinter group of the IRA.
66 Geoffrey Bell, p. 24.

Military intervention placed British security troops in a dilemma in Catholic areas where their forces became targets of the very group they were sent to protect. Viewed as symbols of old-style colonialism, the British troops became a source of conflict rather than a solution. Such a conflict is unwinnable, and it caused British security forces to pay a higher price than their adversaries in terms of manpower, energies and patience.[67]

The British response was to impose controls on the symptoms of paramilitary violence. Such violence was related to sectarianism and aggravated by unemployment, poor economic conditions and Republican nationalism.[68]

British armoured cars patrolling Ulster's cities and country-side have served to increase an already tense political atmosphere. Their presence reinforces attitudes that social-political conflicts are resolved by force of arms. Military activities only serve to cut off constructive dialogue concerning community problems. Political analyst Jonathan Power comments, "The military is too blunt an instrument. It is a highly visible sign of a dominant political presence. Nor does it understand the dynamics of long-term interaction among people."[69]

Yet the government's response to increased IRA terrorism in August, 1971, was to invoke the Special Powers Act, a re-instatement of internment legislation of 1921 - 22, 1938 - 39, and in 1956 - 62. This was an effort to halt paramilitarism as legislation allowed authorities to arrest anyone suspected of terrorist activities. Citing security as a rationale, the government could hold a person for interrogation *in camera* for 48 hours. Then a suspect could contact his family but still be held without due process.[70] Those interned

67 "Secret File," p. 1.
68 Tim Pat Coogan, *On The Blanket: The H-Block Story* (Dublin: Ward River Press, 1980), p. 32. (Hereafter cited as Coogan, *On the Blanket*).
69 Jonathan Power, p. 15.
70 MacEoin, pp. 20 - 21.

were political activists engaged in civil rights protests or suspected of extremist sympathies.[71]

The government's suspension of civil liberties meant that a person could be held for prolonged incarceration and reportedly subjected to various forms of physical and mental torture in the "cages" of Long Kesh Prison outside of Belfast.[72] The effectiveness of the internment policy on terrorism is charted on Tables 13 and 14 showing marked increases in shooting incidents and deaths prior to and after the Special Powers Act was invoked.[73]

Republicans accused the Royal Ulster Constabulary of using internment as a sectarian weapon against Catholics. They saw this as repeating a historical pattern in which Catholics were interned at a larger proportional rate than Protestants. Table 15 shows the imbalances for the 1962 - 75 period. It illustrates an increase of internees and Special Category political prisoners associated with the violence during 1972 - 75.[74] Table 16 presents the growth of security forces and prison population during the re-introduction of the internment. This also reflects an accompanying rise in the crime rate.[75]

Table 17 distinguishes the rate of increase of political detainees over the non-political. This chart indicates that withdrawal of normal due process and implementation of torture techniques did not reduce deviant political-social behavior. Rather, it indicates that repressive methods had the opposite effect and increases anti-government activities.[76]

As a result, in 1973 the Emergency Provisions Act introduced changes in the internment policy under which the initial arrest had

71 Downey, pp. 60 - 61.
72 MacEoin, pp. 251 - 255. Also see: *Report of Amnesty International* (London: Amnesty International Publications, 1980), pp. 310 - 312, and "Northern Ireland Charged With Prisoner Maltreatment," *Matchbox,* (Summer, 1978).
73 Downey, pp. 60 - 61.
74 *Ibid.,* p. 73.
75 *Ibid.,* p. 55.
76 *Ibid.,* p. 87.

TABLE 15

**Roman Catholics as a Percent of Total Prison Population in Northern Ireland
by Type of Offense, 1962 - 1975**

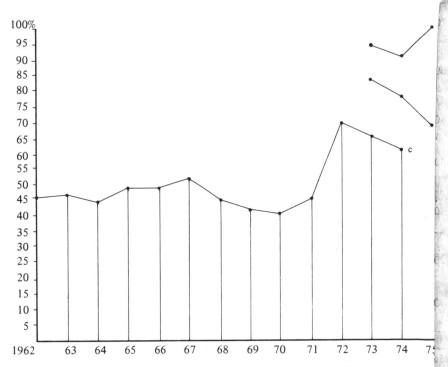

Source: P. A. McConagh, Office of Penal Planning, Northern Ireland Office, Belfast.

a Detainees and internees only
b Detainees, internees, and special category
c All offenders

154

TABLE 16

Northern Ireland Security Forces, Crime Rates, and Prison Populations, 1965 - 1975
(per 100,000 Population)

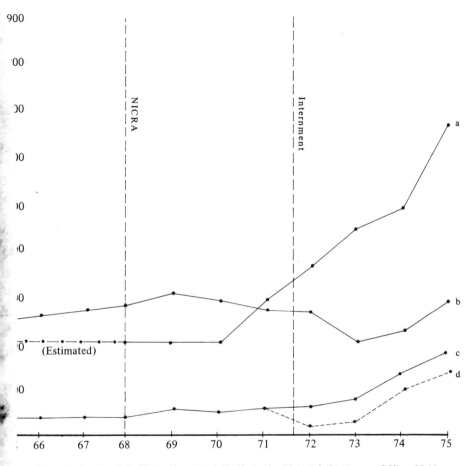

ces: Time-Series A and B, *Ulster Year Book* (Belfast: Her Majesty's Stationary Office, 1965 -
ɔ) Time-Series C and D, P. A. McDonagh, Office of Penal Planning, Northern Ireland Office,
.lfast.

Strength of Royal Ulster Constabulary
Persons found guilty, felony offenses
Prison populations
Prison populations, minus internees

155

TABLE 17

Political and Non-Political Offenders in Northern Ireland Prisons (per 100,000 Population)

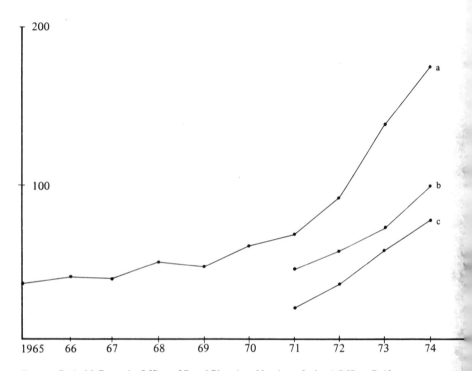

Source: P. A. McDonagh, Office of Penal Planning, Northern Ireland Office, Belfast.

a Total prison population
b Political offenders (1917 - 1972, internees only; after 1972, internees and special category)
c Non-political offenders in prison population

been made by the British Army rather than the police. It also shortened the detainment of suspects to four hours, after which time they were handed over to the police for three more days of interrogation. They were then either released or formally charged.[77] While less severe than earlier detainment procedures, the policy of arrest on mere suspicion remained and resulted only in fostering alienation.

A total of 1,576 were detained within six months after the initiation of internment.[78] The policy failed as Catholic reaction to its application revealed the government's discriminatory application of that policy. Internment backfired on the British with increased Catholic hostility. Roger Hull, American Professor of Law, explains, "Internment only succeeded in uniting the Catholics and showing the world the inhuman depths to which British-Unionist policy had sunk."[79]

As illustrated in Tables 13, 14 and 15, internment only increased the numbers of Catholic prisoners, with no appreciable decline in terrorist activities. This was taken by Protestants as proof that Catholics were responsible for Ulster's problems and that separation was preferable to social integration. This resulted in magnifying ethnic and religious tribalism, in which communal solidarity and acceptance is based primarily upon religious loyalty while outsiders are suspected and feared.

The Problem of Conflicting Loyalties

Because each side practices deliberate disengagement, there is no effective communication during periods of strife. Indeed, rather then increasing communication, it appears the violence only drives

---

77 *Ibid.,* pp. 68 - 69, cited in Great Britain, Her Majesty's Stationary Office, *Report of the Commission to Consider Legal Procedures to Deal With Terrorist Activities in Northern Ireland,* 1972.
78 Roger Hull, *The Irish Triangle: Conflict in Northern Ireland* (Princeton, N. J.: Princeton University Press, 1976), p. 49. (The author is Vice President for Development and Adjunct Professor of Law at Syracuse University. He is an attorney and formerly with the U. S. State Department).
79 *Ibid.*

each community further inward. As previously stated, Catholics only identify with Catholics and Protestants with Protestants.

Catholic provincialism is further compounded by the fear of losing cultural and spiritual identification as well as inherited Catholic values which are part of the Gaelic tradition. Many of them " . . . still believe that Orangemen swear a secret oath to do all in their power to exterminate the Catholics of Ireland."[80]

Protestant loyalists fear the loss of British sympathy and support and the collapse of the British Guarantee.[81] Loyalist politicians see all change as a serious threat to themselves and fear their absorption into the Catholic Republic will mean a dilution of their traditional power base. Because they are " . . . a minority with power all out of proportion to their size," according to Robb, the ascendancy class " . . . assumed an arrogance in the justification of their position."[82]

The ordinary Protestant feels isolated, angry, powerless and misunderstood. Such feelings are generated by what many loyalists see as a British unwillingness to expend the necessary resources to crush Republican terrorism. Loyalists fear that Britain's desire to be rid of the northern problems will prompt her to give in to Republican demands for a united Ireland and evacuate its forces from the scene. Unionists feel that Britain does not sufficiently understand their fears about being drawn into a Catholic state.[83]

Enda McDonagh, Professor of Moral Theology at Maynooth, states, "The basic fear of both Catholic and Protestant is that of absorption by the other and the permanent loss of identity."[84] Because both sides also fear mutilation and death at the hands of the other, there has been little movement toward understanding one another's positions. Indeed, there is little inclination to listen to the other side. "Debate," explains former Peace People Chairman Peter

---

80   Gray, p. 276.
81   See Chapter I regarding this aspect of Ulster-British relations.
82   *Ibid.*
83   "Disturbances," p. 64.
84   Enda McDonagh, pp. 86 - 87.

McLachlan, " . . . never works because this is emotionally grounded and because people in Northern Ireland are very poor listeners."[85] Robb describes Ulster's citizens as having " . . . developed an obsession about the justice of their own viewpoint – with total intolerance of the viewpoint of others."[86]

The Protestant majority has also lost confidence in Britain's government of Direct Rule imposed in 1972. When public safety broke down, responsibility for security shifted to the Parliament in London and out of the hands of the dissolved Parliament of Northern Ireland.[87]

Loyalists also accuse the Northern Ireland Office administering Direct Rule as being unresponsive to loyalist fears and irresolute in putting a halt to the IRA's clandestine war.[88]

The issuance of Britain's White Paper in 1973 increased loyalist fears. It announced Britain's authority over elections as well as security. Unionists believe that the most ominous aspect of the White Paper was the suggestion of some future union with the south.[89] Because it proposed a Council of Ireland that would implement power-sharing and possible unity, the Protestant majority strongly rejected the White Paper.[90]

The Ulster Defense Association, however, seeks an independent Ulster and views the Westminister Government as showing " . . . no qualities of leadership in trying to work out a solution to the violence." According to one of its spokesman, "We are still of the opinion that the United Kingdom will pull out of Ulster within a five year period."[91]

---

85 Interview with Peter McLachlan, Bledheim, Belfast, May 11, 1979. (At the time of interview, McLachlan was Chairman of the Executive Committee of the Community of Peace People).
86 Robb, p. 14.
87 Hull, p. 79.
88 "Ulster and the Tories," *Orange Standard* (November, 1980), p. 5.
89 Hull, p. 78.
90 *Ibid.*, p. 79.
91 Letter from Sam Duddy to Donald Doumitt, January, 1980.

The present situation suggests that the government has lost the confidence of the majority of the populace. This lack of confidence disposes extremists of both sides to forget their political objectives and to resort to force of arms.[92]

Ulster's polarized society views conflict as an essential outlet for built-up tensions. The latter corresponds to the degree to which the social structure has become unwieldy and adverse to change. Such attitudes are even reflected by individuals claiming they can tell Protestant from Catholic by body type, facial feature and name.[93]

Ulster is referred to as a society of "two breeds and two creeds".[94] Segregation in Belfast is exemplified by the "Peace Line" between the Shankill and Falls Road, symbolic of the rift between two cultures and two loyalties. Each has its own social groups and where interaction does take place, the distinctions are ever present. Even friendly relationships exist ". . . with a consciousness of difference."[95]

The ethnic and religious differences exacerbate the fears each group has of the other and affects the competition for jobs. Employment rivalry is so keen that it splits the working class and effectively prevents them from realizing their common interest.[96] Thus, whatever commonality exists is determined by the "our own kind" syndrome.[97] This situation prompted social analysts Barritt and Carter to comment:

> The Protestant working class feel they are more 'decent' than the Catholic working class. Protestant business people and professionals feel they too have a more respectable status. A housewife may be heard saying, after tidying up a room, 'That's more Protestant looking.'[98]

92 *Ibid.*
93 Graham Interview. Also see: Robert Moore's chapter entitled, "Race Relations in the Six Counties: Colonialism, Industrialism and Stratification in Ireland," in *Race*, XIV, pp. 21 - 42.
94 Hurwitz Interview.
95 Barritt and Carter, *Northern Ireland Problem*, p. 58.
96 Parenti, p. 96. Also see: Gerhard Lenski, *Power and Privilege: A Theory of Social Stratification* (New York: McGraw-Hill Co., 1966), p. 64.
97 *Ibid.*, p. 97.
98 Barritt and Carter, *Northern Ireland Problem*, p. 56.

Gary Easthope, a British sociologist, suggests that observers of the Northern Irish situation look beyond economic and power distribution to the symbols and rituals of Ulster politics. He views "the Churches" in conflict as really loyalism and Republicanism, each with its own rituals, symbols and traditions.[99] Constructive dialogue is difficult to promote because Ulster's political climate is dominated by such religious attitudes and characteristics.[100]

A Belfast teacher, burned out of her house, reflected with tragic irony the state of Northern Ireland's sectarian politics. "We are very lucky to have such a beautiful country. We have no disasters like earthquake or floods, just our own personal disaster – Religion."[101]

Religious beliefs are always in the foreground, but, throughout Ulster's turmoil, there has been little evidence that the message of Chrisitan love is being expressed in social interaction and solidarity. While the churches are filled to capacity, the gospel of compassion that is preached from pulpits is not being sufficiently translated into meaningful action. Rather religion has been used by politicians as an excuse to keep people apart, isolated and fearful.[102] Such fears are amplified in the minds of people like the mother whose daughter was caught in the wrong area one night and had her hand broken. Why? Because she was a Protestant.[103]

Such acts promote psychological blocks that are pervasive and ingrained in the religious perceptions of both groups. It is even manifested on intellectual and scholarly levels. Trinity College Fellow, William Kingston, refers to the Republic's Protestant minority of 300,000 as essentially the "social betters" of their Catholic neighbors. Here it appears that bigotry has been accepted as a normal and expected attitude among Protestants in the south as well as in the north.[104]

99 Gary Easthope, "Religious War in Ireland," *Sociology: Journal of the British Sociological Association* 10 (September, 1976), p. 446.
100 *Ibid.*
101 *Ibid.*
102 Beeson, "Can Order Come?" p. 723.
103 Personal Interview.
104 Kingston, "Elements," p. 202.

In an attitudinal study of youth made in August 1971, the willingness to accept violence as a norm of behavior was effectively illustrated. A questionnaire was given to 3,800 children and young adults of both religions. Protestants were asked questions such as "Do you think that people have a right to fight in order to keep Ulster Protestant?" The Catholics were given the question, "Do you think that people have the right to fight in order to bring about a united Ireland?" The word "fighting" in the questions meant bloodshed.[105]

Sixty percent of all the boys interviewed approved the use of violence for political ends while 37 percent rejected it. Data for girls was not reported. Sociologist James Russell concludes:

> Socialization into violent political discord is widespread and effective. That 37 percent reject violence for these goals suggests that permanent political peace without changes in the most basic political attitudes and structures is unlikely.[106]

A similar survey taken in 1975 by the Center for Environmental Studies in London showed an even greater willingness to use violence than the earlier survey. One thousand secondary schoolboys between the ages 13 and 17 were interviewed and 81 percent endorsed the use of violence to achieve a Protestant Ulster or a united Ireland.[107]

As of 1969, there was almost total lack of interaction between Ulster's two populations. Table 18 shows the extent of communication with the "other side", showing percentage responses by area.[108] It indicates a pattern in which the two communities deliberately choose not to interact with one another. This is apparent in the separation of neighborhoods along sectarian lines. Other than special circumstances of economic necessity or business needs, very little opportunity is utilized for inter-group communication.

105 James Russell, "Northern Ireland: Socialization into Political Conflict,"
     Social Studies: Irish Journal of Sociology, IV, (Summer, 1975), p. 111.
106 *Ibid.,* p. 112.
107 *Ibid.,* p. 123.
108 *Ibid.,* p. 432.

TABLE 18

Responses

		Protestant Area	Catholic Area
Catch Bus:	Protestant Road (Shankill)	89	7
	Catholic Road (Falls/Springfield)	7	93
Shop:	Protestant Road	93	10
	Catholic Road	4	90
Visit Sick:	Protestant Area	96	0
	Catholic Area	0	99

Summary. This discussion offers several theories that explain the dynamics of conflict and how they apply to Northern Ireland. Prejudice and discrimination are described as forms of violence. There is a marked relationship between religious prejudice, discrimination, poverty and communal warfare. Extremists inflict human and material losses that are not only tragic, they impede economic progress while aggravating unemployment and discontent. This, in turn, encourages more violence and difficult security problems as paramilitaries on both sides maintain their own ideological justification for war.

For many people, violence hardens attitudes of revenge and retaliation. For others it can be an occasion for soul-searching, reflections and self-criticism. During the decade of the seventies there was some movement among groups toward understanding and reaching out across the religious divide. It is argued that political structures must change before there can be peace, but this cannot happen until there is a more fundamental change in attitude. The following chapter discusses this problem as it relates to changing attitudes and arriving at a peaceful resolution of the conflict.

CHAPTER IX

Attempts to Alter Historical Pre-Conceptions

The observers cited so far stress the historical conditions that have promoted social alienation and allowed for open conflict. The nature of the conflict is one in which, after years of struggle, no solutions have been achieved. Unemployment and under-employment are cited as forms of oppression. The victims of discrimination in Northern Ireland are easily manipulated because of their hostility created by their situation. The solutions advanced are political, social and economic reforms permitting all groups in Ulster to share in the governing process.

The problem of the present violence can only be solved by the people of Ulster. This is not possible, however, until the native populace changes its attitudes. Unless this happens, little reason for optimism exists. As long as deep fears and feelings of alienation exist, peace formulas have little hope of success. Efforts have been made by individuals, groups, the churches and even some para-militaries to change the mind-set of the populace. Their efforts have been attempts to seek solutions to Northern Ireland's internecine war. These efforts will be examined in this chapter.

The Sterling Workshop

This project, which is also called the Travistock Workshop, was initiated by two American researchers from Yale University, William Foltz of the Department of Political Science and Leonard Doob of the Department of Psychology. Their purpose was to demonstrate that in Northern Ireland deeply engrained sectarian prejudices could be dispelled if only a positive and sustained involvement between groups were to take place.

It was determined that the workshop should be held on neutral ground free from the social limitations that would normally exist in the participants' own neighborhood. So 56 Protestants and Catholics of Belfast were transported to Sterling, Scotland, where the workshop was held. The participiants were mainly lower to lower middle classes, between the ages of 16 and 60. Three-fifths of them were male.[1]

They were placed in mixed groups and presented issues to which they were encouraged to respond in a spirit of openness and genuine honesty. They were urged to dialogue with one another, i.e., to listen to differing points of view with mutual respect and to examine seriously the validity of their own feelings toward one another. It was learned that several participants had never spoken with persons of the other faith, much less visited them in their homes. Having come from Northern Ireland's dichotomous population, each group was seen to view the other as monolithic and threatening and themselves as divided and weak.[2]

The Sterling Workshop proved to be a positive experience for all participants. Doob and Foltz noted this when they returned to Belfast nine months later to discern for themselves the impact of the experience on the participants. It was discovered that workshop members changed their negative attitudes about themselves as well as their perceptions of others. Protestants and Catholics acquired a greater self-awareness and self-confidence and became more reflective on the issues. They also felt less threatened, possessed more self-control and were less aggressive.[3]

It was further observed that various degrees of interpsychic changes did influence their overt behavior. They were more concerned with facts and less involved in emotionalism and aggressive outbursts. These changes came after some intra-personal self-analysis that lasted from two weeks to two months.[4]

---

1 Leonard W. Doob and William J. Foltz, "The Impact of a Workshop Upon Grassroots Leaders in Belfast," *Journal of Conflict Resolution: Research on War and Peace Within Nations,* 18 (June, 1974), p. 247. (Hereafter cited as Doob and Foltz, "Impact").

2 Leonard W. Doob and William J. Foltz, "The Belfast Workshop: An Application of Group Techniques to a Destructive Conflict," *Journal of Conflict Resolution: Research on War and Peace Within Nations,* 17 (Sept., 1973), p. 504. (Hereafter cited as Doob and Foltz, "Belfast").

3 Doob and Foltz, "Impact," p. 247

4 *Ibid.,* p. 248.

Doob and Foltz concluded from their study that the positive aspects of the workshop at Sterling could also happen in Belfast and, given time, alter the consciousness of the general population.[5] In spite of social pressures at home, conference participants noted that they had acquired a greater mutual trust which allowed them to grow toward a new objectivity along non-sectarian lines.[6]

The effort at Sterling demonstrated how, in a relatively short space of time, deeply enculturated socio-religious mistrust and bigotry could be resolved. Certainly any change in long-standing feelings and attitudinal stereotypes was painful and required new social and psychological adjustments even in ideal circumstances. Even so it appeared Sterling was an encouraging experiment. Admittedly it involved only a few people, but it showed that it was possible for seemingly rigid individuals to become flexible and open to new understanding.

One can question the feasibility of a Sterling Workshop for the whole of Northern Ireland. But any attempt to promote a massive change in social attitudes must also take into account many problems. These include economic and political inequalities in housing, employment, and political participation and the overriding issue of Ulster's future within or outside the Republic. These matters must be resolved before a viable peace can be achieved. It appears, too, that if there is any hope for equity on the economic and political levels, that hope must take form in an atmosphere of mutual openness and trust. This cannot happen while each religious community sees the other as intrinsically alien to its interests and inter-Christian conflict continues to be perpetrated in the name of God.[7] For this reason, Northern Ireland needs an impetus to stimulate an ongoing spirit of social communication that goes beyond sectarian prejudices. As has been stated, whatever will work to " . . . focus away from sectarian consciousness will be in the long-term interests of the country."[8]

5 *Ibid.*, p. 250.
6 *Ibid.*, p. 255.
7 Beeson, "Impotence," p. 888.
8 Boserup, p. 62.

167

In addition to the Sterling Workshop are the efforts of 60 or more peace groups, nearly half of which are in Belfast. These include *Protestants and Catholics Encounter, Women Together, Peacepoint, People Together,* and others which have functioned since 1969.[9] Their work is aimed at building an atmosphere of trust, which they describe as the "politics of reconciliation."[10]

The Peace People Community

The most widely known of the peace groups is the Peace People Community, formed in 1976 after three children were killed in Belfast following a clash between the IRA and security forces.[11] This group was established by Catholics Betty Williams and Mairead Corrigan and Protestant Nancy McDonnell. They believed that Northern Ireland's violence was an insanity that had no place in civilized society. Extremist methods were condemned as fruitless exercises in twentieth century barbarism and irrationalism that could never achieve justice, much less communal solidarity.[12]

Large numbers of Protestants and Catholics joined the Peace People out of disgust with the IRA, the UDA, the UVF, and "all men of violence."[13] One survey taken as early as March, 1972, showed that 85 percent of Ulster's Catholic population had rejected IRA methods for achieving unity with the Republic.[14] According to another estimate, two-thirds of the Northern Protestant population in 1979 did not agree with Ian Paisley's methods. Citizens are said to be mortified by what has been called "Paisleyite madness."[15]

9   Andrew Boyd, "The Success of the Peace People," *Nation,* 235 (April 16, 1977), p. 454.
10 David Bleakley, *Peace in Ulster* (London: Mobrays, 1972), pp, 15 - 17.
11 Eileen Evason, "Northern Ireland's Peace Movement: Some Early Reflections," *Community Development Journal,* (April, 1977), p. 108.
12 Kennedy and Klotz-Chamberlin, p. 746.
13 Boyd, p. 454.
14 Conor Cruise O'Brien, *States of Ireland* (Bungay, Suffolk, England: The Chauser Press, 1974), p. 187.
15 Hurwitz interview.

Unprecedented numbers of citizens protested against social injustices and the protracted conflict that deepen sectarian divisions. Organized peace marches and massive demonstrations in both Belfast and Londonderry in 1976 - 77 dramatized the appeal of the Peace People. Thousands sang and prayed together in inter-religious gatherings in what was described as an outpouring of love and compassion.[16] This method was found useful in bringing the people together. It was believed that people of the two faiths were discovering a new openness and freedom to express themselves by means of outward affection towards one another in public.[17] This movement is considered religious in nature, as many people working for peace feel they are doing the work of God. For example, the approximately 25-member staff at *Bledheim* (the Norwegian word for Peace House) has observed frequent five and ten minute silences in its library since June, 1977, and holds an occasional non-denominational service.[18] The Peace People Community's active membership is believed to number 8,000 and is essentially a political pressure organization. It works for political and social reform rather than for spiritual goals.[19] It describes itself as a catalyst for change in the whole field of social relations, arguing that even if hatred is firmly instilled into young peoples' minds as part of their intellectual training, there is hope for genuine reconciliation.[20]

The charismatic spirit of the Peace People Community encourages better rapport between large segments of the population. This practice of uninhibited dialoguing and sharing of values appeared to be breaking down psychological blocks and religious barriers. Ciaran McKeown, who edited the movement's fortnightly news-

---

16   Evason, p. 109.
17   Kennedy and Klotz-Chamberlin, p. 748.
18   *Ibid.,* p. 750
19   George Sloane, private interview held during meeting of the Cork Peace Council, Cork, Ireland, May 1, 1979. Sloane is a Methodist Minister.
20   Betty Williams, Talk given during the Cork Peace Council, Cork, Ireland, May 1, 1979. (Williams is a founder of the Peace People Community and Nobel Peace Prize recipient. Hereafter cited as William's talk).

169

paper *Peace By Peace* in 1976, described the interaction quite pointedly when he said, "Nothing is more political than an act of friendship."[21]

The 1976 - 77 phase of the Peace Peoples' efforts was considered valuable as it stimulated intercommunication and dialogue. This was a period in which Protestant and Catholic members appreciated their fears, beliefs and experiences. This seemed to weaken long-standing stereotypes of one another.[22] Thus the community now provides opportunities for individuals to change their relationships. Former Peace People Chairman Peter McLachlan, asserts that total change sometimes may take only five minutes, depending on the circumstances. He suggests that attitudinal changes involving group interaction have taken place in two ways:

  1. The "Network Method," involving continued contact in a non-threatening situation.
  2. The "Abrasive Method," wherein distinct differences in attitudes concerning controversial questions are confronted and challenged.[23]

McLachlan reveals a sensitivity about the problem of collective prejudice and illustrates the Peace Peoples' awareness that attitudinal changes are crucial if a lasting peace is to be acomplished.

Like the Sterling-Travistock Workshop, the peace movement possesses a potential for creating a learning experience involving attitudinal change on a large scale. At least during its first few months of existence, the Peace People Community generated a confidence that its enthusiasm alone could serve a useful function in the process of social change. Hopes were high that its members could actually transform Northern Ireland's political consciousness. Especially was this apparent among those who had suffered most from the social polarization, e.g., the families of the victims of violence, the business people whose shops and homes were bombed, those who had been blackmailed, the hundreds who had become

21 Jonathan Power, p. 504.
22 Evason, p. 111.
23 Peter McLachlan. Interview held at *Bledheim,* Belfast, Northern Ireland, May 10, 1979.

unemployed, or the many people who felt threatened by any one of these experiences because of the conflict.[24] Insofar as their stated mission is to alter Northern Ireland's intellectual consciousness and " . . . to broaden Ulster's narrow world view," the Peace People had good reason to be hopeful.[25] Mairead Corrigan stated it more dramatically when she said, "Let us dedicate ourselves to a new form of battle that can turn Ireland back into a land of saints and scholars."[26]

It soon became apparent that the peace movement could not depend on massive demonstrations alone. The social and political realities had also to be addressed.[27] "They were marching everywhere for peace," says peace advocate Cecil Hurwitz. "You can march them from here to Timbuktu but it won't stop the bombing!"[28] The charismatic and idealistic behavior of Northern Ireland's peace forces needed to develop concrete reforms. A blending of the idealistic and practical was essential so as to make them mutually supportive and engender positive results. Hurwitz, for example, argues that inter-sectarian cooperation on practical matters such as employment and housing is no less important than producing a permanent change of heart and strengthening the movement's intellectual foundation.[29]

Irish journalist Jonathan Powers recommends that the peace movement become thoroughly familiar with the problems that have produced tensions, be they economic, political, or social at the local level. It must develop an awareness of the causes as well as the symptoms of social unrest. Powers urges that Ireland's peace groups adopt Martin Luther King's tactic of concentrating on micro-situations so as to dramatize injustices in certain areas. As he points out, the strategy of using the media to amplify individual injustices while not distorting them, proved successful in places like Selma and Montgomery, Alabama. There, an individual murder, beating

24 James Gilhooley, "On the Road to Drogheda," *Commonweal,* CIV (March 18, 1977), p. 180.
25 Kennedy and Klotz-Chamberlin, p. 750.
26 Power, p. 12.
27 *Ibid.*
28 Hurwitz interview.
29 *Ibid.*

or institutionalized injustice was kept in the forefront as a human rights issue. These problems were rarely allowed to escape from the public eye. In time a sense of moral outrage was so clearly developed that the President saw that it was politically expedient to intervene.[30] Eileen Evason also suggests that this strategy could be successful in Northern Ireland if it were consistently applied to established discrimination and problems involving the denial of basic rights, unemployment, poverty and harassment by security forces.[31]

Accepting this recommendation, the Peace People developed an emphasis on practicality shown in their officially stated program:

> To advance the cause of peace and reconciliation in Northern Ireland by promotion of education, information, and publicity relating to such cases and by establishing, developing, supporting, assisting and carrying on industrial, manufacturing, and commercial enterprise, business and trades.[32]

By 1977, Northern Ireland's Peace People Community included 162 local groups and 8,000 field workers.[33] Each group focused on the causes of violence in its area. For example, they formed youth groups and community centers and worked to include Peace and Conflict Resolution studies in secondary schools throughout the six counties.[34]

This practical approach included in some measure the strategy already mentioned of transforming micro-problems into macroproblems. They have dramatized many social and economic inequities that stem from sectarianism. For example, a 20-foot-high barbed-wire fence or "peace line" separating the Protestant and Catholic areas in Belfast became a macro-problem. Viewing this

---

30 Power, p. 13.
31 Evason, p. 110.
32 Peace by Peace Ltd., and the Peace People Charitable Trust Report on the Period From Their Establishment to March 31, 1978, p. 1.
33 Kennedy and Klotz-Chamberlin, p. 742.
34 Tom Donaghy, Interview held at *Bledheim,* Belfast, Northern Ireland, May 10, 1979. At the time of interview Donaghy was Assistant Chairman of The Executive Committee of the Community of Peace People. (Hereafter cited as Donaghy interview).

as a symbol of sectarian division, the Peace People launched a campaign against it until it came down.[35]

Although suffering occasional physical and verbal abuse, the peace activists have achieved some success in such areas as making available abandoned housing for hard-pressed families, using the media to highlight social ills and calling attention to many other social action projects in which they have become involved. The groups also have set up co-ops, a neighborhood law firm, pre-schools, family counseling programs, summer camps and sport programs such as the Peace People Junior Football League.[36] In attacking the 38 to 41 percent unemployment rate, the peace groups cooperated in developing small craft industries such as a stationary plant, a leather factory and others with growth potential.[37]

In 1976, Betty Williams and Mairead Corrigan received the Nobel Peace Prize. The Prize money of £202,684 plus other contributions were placed in the Peace People's Charitable Trust Fund to carry out their work.[38] These funds have been used in the form of loans and grants to fund projects and to develop business enterprises.[39] Whenever an investment became profitable, the money was repaid to the fund to be used again for other projects. This program has realized a 70 percent success rate.[40]

All the programs cited needed continual Protestant-Catholic co-operation. Project development aimed at achieving stronger social bonding and communal identity wherein the sectarian groups would discover their rights and freedoms were best protected in communal peace rather than in terrorism.[41] The various neighborhood social action projects have continued to function in cooperative effort between Protestants and Catholics. However, the Peace People sees its objective of peace throughout Ulster as slow in coming. "To

---

35 Hurwitz interview.
36 Power, p. 14. Also see: "Peace Cup Highlights Season," *Peace by Peace* (May 9, 1980), p. 1.
37 *Ibid.*
38 Donaghy interview.
39 *Ibid.*
40 Hurwitz interview.
41 Donaghy interview.

grow a plant takes a long time," asserts Peter McLachlan, "but the Peace People prepare the soil for long-term growth."[42]

The peace movement views IRA nationalism as a critical barrier that negatively affects the practical side of their efforts. Says former Assistant Chairman of the Peace People Executive Committee, Tom Donaghy:

> Even if we eliminated unemployment, inequality, and poor housing, even if the ghettos were wiped out, there would still be IRA nationalism. We have no quarrel with nationalism, but we want people to talk and argue, and reason instead of resorting to violence. This is crucial in Northern Ireland where parties will not talk unless others agree with them on key issues.[43]

IRA nationalism is culturally Catholic, and it contains its own united Ireland momentum, independent of religious loyalties. It does not agree with peace forces that the basic issues lie in the elimination of societal prejudices that call for a change in attitude. As has been pointed out, the IRA sees sectarian politics as peripheral to the real problems which are the British presence and the division of Ireland. Any compromise with these key issues is described as a sellout and a " . . . peace at any price."[44]

However, peace forces also reject the notion of peace at any price, i.e., acquiescing to demands of Protestant and Catholic extremists. Instead, they envision peace as a long-term objective. The process involves getting people from all ages and walks of life to discuss openly problems relating to prejudice and nationalism. This also means discussing the issues with paramilitaries on both sides. McLachlan sees some successes and failures here:

> So far it has been impossible to get extremists to talk while they are using violence. So far the Ulster Defense Association, the Ulster Volunteer Force, and the Official IRA have all produced good, viable political documents that are worthy of serious study. The Provisional IRA has not done this but we hope to get them politicized and talking in a non-threatening atmosphere.[45]

42 McLachlan interview.
43 Donaghy interview.
44 McAuley interview.
45 McLachlan interview.

There have been mixed reactions regarding the Peace People Community since it began in 1976. Its social activity is described as low level and no longer possessing any strong influence. The days of the big demonstrations are gone and so is the emotional expression. The UDA asserts that the movement's emotionalism exaggerated its ability to bring peace. According to Sam Duddy, UDA Information Officer:

> The Peace People managed to convince the world that they speak from a position of power, but the opposite is true. They are in a very false position because they pretend to speak for the great majority of people in Ulster.[46]

Protestant paramilitaries also suspect the Peace People of not coming from the working class and therefore not understanding the latter's problems. The UDA described Peter McLachlan, Peace People's chairman in 1979, as representative of the well-dressed intelligentsia who made up the movement's leadership and rank and file. A UDA spokesman further describes members of the peace movement as possessing qualities more respectable to the ascendancy business class. One criticism of McLachlan was " . . . his upper class British accent which did not help his image with the workers."[47] In addition, Betty Williams and Mairead Corrigan, who founded the Peace People Community, were often criticized for spending too much time traveling abroad and not giving enough attention to grassroots problems at home.[48]

The Provisional IRA also has mistrusted the Peace People since August of 1976, when the latter declared its support for the security forces and Britain's Direct Rule. The Provisionals believe this blunder cost the Peace People much support.[49] Their feeling is that the Peace People are really pro-British and have British backing.[50] It appears the average Ulsterman, too, is not optimistic about the peace forces achieving any lasting results. Their basic weakness lies in not develop-

---

46 Duddy interview.
47 *Ibid.*
48 *Ibid.* (Betty Williams broke away from the Peace People at *Bledheim* in 1980 to form another peace group).
49 McAuley interview.
50 Graham interview.

ing a broad political base. Thus peace groups are viewed as representing only a small percentage of the population, whereas the vast majority still votes conservatively on issues that are based on sectarianism. The British elections in 1979 showed a general hardening instead of softening of political positions in Northern Ireland. Not only did Paisleyites gain over the moderates in the election, but there were also indications that Britain's Conservative Government would tighten security throughout Ulster. For these reasons the Peace People's movement has been called ". . . a spent and beaten force."[51]

It must be noted, however, that according to political analyst William Graham, large numbers of citizens approve of what the Peace People are doing because they provide a useful forum for discussion and are an asset in the province's ongoing state of tension.[52] Their efforts were to initiate dialogue involving contending Ulster factions. In 1979, McLachlan called for a conference of 1,000 people to discuss " . . . a new political order."[53] He acknowledged several new and positive ideas, even from the paramilitaries, aimed at a truly democratic society. While indicating a need to study them carefully, he said those groups which advocated violence would not be invited to such conferences.[54]

McLachlan called attention to the Provisional IRA, which in 1979 was alleged to be committing 99 percent of the murders and bombings. The UDA, on the other hand, remained relatively inactive in accordance with its decision in 1976 to halt sectarian killings. Observers feared that any retaliation from the Protestant side could seriously escalate the conflict. At that time the Peace People were hopeful that the very low profile of both the UDA and the British military would cause the Provos to lose ground both materially and psychologically.[55] While this did not happen, there was a feeling that any renewal of Protestant retaliation such as occurred during the early

51 *Ibid.*
52 *Ibid.*
53 " 'No Pleasure in Vote,' Says Peace Leader," *Sunday Times,* April 1, 1979, p. 6.
54 *Ibid.*
55 Betty Williams talk.

and mid-1970s, and/or stepped-up British security involving restrictions on the Catholic population, would renew credibility and support for the Catholic extremists.[56]

The Presbyterian Study

In recent years churches have shown a growing concern for the province's volatile condition. They are now willing to probe within themselves for solutions rather than to simply place all the blame on the other side. This could indicate that the concerned citizenry sees the conflict as so pervasive that all must share some responsibility. In this spirit two Presbyterian Church reports were written, one in 1973 and the other in 1977.

The first report concerns attitudes within the Presbyterian Church, whose membership of 413,000 is 29 percent of the Ulster population.[57] The Committee on National and International Problems, an organ of the Presbyterian Church and author of the report, explains the lawlessness and assassinations of communal warfare as coming from deeply-rooted attitudes of fear and hatred. The study based on questionnaires to Presbyterian churches and entitled *Christians in a Situation of Conflict,* suggests that destructive attitudes have undermined Northern Ireland's society leading to the breakdown of the populace's moral fiber.[58] The Committee points out that violence and intimidation have been perpetrated by the Protestant as well as the Catholic side. No one is innocent; both sides are to blame. The Committee states:

56 Hurwitz interview. (IRA-INLA assassinations of prominent British citizens such as Airey Neave, the former Secretary of State for Northern Ireland in March, 1979, and Lord Louis Mountbatton in September, 1979, may have provoked a resurgence of Protestant countermeasures in the form of sectarian assassinations).

57 Fair Employment Agency. (Figures were taken from the 1971 Religious Tables of the Northern Ireland Population Census, p. 2.)

58 *Report of the Committee on National and International Affairs to the General Assembly of the Presbyterian Church on Christians in a Situation of Conflict,* Belfast: Church House Publications, 1973, p. 189. (Hereafter cited as Report on Christians in Conflict).

There are reports of Roman Catholic families being intimidated by Protestants and of Protestant families being intimidated by Roman Catholics: of Roman Catholics intimidating one another, of Protestants doing the same.[59]

The report documents the inflammatory propaganda that has led to business boycotts. Such diatribes have disrupted communal peace and prosperity:

Business has been upset after some outrage, and irresponsible political speeches have often led to disturbances among workers. Boycotting would seem to be confined to certain areas. There is not much evidence of it in areas across the border.[60]

The adverse psychological effects of "the troubles" on the younger generation are also discussed. Reportedly, " . . . gangs of teen-agers dominate urban streets at night and people are afraid to go out of their houses or even to open their doors."[61]

This first Presbyterian Report calls attention to such positive actions as the interdenominational efforts toward goodwill and cooperation. Some Protestants and Catholics from a broad spectrum of life formed prayer groups that met together. During the times of trouble beginning in 1969, there was a genuine expression of interdenominational sympathy and support for the families that suffered, regardless of their religious differences.[62]

According to the report, some Presbyterian groups questioned the necessity of linking Protestantism with the Unionist Party, as the Paisleyites had often encouraged them to do. The Committee also calls attention to several positive ways of communicating so as to achieve better Protestant-Catholic understanding. The committee states:

There is a great need for intermingling by the communities for dialogue and for increasing inter-communication. The means advocated for this were varied. High on the list was integrated education. Others thought

---

59 *Ibid.*, p. 190.
60 *Ibid.*
61 *Ibid.*
62 *Ibid.*

178

that local discussion groups, prayer groups, Bible study, and raising of matters of social and economic concern were of great value.[63]

The report also notes several areas where Protestants and Catholics are sharing their activities and where secular cooperation serves in a limited way to bridge the religious divide. The committee report outlines them as follows:

1. Development of village associations that work for the improvement of sectarian relations.
2. Efforts to aid the handicapped and the underprivileged, e.g., the aged, the blind, and cancer victims.
3. Cultural activities in dramatic and musical societies.
4. Debating clubs
5. Sports
6. Cooperatives[64]

Some committee members suggested that the many activities should be in "neutral," non-church buildings and that discussion be directed to correcting misrepresentations and distortions. This is seen as a positive way to gain a valid perception of one another. More specifically, members requested educational study groups and favored an integrated public school system staffed by teachers who taught secular subject matter and whose training was secular rather than denominational. The Irish Catholic clergy insists on parochial education. According to the study, an intellectually neutral ground would be less likely to alienate anyone.[65]

In respect to religious study, some Presbyterian congregations sought teaching on the following items:

1. Why are we Presbyterian?
2. What is the difference between us and other churches and what about the considerable common ground we share?
3. What is the Roman Catholic Church as it really is, and especially as it is after Vatican II?
4. A special course on the "troubles" (in Northern Ireland) and a Christian assessment.[66]

63 *Ibid.,* p. 194.
64 *Ibid.,* p. 191.
65 *Ibid.,* p. 193.
66 *Ibid.*

The Presbyterian study also notes renewed efforts to change attitudes toward Catholics and violence, although not all member participants agreed to the following position statement:

> There should be a new realization that Christian love and Christian justice know no barriers and that these are fundamentals of the Christian faith. Tolerance should be taught and a new "radical" approach to put prejudice and bitterness behind us, to live for others and to bear one another's burdens, including those of Roman Catholics.[67]

> Violence is a sin: Violence should never be used to attain political ends. Church courts and ministers should be careful to avoid any utterance which may seem to justify violence. Churches individually should refrain from making statements that reflect only their own particular viewpoint.[68]

The report also mentions the need to promote a new "politics of reconciliation" which must replace the "politics of division." It stresses the divisiveness of party politics as natural, stemming from differences of opinion. An essential element of the democratic process is to " . . . agree to differ," to accept the loyal opposition, and to respect opposing points of view. Reconciliation can only come through respect and tolerance, not aggression.[69]

Spiritual renewal is noted as a crucial element in interchurch co-operation:

> The politics of reconciliation would be the hard, demanding job of men with the mind of Christ (and all that it means) who will stand, work, and if need be suffer together for justice and righteousness. Because we believe in God we therefore refuse to believe that such politics are not possible.[70]

The General Assembly of the Presbyterian Church in Ireland describes a pluralistic society as an ideal which guarantees the civil and political liberties of all groups, regardless of how they may differ. The answer to conflict is found in a mutual acceptance and respect for differences in individuals and groups. This does not mean having to conform to the values of a single dominant group, but remaining faith-

---

67 *Ibid.*
68 *Ibid.*, pp. 194, 199.
69 *Ibid.*, p. 196.
70 *Ibid.*, p. 197.

ful to one's cultural and religious heritage. The report further stresses that both groups should aim at doing together all those things which lead to harmony and which conviction does not compel them to do separately.

The 1973 Presbyterian Committee Report makes no mention of economic discrimination. However, the 1977 follow-up study by the same Presbyterian Church committee blames discrimination in housing, industry and employment as perpetuating a ghetto mentality and a segregated society. This encourages prejudice and violence. The report is vague about solutions. It expresses confidence that a brighter economic future is possible with fuller employment. An improved economy can encourage trust in government and greater interaction between Protestants and Catholics.[71]

The 1977 committee report states that even though Ulster's Protestant and Catholic cultures choose to live apart, it is still possible to form a pluralistic society. This must be based on agreement to support the common good by upholding justice for all citizens and respecting Christian values.[72] Meanwhile, the Church committee warns its members not to heed "power-hungry persons," "ambitious powerseekers," and "political Protestants — none of whom need any encouragement."[73]

While some cooperation resulted from these reports, the activities such as interdenominational Bible study and discussion groups met with opposition. Many church members strongly opposed the idea of initiating any relationship between Protestants and Catholics with the arguments that such action would be misunderstood and were difficult if not impossible because of theological disagreements. Many people insisted on identifying Roman Catholicism with IRA extremists. Some congregations feared integrated sporting activities would create special friendships that would lead to inter-marriage.[74]

---

71 *Report of the Committee on National and International Affairs to the General Assembly of the Presbyterian Church on Pluralism in Ireland,* Belfast, Northern Ireland, Church House Publications, 1977, pp. 2, 11, 13.
72 *Ibid.*
73 Report on Christians in Conflict.
74 *Ibid.,* p. 190.

Other Presbyterians have refused even to discuss the sensitive issues that keep Ulster divided.[75] Protestant leaders other than Presbyterian also have taken up the peace cause. They include Church of Ireland, Methodist and Baptist churches. Their congregations, however, still adhere to the psychological barriers of the past and remain unmoved.[76] Clergymen who have strongly condemned violence and made repeated appeals to extend social and political privileges to the Catholic minority have been largely ignored.[77]

Some churchmen call for the citizens to be outraged with those who perpetrate murder and destroy property. In his presidential address to the Diocesan Synod of the Church of Ireland, the Most Reverend Dr. A. R. Caird stated that his condemnation of such acts stemmed from a Christian duty. His message applied to Protestant Unionist as well as Roman Catholic nationalists. He explained that no political solution could be hoped for without constant prayer and effort.[78]

The Church of Ireland Primate, the Most Reverend John Armstrong, also condemned the irrationality of continued conflict:

> An escalation of street violence and heightened terror displays are possible. So is renewed support for the whole campaign of violence . . . Enough desolation has been perpetrated on Irishmen by Irishmen. Any escalation can only be futile.[79]

The Roman Catholic Church cites its long history of condemning violent change. This has been especially true in the history of Irish nationalism, where the traditional stand of the Irish bishops was to oppose the use of physical force. The Church stood against violence during the French Revolution and, according to Irish Church Theologian Enda McDonagh, continues to condemn the extremism associated with IRA-INLA activities.[80]

75 *Ibid.*
76 Beeson, "Northern Ireland," p. 723.
77 Beeson, "Impotence," p. 888. (For further discussion of this matter see "Who Gets Housing Priority?" *Orange Standard* (November, 1980), p. 5.
78 "Protestant Rivival in Meath, Kildare," *Orange Standard* (November, 1980), p. 5.
79 "Primate Critizes Hunger Strikes," *Orange Standard* (November, 1980), p. 8.
80 Enda McDonagh, p. 86.

Recently former Primate of Ireland Cardinal Conway, his successor, Cardinal Tomas O'Fiaich, and other clergy have denounced extremism and called for peace. When Pope John Paul II visited Ireland in 1981 he made the following plea:

> I wish to speak to all men and women engaged in violence. I appeal to you in language of passionate prayer. On my knees I beg you to turn away from the path of violence and to return to the ways of peace.[81]

Acknowledging the right of self-determination, the Roman Catholic Church sees violence as an addictive and enslaving aspect of nationalism, whether in Ireland or elsewhere. However, the extremists have ignored clerical pleas as McDonagh reports, "To denounce violent nationalism has not been effective, nor has the imposition of law and order resolved anything. Even military repression has failed to pacify the extremists."[82] Because Catholic extremists have not taken Church opposition seriously, many Protestants take this to mean the Catholic paramilitaries enjoy the *de facto* toleration of the clergy.[83] Nevertheless, there exists cooperation between Protestants and Catholics which will be discussed below.

The practice of avoiding issues and thinking the worst of the other side is symptomatic of the endemic hostility and fear. As a result, attempts at conflict resolution appear futile. Indeed, many of those who call for an end to the violence are often those with entrenched attitudes that make peace impossible.[84]

Others argue that the greatest challenge for peacemakers in Northern Ireland is to find ways of replacing fear with confidence and trust. This would require a heartfelt conversion by not only the average citizen, but also men of violence as well.[85]

81 Neil Hickey, "The Battle for Northern Ireland: How TV Tips the Balance," *TV Guide* (September 26 - October 2, 1981), p. 20.
82 McDonagh, p. 86.
83 Crowley interview.
84 Alan Senior, "Master of Garbage," *Peace by Peace* (June 5, 1981), p. 7.
85 Robb, p. 88.

The Joint Commission Study

In 1977, the Irish Catholic journal *The Furrow* published a report entitled *Violence in Ireland.* The document was a joint effort of two groups, the Working Party of the Protestant Irish Council of Churches and the Roman Catholic Church's Group on Social Problems. The two church bodies agreed on several recommendations pertaining to the underlying unrest.[86] Their report was very controversial for Catholic Republican conservatives because it criticized having the Catholic moral law enshrined and unchanging in the south and for Protestants because it discussed the feasibility of a united Ireland and gave encouragement toward ecumensim.[87]

Regarding the problems of extremism, the document states, "No sane politician considers that physical force can bring about the political unity of Ireland." The study went on to blame politicians and churchmen for failing to educate the citizenry on how the peaceful change could some about.[88]

The report recommended the following actions to the Protestant and Catholic churches throughout Ireland.

1. To state that there is no justification for the existence of any paramilitary organizations in Ireland.
2. To take action to promote reconciliation.
3. To remind citizens that they have a fundamental moral obligation to support currently constituted authorities throughout the north and south against all paramilitaries.
4. To promote schemes for developing ways of bringing together Protestant and Catholic young people, e.g., arranging the exchange of teachers and clergy to speak in schools and the sharing of games.
5. To teach religious instruction with an ecumenical dimension.
6. To reject inherited stereotypes of one another.
7. To build a Christian Centre of Social Investigation in Ireland, (CCSI) for the purpose of developing an awareness of the political and social

---

86 Donal Barrington, "Violence in Ireland," *Furrow* (February, 1977), p. 67. The author is a leading constitutional lawyer and President of the Irish Association in Dublin.

87 *Ibid.,* p. 68.

88 *Ibid.,* p. 69.

implications for Christians. That is, the CCSI would research problems that give rise to social unrest.

8. To encourage political leaders to seek just agreements with opponents rather than victory over them.[89]

Recommendations are directed towards peace and greater tolerance. Though Ulster's history is very old, its social and cultural understanding is still in its infancy. "Conference resolutions of the past have failed," asserts Barrington, " . . . because political leaders were prisoners of popular prejudices."[90]

Ecumenism

Dialogue is considered crucial in achieving Protestant and Catholic understanding. Nowhere is this truer than in Northern Ireland. Efforts by Christian theologians to communicate on matters pertaining to doctrines were launched during the pontificate of Pope John XXIII in the early sixties. The purpose of the movement was to open a Catholic dialogue with other Christian bodies and to heal centuries-old wounds which have divided them.[91] In 1968, the late Pope Paul VI and the former Archbishop of Canterbury Michael Ramsey created the Anglican-Roman Catholic International Commission to discuss doctrinal differences and inter-Church cooperation.[92]

Northern Ireland's fundamentalists have reacted negatively towards ecumenism and have warned their congregations against dilution of their Reformation faith and submission to Roman Catholic authoritarianism. Except for the authors of the 1973 and 1977 reports, Presbyterians seem especially skeptical of inter-faith dialogues. They argue that, while talks have been friendly, they have not changed anything:

89 *Ibid.,* pp. 67 - 68. (Also see the Report of the Anglo-Catholic Conference on Marriage and Church-State Relations in the Republic).
90 *Ibid.,* p. 69.
91 Hans Kung, Yves Conger, O.P., Daniel O'Hanlon, S. J., *Council Speeches of Vatican II,* (Glen Rock, New Jersey: Paulist Press, 1964), pp. 145 - 227.
92 "Betraying the Protestant Faith and the Reformation," *Protestant Telegraph,* (September 19, 1981), p. 11.

Tension and Prayers in Northern Ireland

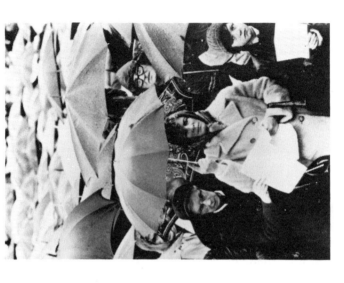

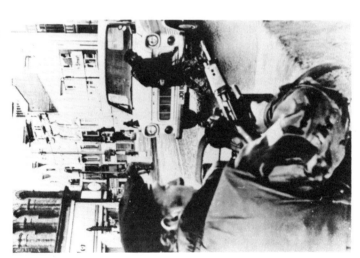

Belfast — With the end of the Irish Republican Army Provisional's cease-fire, tensions returned to the streets of Belfast and other cities in Northern Ireland. At left, a soldier keeps his finger on the trigger while another soldier checks a van for explosives or firearms at a vehicle checkpoint.

At right, people stand in silent prayer during a peace rally at Belfast's City Hall. About 12,000 people turned out for the interdenominational rally, marching through heavy rain. Leading Protestant and Roman Catholic clergymen con-

It is producing very little in the way of changed attitudes in fundamentalism and it remains a cause for unease among those who find it impossible to accommodate to dogmas and practices which are foreign to their beliefs and attitudes.[93]

As William Moody, Deputy Grand Master of Armagh, and spokesman for Official Unionists, told his fellow Orangemen:

Ecumenism can be nothing more than a word while it dabbles in subjects which are divisive for proper reasons and which will prevent a meaningful Church unity because there is a lack of understanding and agreement on Gospel truth.[94]

Ulster Protestants had misgivings about early exchanges involving the former Anglican Archbishop Coggan of Canterbury with Pope Paul VI and Cardinal Hume, Catholic Archbishop of Westminister.[95] Ian Paisley, who speaks for the majority of Presbyterians, has described Cardinal Hume as " . . . the sinister figure on the horizon in England – someone on whom everyone should keep his eye." He has viewed the visit to England by Pope John Paul II in 1982 as a move to overthrow England's Protestant throne.[96]

This hostility seems pervasive. Nevertheless, there is progress in the ecumenical movement. In March, 1980, Reverend Bill Gowland, President of the British Methodist Conference, presented Pope John Paul II with a scroll containing greetings from 500,000 Methodists.[97] The same year, Cardinal O'Fiaich became the first Roman Catholic prelate to attend a service of the Church of Ireland in Armagh since the Reformation. This was the occasion of the enthronement of the Most Reverend John Ward Armstrong as the Archbishop of Armagh.[98]

93 "Comment," *Orange Standard,* (June, 1980), p. 5.
94 "Eire Protestants' Good Citizenship Earns '12th' Praise," *Orange Standard,* (August, 1980), p. 3. (Hereafter cited as "Eire Protestants").
95 "The Archbishop Goes and Comes," *Orange Standard,* (May, 1980), p. 6.
96 Ian Paisley, "Jesuitical Trick to Overthrow Protestant Throne," *Orange Standard,* (September, 1980), p. 3.
97 "The Rush to Rome," *Orange Standard,* (March, 1980), p. 8.
98 "Cardinal Worships With Protestants," *Orange Standard,* (June, 1980), p. 4. (Hereafter cited as "Cardinal Worships").

While such events are unique, meetings between Protestants and Catholics are becoming more frequent.[99] Even though the issues of papal authority and shared communion are unresolved, relations between Anglicans and Catholics are better now than at any time since the Reformation. Protestants are especially pleased over Cardinal O'Fiaich's attendance at an Anglican enthronement and believe this is evidence of an alteration of the Vatican's position on the validity of Anglican Orders. They also hope that the Catholic laity's greater role in Church affairs in recent years will lead to less clerical authority and more democracy within the Roman Catholic Church. They are inclined to applaud this aspect of the Church since Vatican II.[100]

An official position of the Church of Ireland regarding ecumenical dialogue with the Church of Rome was given by Dr. Henry McAdoo, the Church of Ireland's Archbishop of Dublin. He described ecumenism as " . . . the meeting of different traditions in their richness and in their authenticity." This does not mean watering down the faith for the sake of dialogue, but "in seeking a clearer understanding of the Church's teachings since Apostolic times."[101]

Similarly Reverend Warren Porter, a Presbyterian minister, supported ecumenism with a powerful statement of reconciliation to the Orange congregation at Rosenowlagh in August, 1980:

> Our problems in Ulster are not simply political or merely religious in the common use of that word. They have deeper roots and a longer history than most are prepared to admit. Their roots are spiritual, and only a spiritual cure will solve the problems . . . Ulster's needs will not be met by a man be he politician, or preacher, or someone who is both. Ulster's needs will be met only when it returns to Christ. That is the need of the hour. That is the first priority. If that were true of every Orangeman we would be halfway towards the greatest revival Ulster has ever seen . . . A Protestantism which knows nothing but a hatred for Romanism or of ecumenism and is a stranger to practical godliness is a curse. I want nothing to do with a Protestantism of hate and ignorance.[102]

99 "Ulster a Key to Its Own Future," *Orange Standard,* (April, 1980), p. 6.
100 "Cardinal Worships".
101 "Inter-Church Discussions," *Orange Standard,* (November, 1980), p. 8.
102 "Eire Protestants."

188

The desire for reconciliation through peace groups and ecumenical dialogue is a hopeful beginning. Spiritual and attitudinal changes are necessary before effective changes in the political and economic sectors can be considered possible. The attitudinal changes, however, need direction. What follows are descriptions of two attempts that address the political and economic issues.

The Fitzgerald Plan

Numerous solutions for the Northern Ireland situation have been advanced. A recent one worthy of note is that of Dr. Garret Fitzgerald, leader of the *Fina Gael* Party in the Republic. His idea is to make Northern Ireland and the Republic a confederation. Each state would be free to determine its own political and economic policies as well as its relations with other nation-states, including the European Economic Community. The confederation would have its own mutually-agreed-upon constitution guaranteeing maximum autonomy, and a confederally-controlled security force with security jurisdiction in the north and south. Parliamentary leadership would be chosen by direct, free elections of the people of both states.[103] Two important advantages of the plan are:

1. A confederation would alleviate longstanding Unionist fears that they will be forced into union with the Republic; and they would be able to so retain their political representation in relation to their population.
2. It would open the way for an internal political solution for Northern Ireland by means of devolution toward power-sharing with the Catholic minority.[104]

Political analysts view the Fitzgerald Plan as sound and undoubtedly quite workable, but not without special problems in Ulster. That is because Fitzgerald's idea of confederation introduces a political compromise between the loyalists, who want a Protestant Ulster and continued union with the United Kingdom, and the Repub-

103   Liam O'Neill and Peter Martin, "Unionist Interests Guaranteed by Fina Gael," *Cork Examiner,* February 19, 1979, pp. 1 - 2.
104   *Ibid.*

lican nationalists, who want an autonomous united Ireland. Political compromise has always been difficult to achieve in Northern Ireland.

The New Ulster Political Research Group Study

In 1979, the New Ulster Political Research Group (NUPRG), ideological voice of the Ulster Defense Association, published a peace plan entitled *Beyond the Religious Divide.* Ironically, the document came from a Protestant paramilitary group which, until 1976, was involved in sectarian conflict that claimed the lives of several hundred Catholics. Its slogan had been "No surrender!"[105] However, the killing of Catholics was driving them into the hands of the IRA and, as noted, the random killing of Catholics lost the UDA much Protestant support.[106]

The NUPRG peace plan was viewed as a breakthrough in the changing of attitudes. Combining elements of both the United States and British constitutions, the NUPRG prefaced its document with an interesting statement:

> To the people of Northern Ireland . . . we commend the words of Bacon:
> He who cannot compromise is a fool,
> He who will not compromise is a bigot,
> He who dares not compromise is a slave.[107]

The Research Group called for " . . . a proper politics" in which Protestants and Roman Catholics recognized their commonality and formed a strong political unity. Unless this happened, it argued, the two peoples would continue to be manipulated by the sectarian politicians. According to the NUPRG's findings, whenever there was any movement toward unity between the two communities the politicians would always exploit the constitutional differences

---

105 Donaghy interview.
106 Duddy interview.
107 New Ulster Political Research Group, *Beyond The Religious Divide* (Belfast, 1979), n.p. (Hereafter cited as: Beyond The Religious Divide).

that divide them. Therefore, the group believed that its first priority was in settling the constitutional problem.[108]

It must be remembered that the Government of Ireland Act of 1920 included a constitutional guarantee to Protestants that Ulster would always be part of the United Kingdom. There can be no change in the law without the consent of the Parliament of Northern Ireland.[109] The Act was never recognized by Republicans because it divided the country. It also divided Ulster along sectarian lines. The Unionist ascendancy had to rely on the support of the Protestant working class against the Catholic minority so as to control the richest part of Ireland.[110]

In Catholic areas such as Londonderry, Strabane, and Newry, Unionists gerrymandered to maintain an exclusive control of the Stormont Parliament and district councils.[111] Kevin M. Cahill, President of the American Irish Historical Society in Dublin explains:

> The six counties of Northern Ireland were ruled until the 1970s by a closed obligarchy that protected a Protestant monopoly of economic and political power, compounding an inherited legacy of prejudice and bitterness.[112]

The "proper politics" to which the research group referred is a system based on political rather than religious differences. This would necessitate political reforms to eliminate exclusive control by the majority, thus allowing the minority a fair participation in the political process. This would require a constitutional settlement in which all parties would have to agree.[113]

The NUPRG is seeking a compromise solution between the position of loyalism, which leans toward Britain, and nationalism, which leans toward the Republic:

108 *Ibid.,* p. 2.
109 Hume, p. 303.
110 Letter from Professor Joseph McVeigh of the Peace Studies Institute, Manhattan College to Donald Doumitt, October 19, 1980. (McVeigh is a Catholic priest from Northern Ireland. Hereafter cited as: McVeigh letter).
111 Government of Northern Ireland, *Disturbances,* p. 63.
112 Kevin M. Cahill, "America and Ulster: Healing Hands," *Foreign Policy* 4 (Winter, 1979 - 80), p. 87.
113 Beyond The Religious Divide, p. 2.

> It is sufficient to say that principally we found that any proposal which involved London would be rejected by the minority and any proposal which involved Dublin would be rejected by the majority community.[114]

The group sees Britain and the Republic as interfering in Ulster's affairs. They argue that peace will come only when the two populations unite in a common identity to solve their problems. They further believe that negotiating for a non-sectarian pluralistic democracy is achievable in a sovereign state, independent of Britain and Eire. These goals are set out in the following steps:

> 1. A new Constitution and Bill of Rights that offers equality and first-class citizenship to every citizen.
> 2. A new political structure which will allow every representative of the state to participate in decisions and responsibilities.
> 3. Guarantees from Britain and the Republic of Ireland to withdraw all their claims to sovereignty over Northern Ireland.
> 4. International recognition and support for Ulster's national sovereignty.[115]

These ideas of confederation and power-sharing with Catholics are strongly opposed by Ian Paisley's Democratic Unionist Party, which sees this as a step toward unification with the Republic. Paisley demands an evolved government that will retain its links with Britain. Should the British pull out, Paisley's party promises to arm and fight to prevent Ulster from being forced by the IRA into the Irish Republic.[116]

The UDA opposes any confederal plan that will allow both Britain and the Republic to interfere in Ulster's internal affairs. The UDA would like to see Ulster break its tie with Britain and become an independent state. The UDA further states:

> There is an instinct within ordinary Protestant people to keep their powder dry. Though we produced a good document that reflects a changing ideology, we still reserve the right to take up arms . . . Civil war is inevitable if our concept of independence is not given a chance.[117]

114 *Ibid.*, p. 3.
115 *Ibid.*
116 Graham interview.
117 Duddy interview.

192

Summary. The results of efforts towards attitudinal change defy statistical measurement. However, the workshop at Sterling, Scotland, provides evidence that long-held animosities can be weakened by means of inter-group involvement. It worked with a small number of people who were taken out of their normal daily routine and transplanted into a situation in which there were no outside influences. Yet, after nine months of living back in their Belfast neighborhoods, the impact of the experience was still evident among participants.

That similar results can take place without having to leave Ulster is also evident. Political and religious leaders may see the Sterling experiment as a model from which to achieve greater understanding of the psychology of changing attitudes.

Notwithstanding some negative reactions from paramilitaries about the Peace People Community, the group has won a measure of respect and acceptance from journalists, politicians, churchmen and ordinary people. Even the paramilitaries on both sides have tolerated them. In addition to theoretical arguments concerning the resolution of the conflict, the Peace People are creating some practical structures and encouraging dialogue. Gerald Goldberg, the former Lord Mayor of Cork, summed up the community's greatest contribution when he said, "They got the Nobel Prize for reviving hope for peace in Ireland."[118]

The Presbyterian and Joint Commission reports have indicated that the two populations are initiating some communication and working together. As was indicated, some Protestant and Catholic leaders are beginning to go beyond merely condemning violence. They are also speaking to other issues such as unemployment, poverty, and how the politics of manipulation perpetuate bad relations between them.

The Fitzgerald Plan and NUPRG's *Beyond the Religious Divide* pointed to practical and idealistic notions about how best to serve the cause of peace. Yet, neither can be deemed as workable so long as the essential principle of compromise in the two plans is not

118 Statement by Gerald Goldberg at the Cork Peace Council, Central Hall, Cork, May 9, 1979.

acceded to by all parties. As was noted, any political compromise on the key issues of Irish unity, independence, or continued union with Britain is generally viewed as a form of weakness and surrender. For this reason, any successful movement toward a compromised settlement at this time seems highly doubtful. Like many earlier formulas, neither the Fitzgerald Plan nor the NUPRG study has received the attention it deserves.

In spite of its readiness to return to violence, the UDA has shown a willingness to compromise on the single issue of power-sharing. In view of Northern Ireland's political climate, the NUPRG document represents a change in its traditional position.

CHAPTER X

Review of the Literature

Recent dissertations about Northern Ireland focus upon many aspects involving the history of the conflict which is central to Ulster's political life. These include diverse and contradictory forces such as Unionists vs reformists as well as Protestant vs Catholic extremists. Means and ends are totally incompatible and mutually threatening to each other. These studies are valuable to researchers and anyone else interested in becoming informed about the Ulster conflict.

Dissertations

The Feeney Study (1974). This work is a history of the civil rights movement in Northern Ireland. It includes a brief overview of political activity from the early nineteenth century and explains how Protestants and Catholics clashed over political and economic interests.

Protestants maintained that unity with the Republic would end democracy for them because the Catholic majority was alleged to be "blindly subservient" to the Church of Rome. On the other hand, Ulster Catholics saw themselves as an oppressed minority whose only salvation was in political reforms and an all Ireland Republic.[1]

Feeney explains that today one can observe a repetition of the past when Unionists " . . . beat the drums at every election" so as to keep sectarian politics alive. In this atmosphere the real political and economic grievances are ignored.[2] Ulster's political life is explained as involving violently opposing factions. On the loyalist side is the Orange Order whose political power has been a decisive factor since its formation in 1795. The author describes the Order as ". . . the bastion of Protestant anti-Catholicism in Ireland."[3]

---

1 Edward Vincent Feeney, "From Reform to Resistance: A History of the Civil Rights Movement in Northern Ireland," (Ph.D. dissertation, University of Washington, 1974), p. 9.
2 *Ibid.,* p. 8.
3 *Ibid.*

This study describes the Provisional IRA (Provos) as a strong counterpart to the Orange Order. By 1970 the Provos' 800-man force claimed to be the most effective group in protecting the Catholic minority. Feeney contends that the Provos' offensive against British security forces in 1971 failed because that action caused Northern Ireland's government to activate the Royal Ulster Constabulary (RUC) to move against them. More importantly, however, the Provisional IRA failed to see that their paramilitary action strengthened general Protestant resistance.[4]

The author sees the predominantly Catholic Social Democratic Party (SDLP) as a new opening for Irish Catholics whose church had until recently opposed socialism. Now a minority of Ulster Catholics were supporting the left-wing SDLP because its program for full civil rights had gained much support.[5] According to Feeney, the party failed to attract Protestants because "The rule in Northern Ireland was, still that Ulstermen looked at *who* was doing the talking rather than *what* was being said."[6]

Feeney describes the Northern Ireland Civil Rights Association (NICRA) as made up mostly of Catholic working class and dominated by Republicans who favored a united Ireland, while avoiding the issue of political unification. The movement was committed to reform.[7] Yet, loyalists perceived reform as a threat to their positions. They were able to convince Protestants that the NICRA was a clandestine Republican-Catholic and/or Communist conspiracy to destroy Ulster.[8]

The study concludes that Unionists were successful in their efforts "to sectarianize an otherwise non-sectarian movement." Because of this the NICRA was never able to attract a mass Protestant following.[9] Loyalists were further able to discredit the NICRA by pointing to its aggressive wing whose confrontation

4 *Ibid.*, pp. 259 - 263.
5 *Ibid.*, p. 252.
6 *Ibid.*, pp. 251 - 252.
7 *Ibid.*, p. 107.
8 *Ibid.*, p. 103.
9 *Ibid.*, p. 104.

tactics were seen as revolutionary and dangerous. Feeney argues that NICRA's aggressiveness alienated the Protestant workers whom they were most anxious to attract to their movement.[10]

This study is important because it discusses the programs and personalities of Ulster's modern reform movements in the context of history. It explains the opposing strategies used by various groups for initiating political change or for resisting it. The breadth of information involved in this history reflects extensive research in which the author utilizes original sources, including official documents and Northern Ireland's newspaper media. The work is a comprehensive and informative account of political action in Northern Ireland from the turn of the century to 1971.

The Downey Study (1978). James E. Downey writes about the IRA and the NICRA as two dominant groups struggling for political change in Ulster in 1969. They differed radically in their approach as to how this was to be done. The IRA believed the only way to effect change was through violence, while the NICRA insisted on working through the political process.

Downey describes the IRA in the early sixties as weak and unorganized. But the clashes between loyalists and Catholics in 1969 caused the IRA to grow on the blood of its martyrs. It gained new support as defender of the Catholic ghettos.[11] The IRA refused to take part in the political system, however, and did not run candidates for election even in Catholic districts where it had strong support. "Even if elected," asserts Downey, "they refused to take their seats in either Westminister or Stormont." The IRA contended that both parliaments were illegal and did not merit recognition.[12]

The NICRA, on the other hand, was less nationalistic and more attractive to civil rights groups, liberals, Republicans and Northern Ireland's Communist Party. Catholics dominated the organization's ranks; however, many Protestans were also involved. NICRA was described as a ". . . non-sectarian movement in membership and

---

10 *Ibid.,* p. 319.
11 James E. Downey, "Conflict and Crime in Northern Ireland," (Ph.D. dissertation, Bowling Green Universty, 1978), p. 48.
12 *Ibid.*

ideology."[13] The study contends that because the NICRA was crossing the religious divide, "Its success would under-cut the basis of Unionist rule. The regime sought to introduce sectarianism as an issue in the civil rights campaign."[14]

Downey outlines the program of NICRA as follows:

1. To define the basic rights of all citizens.
2. To protect the rights of individuals.
3. To highlight all abuses of power.
4. To demand guarantees for freedom of speech, assembly and association.
5. To inform the public of its lawful rights.
6. To seek out alternatives to violence and be willing to make sacrifices to attain social change.[15]

NICRA's purpose was to challenge the government on the issue of discrimination in the allocation of public housing by Unionists who controlled local housing authorities.[16] Its tactics were to launch a campaign of non-violent confrontation and civil disobedience.[17] Its members demonstrated in the streets and were met with Unionist counter-demonstrations. This led to bloodshed in the Catholic ghetto of Derry-Bogside.[18]

Violence provided an entry for elements on the far right of the Unionists. These were Protestant paramilitaries such as the Ulster Defense Association (UDA), the Ulster Freedom Fighters (UFF), and the Ulster Volunteer Force (UVF).[19]

The purpose of the Royal Ulster Constabulary (RUC) was to impose order, but it was accused of provoking conflict rather than keeping the peace.[20] The stated policy of the British Army was to protect the minority, but Catholics viewed it as more interested in preserv-

13 *Ibid.*, pp. 38 - 39.
14 *Ibid.*
15 *Ibid.*
16 *Ibid.*, p. 40.
17 *Ibid.*, p. 50.
18 *Ibid.*, p. 41.
19 *Ibid.*, p. 42.
20 *Ibid.*, p. 46.

ing the *status quo.* Downey comments, "The army was there not as liberators but as an oppressive force in occupied Ireland."[21]

This study makes the following conclusions:

1. The popular acceptance and respectability extended to the IRA and NICRA by the Catholic population in 1969 polarized Catholics and Protestants.
2. The climate of political confrontation had a major impact on the initial increase in the rate of serious deviance. That is, both the IRA and NICRA contributed to a marked increase in the crime rate.
3. The high incidence of crime encouraged Britain's reinstatement of the internment policy, a system of intensified security which the security forces used to control the IRA. This resulted in a sharp increase in crime while the prison population remained constant. Offenders now repeated their crime after being released from prison.[22]

The Downey Study is important because it traces how group actions on one side triggered countersteps from opposing forces. Moreover, the major impact of each group was an increase in the level of serious crime. Downey writes clearly and is easy to follow. His use of primary government sources, in addition to several authoritative secondary sources, strengthens the study's credibility.

Referred Readings

The Carroll Study (1975). This work by Terrance George Carroll identifies several aspects of Ulster's political life which contributed to alienation among political activists. The author refers to a 1972 census survey involving interviews of 259 political activists from four communities which were predominantly Roman Catholic. The survey explained that in each community the general population harbored bitter and long-standing hostility which favored civil disobedience and violent revolution. Such attitudes stemmed from three main causes:

21 *Ibid.,* p. 47.
22 *Ibid.,* pp. 56 - 59, 66, 83.

1. The long history of conflict that recalled the displacement of the Gaelic-Catholic population from their ancestral lands by Anglo-Scottish Protestant immigrants during the seventeenth century. This involved military defeat of the native Irish population and their subjugation.
2. The inequities of the political system which failed to account for extending a share of political power to Ulster's Catholic minority. Exclusion from power meant being totally dependent upon the will of the Protestant majority.
3. The serious imbalance in the distribution of the national wealth in which Catholics were excluded from social and economic benefits.[23]

Carroll suggests that the bombings and assassinations perpetrated by today's Provos have the support of the Catholic population. He alludes to the Unionists' double standard which today condemns IRA paramilitarism but historically also resorted to violence whenever it served its own interests.

The Malcolm Study (1975). The work by Douglas Malcolm Jr. explains societal harmony and disharmony as not determined simply by the nature of communal politics, nor were they the result of innocent disagreement between well-meaning individuals holding differing points of view. Conflict stemmed from political leaders who consciously stimulated and orchestrated factions which were seemingly incapable of existing together in peace. Elites established perimeters within which some expression of political protest occurred.

Malcolm explains the regulation of conflict as most successful in communities such as Northern Ireland where differences have become irreconcilable. He argues that political terrorism persists because Northern Ireland's leadership consciously failed to introduce compromise and conciliation as a viable alternative.

The study discusses a fragmented society as one which was formed by migrations of peoples to other geographical areas in order to found new settlements. The author calls the new groups "fragments" which imposed their own cultural, religious, ethnic and linguistic modes upon the native people. The relationship between the new and

23 Terrance George Carroll, "Political Activists in Disaffected Communities: Dissidence, Disobedience and Rebellion in Northern Ireland," (Ph. D. dissertation, Carlton University, Canada, 1975), No order number.

the old inhabitants became one of dominance as opposed to subservience.

In Northern Ireland the "fragment mentality" requires the former immigrant Protestant population historically to favor the dominance of a single Unionist Party over any party representing the Gaelic-Catholic minority. Thus was laid the groundwork for irreconcilable differences and hostility.[24]

The Palmer Study (1976). Shirley Adams Palmer discusses how the government of Northern Ireland responded to extremism between 1965 and 1972. She explains that the government's efforts toward reconciliation failed to achieve anything positive because the political leadership lost its credibility with a large minority. Especially when security forces were under attack by extremists, reforms did not strengthen the government's position but weakened it. The passage of reforms did not restore peace. Furthermore, a tiny minority which chooses violence can influence the political climate of the whole society.

On the other hand, radical ideologues can realize a more decisive shift in governmental power if they stress the poor social conditions that give rise to conflict rather than bluntly demanding political change.

As part of the political process, street demonstrations can be effective in calling attention to injustices and gathering popular support. Yet, should parades give way to open conflict, the government can halt it by acting swiftly and decisively. However, authorities will fail to restore order and suffer the loss of credibility whenever they support one faction over another or encourage violence by one side against the other. Thus the way will become clear for an open and direct attack upon all the symbols of governmental authority. Under such conditions no amount of reforms or improvement of the social order can bring about a peaceful solution.[25]

24 Douglas Malcolm Jr., "Conflict Regulation vs Mobilization: The Dilemma of Northern Ireland," (Ph.D. dissertation, Columbia University, 1975), Order No. 77-6661.
25 Shirley Adams Palmer, "The Parliament of Northern Ireland: A General Systems Approach to Conflict," (Ph.D. dissertation, Ohio State University, 1976), Order No. 76-18-021.

Other Recent Studies

The MacManus Study (1967). This comprehensive work, The Story of the Irish Race, embraces the history of Ireland from ancient to modern times. The earlier chapters discuss Gaelic mythology associated with ancient Milesian colonizers who came from Spain about 1000 B.C. Later came the Gaels and Phoenicians to Ireland who were " . . . well acquainted with its ports."[26] Writings of early Gaelic kings and poets offer a comprehensive background into Ireland's Christian and intellectual traditions.

MacManus cites Ireland's development of classical learning to the fifth century when " . . . Scholars from Wales, Cornwall and Brittany were coming to Ireland for schooling."[27]

MacManus' account of the modern movement of Scottish Presbyterians into Ulster in the seventeenth century resulted in the removal of the Irish population from the most productive lands. "Sore indeed was the lot of the poor Irish in the woods, and mountains, and moors."[28] The author describes the Irish rising of 1641 and later rebellions as natural consequences of having suffered injustice under penal laws, the suppression of Irish trade and supremacy of the British Parliament over Ireland's political life.

The study describes Ireland's early nineteenth century struggles for repeal of the union with Britain, led by the political leader, Daniel O'Connell, and emergence of modern Irish nationalism.

MacManus discusses the secret Fenians, whose official name became the IRA, who began in 1858 in Ireland and in the United States. The Fenians's purpose was to make Ireland an independent state. The Easter Rising of 1916 is described as a military defeat for Irish nationalists but a moral victory for Ireland's struggle for independence. Such victory was expressed in the General Election of December of that year which provided strong national support for the Republicans.[29]

---

26 Sean MacManus, *The Story of the Irish Race: A Popular History of Ireland.* (New York: The Devin-Adair Co., 1967), p. 21.
27 *Ibid.,* p. 215.
28 *Ibid.,* p. 407.
29 *Ibid.,* pp. 704 - 705.

MacManus' study is comprehensive, informative, and offers valuable insights into the spirit of contemporary Irish nationalism.

The Coogan Study (1980). The publication, *On the Blanket,* examines the status of Republican prisoners who are convicted of crimes against the Government of Northern Ireland. Coogan explains prisoners protests against being treated as criminals rather than political prisoners, or as "Special Category." The IRA campaign for political status is today expressed in their refusal to wear clothes and in their smearing excrement on the walls of their cells in "dirty protest" and in their refusal to take food.

Prison authorities view the IRA as a criminal terrorist organization and insist that IRA prisoners must be treated as criminals under the civil laws of Northern Ireland. Coogan engaged in extensive research at the Long Kesh prison near Belfast where he interviewed inmates and prison officials and corresponded with Michael Alison, the Minister responsible for Northern Ireland prisons.

As to why the encounter with prison authorities is so ferocious, Coogan suggests the answer can be found in Ireland's history of troubles with Britain. Republicans view the prisons as the final testing of their endurance. The author cites the words of the Republican, Terence MacSwiney, who, in 1919, died in Brixton Prison after a prolonged hunger strike. MacSwiney's statement serves to inspire today's IRA: "It is not those who can inflict the most but those that can suffer the most who will conquer."[30]

Coogan describes the "larger prison" outside the walls of Long Kesh as those of high unemployment and widespread poverty that are aggravated by religious bigotry. These are some of the conditions which have produced unrest. *On the Blanket* is a valuable contribution toward understanding Northern Ireland's prison conditions and intensity of IRA feelings.

The Utley Study (1975). T. E. Utley's publication, *Lessons of Ulster,* is a critical study of British policy in Ulster between 1969 and 1976. The author bases his remarks upon personal observation during several trips to Northern Ireland. He argues that successive British governments have blundered in their attempts to construct

30 Coogan, *On the Blanket.*

a peaceful solution to the Ulster problem. This reflects an " . . . ignorance of Ireland and of the nature of politics itself."[31]

Utley points to the British habit on encouraging moderate-minded politicians to serve in Northern Ireland, only to discover how politically ineffective they were soon to become. He sees an irony in positioning political moderates into an already polarizing situation where extremists direct their attack upon the center.[32] Introducing British troops into the area served to prolong the conflict by solidifying opposing paramilitaries. The British military further jeopardized the safety of the Catholics whom they were supposed to protect.[33]

Utley asserts that the British Government did not really act on the belief that Ulster was part of the United Kingdom. Britain was therefore hesitant to fully utilize its military power against the IRA. Instead, the military acted as though it was putting down a rebellion in one of the provinces. Part of the reason for this attitude about Ulster is because of Britain's separation by the Irish Sea. Another reason is because Northern Ireland's civil war seems to be mainly over religion and about " . . . transubstantiation and the mediating role of the priesthood between God and man."[34] British citizens generally view such issues as having no relevance to them. Ulster is thus treated more like a colonial problem which has no direct bearing on domestic politics.[35]

The six counties of Ulster had since 1921 interpreted the Government of Ireland Act as a guarantee to remain part of Britain. British politicians, on the other hand, viewed the Act as having provided a means for gradual devolution toward union with the Republic. Utley argues that Britain's political center, or moderates, did not face up to the reality concerning Catholic aspirations toward a United Ireland, and Protestant determination to remain a part of the United Kingdom.[36] "In the process," asserts Utley, "they misunderstood

31 Utley, p. 7.
32 *Ibid.*, p. 13.
33 *Ibid.*, p. 14.
34 *Ibid.*, p. 17.
35 *Ibid.*
36 *Ibid.*, p. 25.

the natures both of Catholics and of Protestant Ulster."[37] While Britain's moderation policy was to end polarization, the effect was to intensify even more the politics of extremism, a tragic political irony.[38]

Utley further argues that the citizens in the Republic gave only lip-service in support of a united Ireland. The majority of people in the Republic were repelled at the thought of unity with Ulster. Because of her failure to see this, Britain lost a condition for favorable bargaining with Dublin. Britain could have reaffirmed its 1921 statement not to view unity as an ideal, but as an option for the people of Ulster. Utley sees that such a stance would have been a fair exchange for the Republic's support against the IRA. He asserts, "Through its almost incredible failure to understand southern Irish politics it failed to bargain at all."[39] Major British mistakes were failing to appreciate the internal cohesion and power of Ulster Protestants and perceiving this as weakness. Therefore, Ulster's problem rarely received Britain's full attention.[40]

Utley's summary of British policy is that it failed to understand the political climate in Northern Ireland and the general nature of politics there. The study is a strong and insightful analysis of Britain's policy toward Ulster between 1969 and 1974.

The Hull Study (1975). Roger H. Hull's book, *The Irish Triangle: Conflict in Northern Ireland,* is a study dedicated to peace. The book is valuable in that it attempts to fit the Northern Ireland problem into an analytical framework. Hull argues that Ulster is not another example of ethnic nationalism or religious strife. It is different from other conflicts between Hindu and Moslem, Arab and Jew, or Black and White. Yet the conflict can be viewed as containing some relevance to those struggles.[41]

Hull traces the problem to the year 1171, when the armies of Henry II invaded Ireland. Since that time, many factors, such as

37 *Ibid.*
38 *Ibid.*
39 *Ibid.,* pp. 68 - 69.
40 *Ibid.,* pp. 114 - 115.
41 Hull, pp. 3 - 4.

religion, political ideologies and economic interests have made the Ulster problem particularly complex.

Throughout the book Hull presents historical and political points of view of Belfast, Dublin, and London. He sees the value of including this triangle in every major issue which divides the north. The issues involving civil strife, human rights, political authority, and intervention are discussed throughout his book.

Hull does not wish to make his study another exercise in biased reporting. While striving to be objective in presenting the facts of the conflict, he believes it is important to make personal analyses and observations of the facts concerning the Northern Ireland problem. Hull suggests that the primary responsibility for resolving the Ulster conflict is Britain's, but he believes that a humanitarian intervention by the United Nations would serve the international community. A United Nations role would be to ameliorate the situation.[42]

Hull's conclusions are that the policy of applying a military solution is bound to fail if freedom and justice are not applied simultaneously.[43] His two-step solution includes the following:

1. Extending full equality to all citizens, replacing discrimination with equity and justice to all citizens. This includes the integration of schools so as to break sectarian segregation in education. In the face of anticipated opposition from the clergy, the British Government could reduce funding, pressuring parochial schools to conform.[44]
2. A British request for a United Nations peace-keeping force to replace the British Army, and intervention by the European Economic Community which has a special economic interest in terminating the conflict.[45]

Hull concludes that the first of the two steps appears to be a hard-line approach but he sees this as necessary to " . . . end the eye-for-an-eye brand of sectarianism now and in the future."[46]

The Strauss Study (1951). This study entitled, *Irish Nationalism and British Democracy*, begins with a description of Britain's history

42 *Ibid.,* p. 254.
43 *Ibid.,* p. 255.
44 *Ibid.,* pp. 265, 268 - 269.
45 *Ibid.,* p. 241.
46 *Ibid.,* p. 270.

of conquest of land which made up her empire. In Ireland that conquest was blended with settlement which produced conflicting results. The Republic of Ireland broke away from the Empire as did most of the English descendants who remained in Ireland. But, the Scottish and English descendants living in Ulster remained loyal to the United Kingdom. Strauss states that "Ireland was conquered by force, held by force, lost by force."[47]

Strauss condemns the English land system, the extortion of exorbitant rentals, and acquisition of title deeds by whatever means possible. This was " . . . the root problem of Irish economy."[48]

Armed resistance movements were met with hostile attitudes of the Catholic Church which condemned secret organizations and their revolutionary spirit. The Church's condemnations were intensified when the secret Catholic Defenders group formed an alliance with the largely Protestant United Irishmen shortly before the Rebellion of 1798.[49] Strauss argues the Church's concerns were more with power than with morals: " . . . they interfered with the peculiar relationship of priests with their flocks which was the psychological basis of the power of the Church."[50]

In his discussion on Ulster, Strauss states that by the eighteenth century that province was already " . . . the main battlefield of powerful but contradictory political and religious tendencies."[51] At this point in Irish history the Scottish Presbyterians who were also subject to the English ascendancy's overlordship, might have just as well sided with the Irish Catholics in revolution against Britain.[52] But, the pressure of population and competition for suitable farmland increased frictions between the two populations which kept them apart.[53]

47 Eric Strauss, *Irish Nationalism and British Democracy* (New York: Columbia University Press, 1951), p. 3.
48 *Ibid.,* p. 9.
49 *Ibid.,* pp. 17 - 18.
50 *Ibid.,* p. 18.
51 *Ibid.,* p. 23.
52 *Ibid.,* p. 25.
53 *Ibid.,* p. 24.

The Rebellion of 1798 against British rule also contained a definite anti-Protestant bias. The British Government suppressed it with the backing of the Protestant and Catholic upper class which was opposed to any attack on the *status quo.* The Anglo-Irish ascendancy was strengthened by wealthy Catholic collaboration, and proceeded to use Orange terrorists to exploit divisions among the Protestant and Catholic people.[54]

The practice of dividing the conquered was a long-established method of British rule. Strauss states:

> The Irish Government was well aware of the crucial importance of Ulster and concentrated both on disarming the Ulster revolutionary movement and on encouraging all signs of anti-Catholic and anti-nationalist prejudice, and in particular the nascent Orange society. The eventual success of this policy in Ulster guaranteed the survival of British rule over Ireland in the greatest crisis which had confronted it for centuries, the Napoleanic Wars.[55]

The Catholic middle business class continued to be disinterested in the impoverished peasantry, and left Ireland during the Great Famine which struck that nation in the mid-nineteenth century. Irish industry that collapsed due to hard times and English competition caused many Irish business people to leave Ireland. Those who could manage, assimilated into the British circle of journalists, administration, soldiers, and colonial professions.[56]

Strauss sees a relationship of Ireland's social, political, and religious history with its economic history. He uses the Ulster leader, Lord Carson's description of this history of Irish nationalism as a class conflict being waged by the lower class "have-nots" against the upper class "haves." This calls attention to a condition of which Britain has historically taken advantage.[57]

Britain's colonial policy was one of expediency and responding to what it believed was in its national interests even if this meant weakening Ireland's economic life. Britain's willingness to make concessions depended upon a hard headed practicality. Strauss asserts:

54 *Ibid.,* p. 55.
55 *Ibid.,* pp. 25 - 26.
56 *Ibid.,* p. 142.
57 *Ibid.,* pp. 25 - 26.

208

As soon as the growth of democracy and the shift in Britain's economic position made imperialist rule over Ireland more difficult and less profitable, the economic bonds between the two countries weakened from year to year.[58]

This study is comprehensive and adequately treats the history of people and events which shaped colonial rule and Irish politics over the last two-hundred years.

The McCaffrey Study (1979). This book is a relatively updated, concise, and easy to read history of Ireland. It begins with the Norman-English conquest of 1169 of a people who were " . . . united culturally but not politically."[59] The author sees the lack of political cohesiveness as a major weakness in Ireland's ability to resist foreign invasion. By the fourteenth century the Irish had adopted military tactics and weaponry of the invaders and had an opportunity to expel the enemy, by then demoralized by the dreary winters. Yet, Irish tribal divisions made it impossible for them to exploit the enemy's weakness.[60]

McCaffrey discusses the origins of the Irish Question by tracing the influences of the Protestant Reformation and how events of the sixteenth and seventeenth centuries served to demoralize Irish Catholics. He also discusses this in relation to the Penal Laws and ascendancy of Protestant power.[61] Though their grievances were real, Irish Catholics were unable to launch an effective liberation movement. As McCaffrey points out:

> They were too depressed and degraded for effective political action . . . most secret societies continued to confine their protests to rents, tithes, and excessive clerical dues.[62]

Discussion is given to early nineteenth century Irish patriots such as Robert Emmet, Daniel O'Connell, Wolf Tone, and a list of martyrs to the cause of Ireland's freedom. The author discusses the rise of

58 *Ibid.,* p. 205.
59 McCaffrey, p. 1.
60 *Ibid.,* p. 2.
61 *Ibid.,* pp. 13 - 34.
62 *Ibid.,* p. 39.

modern Irish political nationalism exemplified in the Young Ireland movement and nineteenth century European nationalism.

McCaffrey describes the Great Famine of 1845 - 1849 as further destructive of Irish morale. "The Famine was the Irish holocaust. As the Jews were in the Third Reich, the Irish were victims of ideological murder, no popery and *laissez faire*."[63] The famine caused about four million Irish immigrants to leave their country for Britain, Canada, the United States and Australia.[64]

The 1916 Easter Rising in Dublin is viewed as the take-off point for Irish national liberation from Britain. McCaffrey quotes Irish poet, William Butler Yeat's poem, "Easter, 1916," where the execution of patriots won popular support. " . . . all changed, changed utterly: a terrible beauty is born."[65]

McCaffrey names his chapter about Ulster, "The Northern Specter." Together with his conclusion he discusses current history and analysis. He ends his study by describing Northern Ireland as possibly:

> Britain's inferno where contemporary politicians disentangle the threads of centuries of ill-conceived and selfish Irish policies, always to be hopelessly thwarted by the duplicity of their ancestors.[66]

The De Paor Study (1970). The author's book, *Divided Ulster*, traces the history of conflict in Ulster and describes sectarian politics and civil rights for the Roman Catholic minority as very complex issues. De Paor says that the suffering of poor Protestants is almost equal to that of Catholics, yet the Protestant moderates fought Catholics with as much enthusiasm as the followers of Ian Paisley.[67]

De Paor argues that the Northern Ireland problem is essentially colonial in character rather than religious. The so-called 'racial' distinction is really a myth. The imagined difference " . . . between the colonists and the natives is expressed in terms of religion."[68]

---

63 *Ibid.*, p. 73.
64 *Ibid.*, p. 89.
65 *Ibid.*, p. 141.
66 *Ibid.*, p. 193.
67 Liam De Paor, *Divided Ulster* (Middlesex, England: Penguin Books Ltd., 1970), p. 2.
68 *Ibid.*, p. 3.

The distinction is maintained in order to perpetuate societal divisions.

The author says any tendency for native Irish and Scotch Presbyterians toward integration was halted and reversed nearly two centuries ago by the capitalist and landlord classes who believed it was in their interest to keep Ulster divided.[69] Ulster Unionists attacked and defeated the Home Rule Bill which would have obtained considerable autonomy for Ireland within the British Commonwealth. Protestants claimed Home Rule would spell disaster for democracy. It was, according to the convenant in 1912, " . . . subversive of our civil and religious freedom, destructive of our citizenship and perilous to the unity of the Empire . . ."[70]

Unionist opposition to the third Home Rule Bill almost resulted in a civil war. De Paor claims that enemies of Home Rule, beginning in 1885, were not Ulstermen:

> . . . the officers and gentlemen of the English ruling class. They 'played the Orange card' and worked to widen divisions in the community which resulted from different religious and cultural traditions.[71]

De Paor describes the events which resulted in the formal separation of the six counties from the south and how Ulster's sectarian politics successfully kept the Protestant and Catholic working class from integrating into a harmonious community. To do this, Unionists relied on a system which employed a facade of moderation, but was in fact, totalitarianism under the guise of Protestantism.[72]

The Northern Ireland Civil Rights Association (NICRA), founded in Dungannon in 1964 was characterized by Paisleyites as communist-dominated and supportive of IRA terrorism. The attack on unarmed civil rights marchers at Burntollet in 1969 by the Royal Ulster Constabulary showed how police " . . . abandoned pretence of impartiality, joining openly with the Protestant mob."[73] De Paor

---

69 *Ibid.*, p. 74.
70 *Ibid.*, p. 80.
71 *Ibid.*, pp. 102 - 103.
72 *Ibid.*, p. 141.
73 *Ibid.*, p. 191.

argues that from that point on, police in Derry " . . . were regarded as totally partial, criminal, and sectarian."[74]

This study concludes with a warning from the Irish socialist James Connolly, that, given the eventual creation of a sovereign united Ireland. England will still rule through capitalist institutions which were planted during the colonial period.[75]

De Paor's analysis of a divided Ireland is a valuable contribution toward an understanding of Northern Ireland where divisions have caused ordinary Protestants and Catholics to suffer.

74 *Ibid.*
75 *Ibid.*, pp. 204 - 205.

CHAPTER XI

Summary, Conclusions and Recommendations

Chapter IX discusses those who believe a resolution of the conflict is possible. The several organizations' activities and studies mentioned give further indications of the many efforts toward peace. Such efforts have come from a broad and diverse spectrum of the population. This is important because in Northern Ireland, where opposing positions are clearly defined, concession-making for peace can be at risk of one's life.

But the formulation of peace plans involving compromise and inter-faith communication are indications that in Northern Ireland there is a possibility of reconciliation.

Summary of the Research

The recent history of the Northern Ireland conflict is described in terms of Britain's efforts to control that country. It points to the way in which the Protestant minority in Ireland became a defensive majority in Ulster and successfully resisted attempts by the Catholic population to displace it.

The rise of modern Irish nationalism was treated in relation to the Celtic literary movement, the Easter Rising and the war with Britain in 1919, which ended in the partition of Ulster from the rest of the island. The British provided a guarantee to Protestants that Ulster would remain part of the United Kingdom. According to this guarantee, union with the Republic would require the approval of the electorate of Northern Ireland. To prevent such a possibility, Ulster's loyalist majority excluded the Catholic minority from exercising any effective power in the political process.

Ulster's Catholics continued to agitate for equality and sought union with the south. In 1969, the non-sectarian Northern Ireland Civil Rights Association launched massive demonstrations for election reforms and the removal of political discrimination.[1] This was coun-

1 MacEoin, p. 223.

tered by Unionists with the help of the RUC and "B" Specials. Such events encouraged a revival of the IRA, on which the Catholic population depended for its security. Thus, Ulster's population has continued to be divided and mutually antagonistic.

The Celtic literary movement or literary renaissance provided an intellectural framework for modern Irish nationalism. The poets and playwrights at the turn of the century wrote for the entire people of Ireland regardless of their religion or ethnic origins. The rise of Irish nationalism was in response to having to live under British imperialism. Loyalism, too, emerged in Ulster to protect Protestant interests there.

Though many of Ireland's writers came from the Anglo-Irish ascendancy and non-Catholic background, their works had a greater impact on the much larger Catholic population. The literary phase of Ireland's struggle for independence parallels the nineteenth and early twentieth century romantic nationalist movements in Europe.

The Irish population had for generations been influenced by British overlordship which extolled England's cultural and moral superiority. Overlordship justified racism and religious bigotry, evils which did serious damage to the national consciousness. By dramatizing a literary superhumanism in mythical characters, the intellectuals countered the feelings of powerlessness and inferiority which the Irish people experienced under Britain.

Poems and plays romanticized Ireland's cultural past, yet they were critical as well as laudatory. Some writers condemned violence as a way to achieve Ireland's independence from Britain, while others believed that violence was the only option when everything else failed. Understandably, the people were divided over this issue as the Celtic Renaissance elicited conflicting reactions between moderates and those who opted for violent revolution. The "apoliticals" were conservative, introspective and mystical. They were repelled by aggressive nationalism. The "action" intellectuals were more doctrinaire. They wrote about social injustice, political freedom and the inevitability of violent change. "Without the shedding of blood, there is no redemption."[2]

Both apolitical and action writers such as James Connolly, helped to shape the attitudes of IRA Republican nationalists in Ulster, where today they make clear distinctions between good and evil, are reluctant to compromise, and willing to resort to violent solutions. Like their predecessors who led the 1916 Rising and the Anglo-Irish War (1919 - 1921), the IRA continues to view the British presence as an evil with which there can be no compromise. This is especially true in regard to a united Ireland. Only on lesser issues such as agreeing with Protestant paramilitaries to halt pub bombings in exchange for an end to sectarian killings have the IRA Provisionals shown any flexibility. Here compromise was justified as a tactic and not as a principle on which a continuation of its war against the British is based.

Provisionals justify their clandestine war with a dogmatic assurance that what they are doing is necessary and right. IRA spokesman, Richard McAuley asserts, "The killings will go on until Britain gets out!"[3] The UDA also reflects this spirit when it promises that a bloody solution is necessary and inevitable " . . . if its concept of independence is not given a chance."[4] Both sides express what seems to be a compulsion for purification through blood sacrifice expressed by leaders of 1916. It is as though Ulster were under the spell of a collective death wish or death instinct as though reflecting the attitude that "We have always sought violent solutions. We have always done it that way."

The constant use of the printed word and reliance on the press by all parties to the conflict is evident in a variety of newspapers. The necessity for parties to inform readers of their political position is a continuing aspect of the literary tradition.

The Irish socialist James Connolly wrote about social and economic inequities and conditions of life. Today sectarianism influences

---

2 C. D. Greaves, *The Life and Times of James Connolly* (London: Laurence and Wishart, 1961), pp. 318 - 319.
3 McAuley interview.
4 Duddy interview.

215

who gets jobs and housing. Unemployment among males is four times higher there than anywhere else in Britain. As most councils are controlled by Protestants, it is the Catholic ghettos that have suffered most from this problem. The Protestant and Catholic working class has traditionally pressured the government to initiate changes in the housing policy so as to benefit the unemployed, large families and the elderly. Unemployment is aggravated by a worsening economy that forces the government to reduce its spending on the improvement of living conditions that include health and welfare. Too few jobs and inadequate housing have further depressed economic conditions in which sectarian politics thrive. The practice of gerrymandering also deprives citizens of a peaceful environment that is necessary for an economy to grow. As the American historian Kevin Cahill has asserted, "Without jobs there can be no dignity and there will be no peace."[5] Yet, even with full employment, the divisive issues of IRA nationalism and sectarian politics would remain a problem.

Protestant grievances are in having to live under the gun of IRA nationalists whose objective is to create a united Ireland. Catholic grievances are in having to live as second-class citizens within a Protestant state. Both groups have developed a scapegoat mentality, blaming each other for the condition of their lives. Especially the populations who live in Northern Ireland's Protestant and Catholic ghettos experience a sense of powerlessness.

Theories relating to prejudice, discrimination and inequality were used to analyze the consequences of maintaining an unjust social order. When a system refuses to change, the "in" groups and "out" groups or the "haves" and the "have-nots" fight one another. As was pointed out in chapter VI, the traditional ascendancy class defended lopsided imbalances in the distribution of wealth. The contrast between the poverty of Ulster's workers and the affluency of the propertied class is frequently pointed out. This situation is especially maintained according to class lines and religious differences.

5 Cahill, p. 95.

Theories were used to explain tensions relative to prejudice and discrimination that have led to community warfare. But like most struggles, the war in Ulster is counterproductive. Its violence appears to be nihilistic in nature and moving in a circular direction. Today violence continues to aggravate unemployment and discontent, while poverty and a depressed economy lead to still more violence.

An important source of sectarian tension is in northern Protestant perceptions of the Roman Catholic Church as an advocate of political unity with the south. Many of their criticisms of the Church's influence on political life of the Republic are valid ones. Considering the numerical strength of Catholicism in Ireland, the moral public order, or value system, reflects Catholic teachings regarding sexuality, divorce and mixed marriages. Given Ulster's political orientation, however, there is a tendency to read more into the dangers of "monolithic Catholicism" than is warranted. Protestants mistrust repeated assurances from southern spokesmen that a united Ireland would guarantee the civil rights of its Protestant minority. Because Protestants view Catholic power in the Republic as an important block to unification, the Church needs to re-evaluate its relations with the southern government. In respect to Protestant fears, this would require the creation of a new constitution within which a non-sectarian, pluralistic Ireland could emerge. It could be the "New Ireland" described by Jack Lynch, former *Taoiseach* of the Republic.[6]

A New Ireland would require a change in attitudes, a willingness to objectively explore new relationships. Understanding of social and psychological tensions and exploring ways to resolve them is of primary concern. Should political union follow from this is also of concern if such a union contributes to the resolution of the conflict. Yet, the ongoing problem of bigotry will always be an object of political consideration even though outstanding issues relating to economic conditions and political unity are resolved.

Ulster's Protestant resistance to unity is expressed in hostility toward its Catholic minority. Because many Catholics favor political

---

6 John D. A. Robb, *New Ireland: Sell Out or Opportunity?"* p. 13.

unity with the Republic and sympathize with IRA nationalism, they are seen as disloyal citizens of Ulster and enemies of the State.[7]

On the other hand, there are many Protestants and Catholics who are saying that Ulster's real enemies are not one another but rather extremists who have contributed to their divisions; that Ulster's ordinary people have been the victims of sectarian manipulation. Peace groups and clergy of various denominations have been calling attention to this problem. They are also saying that this exploitation of societal fears is possible because of the historical failure of Northern Ireland's segregated school system and churches to work for peace.

There are other efforts to bring about peace. One is the Sterling Workshop, which proved that it is possible to change prejudices. Another involves church groups which have shown that people of the two faiths can cooperate in a broad range of activities. Inter-denominational groups have produced studies and sent them to all the churches in Ireland. These have contained recommendations for developing mutual understanding and inter-church cooperation on many issues. Such activities have been augmented by the Ecumenical Movement, which initiated talks between the Church of Ireland and Roman Catholic leaders. These talks brought about understanding on several traditional differences as well as promoted cooperation.

In addition to these efforts, the Peace People Community has especially concerned itself with a variety of social and economic activities that involved Protestants and Catholics working together. Noteworthy has been its quiet albeit limited success in encouraging extremists to talk and to substitute political action for violence.

7 "Protestant-R. C. Attitudes on Ulster Options," *Orange Standard* (August, 1981), p. 4. (The *Orange Standard* cited an opinion poll published by the *London Times,* June 28, 1981, which showed that 58 percent of Catholics living in Ulster favored full integration with the Republic while 39 percent favored integration with the United Kingdom. Hereafter cited as "Protestant-R. C. Attitudes").

Conclusions

Economic Change as a Partial Solution

This study contends that violence feeds on poor economic conditions and deprivation due to discrimination. However, the non-parochial aspects of multi-national corporations may weaken though not entirely eliminate sectarianism. Observers argue that foreign firms locating in Ulster are not concerned with sectarian issues and will employ people according to the needs of the company rather than religious differences. An example is the now defunct De Lorean Motor Car Company, many of whose 2,000 employees came from the United Kingdom and the Republic since both countries are members of the Common Market.[8]

Due to the conflict, Britain's annual subsidy of approximately £2 billion in addition to its increased security burdens, has failed to create an investment atmosphere for Ulster's economic growth. Multi-national corporations already in Northern Ireland are there under the shadow of near-war and at their own risk. Property damage from the bombing of business establishments has cost the government an annual £400 million in repairs, a situation which has discouraged foreign investment.[9] Continuing decline of the province's basic industries has increased unemployment. Economic deterioration has also stimulated the talk of an expanded sectarian civil war in which the working class would bear the brunt. "The real question may again be evaded with disasterous consequences."[10] The powerlessness which the average citizen experiences in this situation encourages paramilitaries and demagogues to exercise a strong influence on the public consciousness.[11]

Developments and future economic projections for the Republic as were mentioned in chapter VI are seen as especially important

8 "Eire Workers for Delorean", *Orange Standard* (April, 1981), p. 2.
9 McVeigh letter.
10 Archie McKeown, "The Shipyard," *Ulster*, (July, 1979), p. 5.
11 "£400 Million Damage," p. 3.

insofar as future relations with Northern Ireland are concerned. Ironically, loyalists have often used economic reasons as well as others to resist being drawn into a political union with Ireland. Until recently, Eire's economy and standard of life have lagged behind Northern Ireland's and seemed to have little hope of matching it. Loyalists saw unity as a step downward to a "begging bowl" economy. Today, because Ulster's economic future could appear less than bright to its southern counterpart, practical-minded northern Unionists may see their natural economic interests as coinciding more with the Republic than with Britain.[12] Thus, their economic reasons for separation may be becoming less important.

If economic partnership is entered into with a spirit of good faith, whatever success that may result from this relationship may be a basis on which unemployment and the principle problems of sectarianism and IRA nationalism can be handled. That this is thought possible was indicated by American willingness to extend its political support and to make the Irish problem the subject of a new Camp David-like initiative from the highest levels of the United States government. To encourage a peace momentum toward a political settlement, the United States made commitments of substantial financial aid in 1979 for Ulster's economic recovery.[13]

By retaining its tie with Britain, Ulster may remain as an economically-depressed province and a society at war with itself; to avoid this, its people may find living in an autonomous state or some sort of provincial confederation with the south more rewarding economically. Strong economic north-south cooperation may create a climate so favorable as to make discussion of a confederal system possible.

Similarly, Britain no longer sees much economic advantage in continuing its close ties with Ulster. Unionists have noted Britain's coolness toward the Commonwealth since it joined the Common Market and, more important, a weakening of its enthusiasm for Northern Ireland.[14] In addition to providing relief from her financial

12 "Southern Irish Begging Bowl Economy," *Ulster* (August, 1981), pp. 12 - 15.
13 Cahill, pp. 97 - 99.
14 John Hume, " The Irish Question," p. 312.

and manpower burdens, a British withdrawal also would spare her much negative world opinion due to her inability to achieve a political solution. Northern Ireland's running sore inside the United Kingdom remains a source of great embarrassment to Britain.[15]

The intervention of a neutral third party such as a United Nations peace-keeping force may be a viable option so that an Irish peace process can begin. This would relieve Britain's security obligation and facilitate a British withdrawal.

On the other hand, any premature withdrawal of British troops would create a security vacuum so serious as probably to spell disaster for the whole community. Because the sorrow of Northern Ireland is partly a consequence of British imperialism, Britain remains responsible for sharing much of the cost for economic recovery. Ulster would require massive economic assistance from Britain, the United States, the Irish Republic, the EEC and elsewhere to bolster its agricultural-industrial system. It is hoped such aid would accelerate a more productive and dispersed national economy so that affluence can assist Ulster out of its dilemma.[16] The ultimate responsibility for settling problems, however, would fall on the people of Northern Ireland where it has always belonged.

This is not to imply that political unity is the best and only solution or, in fact, that it constitutes a necessarily viable solution to the conflict. After twelve years of warfare involving over 2,000 deaths and many more bereaved and injured, Protestant resistance to union with the Republic remains unabated. The truth of this is strongly evident in public statements and in journals whenever Protestant writers refer to the question of north-south unity. This goes far in supporting a position held by Conor Cruise O'Brien. The former Minister for Communications in the Republic explained that so long as the Provisionals continue their war of attrition, there can be no hope for the creation of a united Ireland.[17]

15 "EEC Weakened Bonds With Dominions," *Orange Standard* (April, 1981), p. 3.
16 Cahill, pp. 97 - 99.
17 Dervla Murphy, "A Return," *Ulster* (n.d., 1980), p. 17.

In addition to Ulster's two-thirds Protestant majority who oppose political union, there is evidence that no clear majority taken together on the whole island actually favors political unity. O'Brien refers to a survey conducted by the Dublin-based Economics and Social Research Institute (ESRI) to show how the northern, southern and British people feel about political integration:

1. 72 percent of the whole population of Northern Ireland wishes to remain in the United Kingdom. Of this, 83 percent were Protestant.
2. 16 percent of the population of Northern Ireland favor a united Ireland. Of this, 3 percent declared themselves Protestant and 39 percent declared themselves Catholic.
3. The ESRI shows that in the Republic, 68 percent of the people favored unity, but for the Republic and Northern Ireland taken together, between 48 and 52 percent of the population actually desired political union.
4. Only 25 percent of Britain's population favored continued union with Northern Ireland.[18]

A *Sunday Times* of London poll further indicates what the population of Northern Ireland believes about several more key issues relating to integration, partition, independence, power-sharing and security:

1. 91 percent of Protestants and 39 percent of Catholics favored integration with the United Kingdom.
2. 70 percent of Protestants and 62 percent of Catholics favored union with a United Kingdom with its own assembly and guarantees for Catholics.
3. 9 percent of Protestants and 22 percent of Catholics favored a repartition of Ulster according to religion.
4. 13 percent of Protestants and 58 percent of Catholics favored repartition of Ulster with an assembly and guarantees for Protestants.

18 Conor Cruise O'Brien, "Hands Off," *Foreign Policy* (Winter,1979),pp.110, 102 - 104.

5. 16 percent of Protestants and 10 percent of Catholics favored independence.
6. 6 percent of Protestants and 58 percent of Catholics favored full integration with the Republic.
7. 18 percent of Protestants and 53 percent of Catholics strongly approve of power-sharing.
8. 35 percent of Protestants and 24 percent of Catholics tend to approve of power-sharing.
9. 14 percent of Protestants and 9 percent of Catholics were neutral on the question of power-sharing.
10. 57 percent of Protestants and 30 percent of Catholics agree that the British Army should stay in Ulster.
11. 87 percent of Protestants and 34 percent of Catholics disagree that the British Army should announce the day of its withdrawal from Ulster.
12. 75 percent of Protestants and 66 percent of Catholics agreed that Protestant and Catholic children should attend school together.[19]

The above opinion polls can be given a wide range of interpretations. The relatively large percentage of Catholics who favored integration with the United Kingdom rather than joining the Republic is undoubtedly concerned about the risk of a violent civil war that might follow any political unification. Both peoples showed very little interest in the creation of an independent Ulster, while only 18 percent of Protestants favored power-sharing with Catholics. This perhaps indicates that most Protestants preferred to retain their monopoly of the decision-making process so as to safeguard the political *status quo*. In all, the population showed some common ground on matters relating to union with the United Kingdom, independence, and school integration. Their political views remained deeply divided, however, on repartition of Ulster, a united Ireland, and power-sharing.

19 "Protestant-R. C. Attitudes."

Economic Influences on Political Attitudes

The *Sunday Times* poll includes key issues to which political propagandists continue to speak. As was explained in chapter VIII,
during times of insecurity brought on by depression, war, high
unemployment, and crime, people feel powerless to alter their
situation except by following a demagogue who appeals to mass
emotions. "They took your job!" "They are going to take your
job!" "They are causing you to suffer!" "They are threatening your
survival!" Such rhetoric seems especially palatable and believable
under trying conditions. Parallels can be seen in Czarist Russia during
the nineteenth century and in 1917, prior to the Bolshevik Revolution.[20] It was also apparent in Germany in the 1920's, during the rise
of the Nazi Party.[21]

Ulster's uncertainties have created conditions that make it difficult
for political democracy and liberal values to survive, much less to
grow. They have contributed to the retreat of liberalism that is
reflected in continuing disparities between the rich and the poor and
in sectarian conflict.

The demagogues thrive best in situatuons of crisis, but are less
successful in affluent and pluralistic nations. Examples are western
European countries, where voting patterns reveal a strong disdain for
political extremism.[22] Demagogues are discredited and largely ignored and are unable to gain a popular following. Moreover, if the
economic inequities disappear, the paramount issues of IRA nationalism and Paisleyism may no longer seem so important.

Although it is unlikely that economic prosperity will eliminate
either IRA nationalism or sectarian politics, it may serve to amelio-

20 J. P. Nettl, *The Soviet Achievement* (n. p., Harcourt, Brace, & World,
Inc., 1967), pp. 27 - 54.
21 Alan Bullock, *Hitler, A Study in Tyranny* (New York: Harper and Row,
1964), passem, pp. 58 - 88.
22 Hannah Arendt, "Ideology of Terror: A Novel Form of Government,"
Enduring Questions of Politics, Ed.,Werner Feld, Alan T. Leonhard, Walter W. Toxey, Jr. (Englewood Cliffs, N.J.: Prentice-Hall, Inc., 1969), pp.
61-78.

rate Northern Ireland's social environment so as to allow for more communication between Protestants and Catholics.

Northern Ireland may put an end to paramilitary politics when its economic life improves to the level of full employment and better conditions for everyone regardless of their social class. Nevertheless, the possibility for successful economic growth is remote until the violence ends. The purpose of security forces is to control terrorism, but their very presence is believed to encourage even more terrorism. In these circumstances, neither political nor economic solutions are possible. The problem is seen as a self-defeating tautology leading nowhere.

This causes observers to conclude that there is little hope for peace in a conflict so deeply rooted in history. Ulster is perceived as coming "straight out of past centuries, as belonging to another age," and fated to remain a prisoner of its own complex circumstances.[23] The dilemma is well stated in the epilogue of the novel *Trinity,* where the American writer Leon Uris comments, "For you see, in Ireland there is no future, only the past happening over and over."[24]

The economic argument does not imply that peace will come to Northern Ireland because its people will respond to a given economic stimulus. Its collective behavior is not solely determined by the conditioning of social engineers and politicians who know what is best. New industry and science can influence social and economic change by relieving the symptoms of unemployment and poverty, but this alone cannot instill social flexibility or justice, or entirely eliminate sectarianism and IRA nationalism.

23 Paul Elmen, "Special Report," *Christian Century* (February 3, 1971), p. 170. (Article was written when Elmen was on the faculty of Seabury-Western Theological Seminary in Evanston, Illinois).
24 Leon Uris, *Trinity* (Garden City, New York: Doubleday & Co., 1976) p. 751.

Peace cannot be obtained through solutions involving single issues like economic change or political reforms. It will come by means of long-term dialogue and close cooperation with parties on practical matters. It is hoped that over time this approach can encourage an open and non-threatening atmosphere in which real problems can be debated. Rigid positions appear to be in the nature of the conflict and help to explain why it is so frustrating. Republican nationalism and/or power-sharing are issues which must be confronted in an on-going debate. Moreover, the concerns and fears of the Protestant majority regarding a united Ireland can no longer be ignored or disregarded by Republicans. Should there be no compromise on these issues, the government must be prepared for a protracted, expensive and inconclusive civil war. Yet no solution can be achieved by force. Any attempt by either side to impose its will on the other deepens the problem.

Because of this, extremism seems to be trapped in a military-existential fix. The IRA will find little reason to throw down its arms because it is asked to do so. Its strategy is to use violence to force a British withdrawal.[25] Neither are the loyalists or the UDA prepared to surrender one inch of Ulster's sovereignty to the Republic without a war that they promise would spread into the Republic. But reliance on a simplistic military victory by one side or the other, even were this possible, is no solution. This is stated pointedly by the Jesuit sociologist Michael McGrail: "We want no solution that comes from coercion, whether from the Paisleyites or the Provisionals. We don't want a victory, we want a solution."[26]

Peace plans contain points which can be discussed at length by all parties. They are not meant to be all things to all men. Whenever combinations of peace formulas are given serious attention, there will

25 McAuley interview.
26 Michael McGrail, S. J., "A Civil Rights Movement for Protestants?" *Orange Standard* (March, 1981), p.1. (McGrail is a lecturer in sociology at St. Patrick's College, Maynooth, Ireland).

inevitably be differences of opinion and interpretation. Discussion and debate are useful so long as opposition parties and their views are given ample respect and consideration. Without mutual respect there can be no hope that discussions can lead to any constructive action.

On this note, part of sociologist Thomas Schelling's tactical approach may be useful, which is to be aware of the power of public opinion and to utilize that power whenever possible to support one's position.[27]

As has been shown in the *Sunday Times* poll, public opinion in Ulster tends to favor constitutional guarantees for Catholics. It also favors greater social integration in the hope that this will lead to better understanding.[28]

Sociologist S. S. Komorita cautions that holding fast to rigid positions in bargaining will lead only to failure.

> The concept that, 'It pays to be tough' is basically irrational because it pre-empts any cooperative solution. It increases suspicions and destroys mutual trust without which no agreement can take place.[29]

A deadlock between parties can only be broken when one side is willing to make a small concession and then, in its turn, receives one from the other side. The process of taking small single steps is likely in time to gain an accumulation of concessions from both sides which will lead to a final agreement.[30] Whatever peace plan is focused upon, this approach is suggested for resolving deadlocks. But in Northern Ireland there is an unwillingness for extremists and moderates to meet to discuss their differences. Another approach is needed to cope with this problem.

27 Thomas C. Schelling, "An Essay on Bargaining," *American Economic Review* n. v., (June, 1956), p. 278.
28 "Protestant-R. C. Attitudes."
29 S. S. Komorita, "Concession-Making and Conflict Resolution," *The Journal of Conflict Resolution: Research on War and Peace Between and Within Nations*, 16 (December 4, 1973), pp. 746 - 747.
30 *Ibid.*

An Ulster peace requires major changes in human consciousness and in social-political institutions. This means that national priorities must include the negation of sectarian attitudes by Protestants and Catholics in favor of a more open and pluralistic society. Unless Ulster has the courage to do this and make peace with itself, any peace formulas or constitutional settlements will be meaningless. Political scientist Benjamin Hourani describes this consciousness as " . . . today's single basic phenomenon," in reference to the world community and the ever present nuclear impasse.[31] However, his view is just as valid when applied to Northern Ireland's political impasse and threat of a spreading conflict.

Violence cannot be eliminated by imposing more security. Law and order alone will not treat Ulster's deeper social-economic sickness. It merely treats the most visible symptom of this sickness and ignores the causes of tensions which in time may explode into a full-scale war.

It appears that Northern Ireland has become England's Vietnam, where the escalation of security forces only intensifies the struggle. Understandably, a British withdrawal is fraught with dangers. Yet, Northern Ireland has an opportunity to take decisive action to prepare for this eventuality. The conflict is no different from many others in that if the disease is not treated, it will kill the victim.

This study has shown that the general population in the north desires a peaceful solution. Whether the Peace People Community at Bledheim can become the chief instrument for this is something to consider. Were it to become a non-sectarian "Peace Party," it could receive support from both Protestants and Catholics. As it has attracted both Protestants and Catholics, including liberals and conservatives, a peace party might likewise win moderate church support. The community has resisted ever becoming a political party, because of the divisive nature of party politics. Instead, it has concentrated on the broad aspects of social interaction that were

31 Benjamin Hourani, "On Global Man," paper presented at the 2nd Futurology Symposium, Cincinnati Ohio, July, 1974.

discussed in chapter IX. But the organization contains an infrastructure manned by talented and courageous people who can articulate the issues and work on problems that divide the province. As they are willing to rise above old habits of thinking, so innovation and political creativity seem to be their greatest assets.

Were it to become a political party, the Peace People will have already developed a democratic system of changing its executive leadership with regular frequency so as to prevent a cult of personality from emerging. This policy has created an impressive pool of experienced leaders who have shown initiative in opening up dialogue with extremists. They have done this for the purpose of getting paramilitaries to talk and convincing them that the best way to achieve their objectives is through compromise.

John Cushnahan, a political moderate with the Alliance Party favoring power-sharing, makes the following point on the nature of compromise in Northern Ireland:

> We believe you've got to start from the present position and see what you can build that would be acceptable, and acceptable is the word, for you're not going to get a solution which is what both sides want.[32]

The changing of attitudes has been discussed mainly in regard to inter-church communication. Cooperation between Protestants and Catholics is crucial. Yet, a growing number of clergy and laity on both sides are saying that genuine change also requires a spiritual foundation that must be laid by the Irish people. Peace advocates argue, there is a tremendous evil in the north where satanic forces have to a great extent influenced the entire situation. Hurwitz has stated:

> Prayer and sacrifice can exorcise the evil and move Ulster toward a religious as well as an intellectual renewal. Any other solutions that are attempted *apart* from this are described as putting the cart before the horse.[33]

Though still in its infancy, the above holistic approach is today functioning in many parts of the Island where Protestants and Catholics

---

32 "The Moderate Voice", *Peace By Peace* (September 18, 1981), p. 4. (At this writing, John Cushnahan was General Secretary of the Alliance Party since 1974).
33 Hurwitz interview.

who share in the same God come together in prayer. "Mystical politics" may be viewed by skeptics as a subject that need not be taken seriously. But for many people in the north and south, a spiritual approach of interdenominational prayer groups has become essential for effecting a change of heart.[34]

As a victim of history, Northern Ireland's social-political lag can be portrayed as a society dragged "kicking and screaming" out to the past and into the twentieth century, its sectarianism as one of intellectual and emotional maladjustment to the modern world.[35] Yet, the Northern Ireland problem is very contemporary in that it has been compared to Vietnam, the Middle East, and South Africa.

Finally, it would be premature at this time to conclude that, because peace has not yet been achieved, the forces of peace have been defeated and their program is a failure. Violence goes on, but so does the struggle for peace. As was mentioned earlier there is a willingness among many Protestants and Catholics to study one another's positions and to come together in the interest of the common good. The peace movement and inter-faith meetings are examples of this. Unfortunately, economic changes alone cannot be expected to persuade Ulster Protestants to give up their political advantage and abandon their anti-Catholicism. Yet, in a depressed economy the methods for determining who get jobs and housing and who do not is crucial.

As religious bigotry cannot be eliminated by passing laws against it, an expanding and thriving economy may make sectarian decisions relating to jobs and housing seem less important so long as there is adequate employment for all. Such conditions may diminish the power of political demogogues. A healthy economy may render sectarian propaganda as less convincing and less listened to by the unemployed than is presently the case.

Nevertheless, sectarianism will continue to be a problem to be resolved by a combination of social, economic, political, educational, and spiritual factors working together to break down Ulster's psychological barriers. The greatest challenge for Northern Ireland

34 *Ibid.*
35 Crowley interview.

would be to activate all facets of the political community, including schools, media, churches, political and commercial elements to help create a new environment for bringing the entire community together. Until this happens, Northern Ireland will remain an arena of conflicting forces pulling in opposite directions. And the politics of extremism will continue to dominate the landscape as a normal and acceptable way of life.

Recommendations for Future Study

The research presented in this work includes cultural, political, economic, socio-psychological, and religious aspects of nationalism, violence, and the resolution of conflict in Northern Ireland. It does not discuss the following areas which are recommended as further avenues of study:

1. Investigate the extent to which American and other outside groups are involved with providing money and supplies to Catholic and Protestant paramilitaries.
2. Research the extent of collaboration between the IRA' and other international paramilitary organizations, particularly the Palestine Liberation Organization and foreign governments.
3. Investigate the development of relations between the Northern Unionists and the British Government and their attitudes regarding future relations.
4. Determine the numbers and condition of the Protestant minority in the Republic of Ireland. To what extent have their numbers in Eire decreased over the past three decades and what are the reasons for this? Research would prove or disprove loyalist allegations that the Protestant minority has experienced discrimination affecting their security and economic condition.
5. Study the extent of direct and indirect involvement by Catholic clergy in IRA-INLA activities. Research should validate or refute loyalist contentions of clerical support of Catholic paramilitarism.
6. Study the history and methodology of IRA hunger strikes and their influence on Irish nationalism, British policy and world opinion.
7. Make a comparison of Protestant and Catholic nationalist literature in Northern Ireland since 1921 and determine how this has reflected the nationalism of each group.
8. Investigate the weaponry and order of battle of British security forces in their response to terrorism in Ulster and assess their effectiveness against the IRA.

Bibliography

Books

Arendt, Hannah. "Ideology of Terror: A Novel Form of Government." In *Enduring Questions of Politics,* ed. by Werner Feld, Alan T. Leonhard, and Walter W. Toxey, Jr. Englewood Cliffs, N. J.: Prentice-Hall, Inc., 1969.

Barritt, D. P., and Carter, C. F. *The Northern Ireland Problem: A Study in Group Relations.* London: Oxford University Press, 1962.

Bell, Geoffrey. *The Protestants of Ulster.* London: Pluto Press Ltd., 1976.

Bell, J. Bowyer. *The Secret Army: The IRA, 1916 - 1974.* Cambridge, Mass: The MIT Press, 1974.

Bleakley, David. *Peace in Ulster.* London: Mowbrays, 1972.

Brinton, Crane. *The Anatomy of Revolution.* New York: Random House, 1965.

Brown, Bruce. *Marx, Freud, and the Critique of Everyday Life: Toward a Permanent Cultural Revolution.* New York: Monthly Review Press, 1973.

Brown, Malcolm. *George Moore: A Reconsideration.* Seattle: University of Washington Press, 1955.

Bullock, Alan. *Hitler, A Study in Tyranny.* New York: Harper and Row, 1964.

Camara, Dom Helder. *Spiral of Violence.* Trans. by Della Couling. Denville, N.J.: Dimension Press, 1971.

Canfield, Curtis. *Plays of the Irish Renaissance, 1880 - 1930.* Plainview, N.Y.: Books for Libraries Press, 1974.

Chubb, Basil. *The Government and Politics of Ireland.* London: Oxford University Press, 1970.

Coogan, Tim Pat. *On the Blanket: The H-Block Story.* Dublin: Ward River Press, 1980.

— *The IRA.* London: Pall Mall Press, 1970.

Coser, Lewis. *The Functions of Social Conflict.* New York: The Free Press, 1956.

Cottrell, Alvin J. and Dougherty, James E. *The Policies of the Atlantic Alliance.* London: Frederick A. Praeger, 1964.

De Leon, Daniel. *The Socialist Reconstruction of Society.* New York: New York Labor News Co., 1968.

De Paor, Liam. *Divided Ulster.* Baltimore: Penguin, 1970.

Devlin, Bernadette. *The Price of My Soul.* London: Andre Deutsch, 1969.

Edwards, Owen Dudley. *The Sins of Our Fathers: Roots of the Conflict in Northern Ireland.* Dublin: Gill and MacMillan, Ltd., 1970.

Elliot, R.S.P., and Hickie, John. *Ulster: A Case Study in Conflict Theory.* London: Longman Group Ltd., 1971.

Freeman, T.W. *Ireland: A General and Regional Geography.* London: Methuen and Co., Ltd., 1972.

Freemantle, Anne, ed. *The Social Teachings of the Church.* New York: New American Library of World Literature, Inc., 1963.

Fromm, Erich. *Escape From Freedom.* New York: Farra and Rinehard, Inc., 1941.

Gilbert, Martin. *Winston S. Churchill: The Stricken World, 1916 - 1922.* 4 vols. Boston: Houghton Mifflin Co., 1975.

Gray, Tony. *The Orange Order.* London: Bodley Head, 1972.

Greaves, C. D. *The Life and Times of James Connolly.* London: Laurence and Wishart, 1961.

Hass, Eric. *Socialism: World Without Race Prejudices.* New York: New York Labor News Co., 1945.

Herzl, Theodor. "The Rise of Israel." In *The Middle East: Selected Readings,* ed. by Don Peretz. New Jersey: Houghton Mifflin Co., 1973.

Holt, Edgar. *Protest in Arms: The Irish Troubles. 1916 - 1924.* New York: Coward-McCann, 1961.

Horowitz, Irving Louis. "Transnational Terrorism, Civil Liberties, and Social Science." In *Terrorism,* ed. by Yonah Alexander and S. M. Finger, New York, John Jay Press, 1977.

Howarth, Herbert. *The Irish Writers: 1880-1940.* New York: Hill and Wang, 1958.

Hull, Roger. *The Irish Triangle: Conflict in Nothern Ireland.* Princeton, N. J.: Princeton University Press, 1976.

Jeffares, A. N., and Knowland, A. S. *A Commentary on the Collected Plays of W. B. Yeats.* Stanford, Calif.: Stanford University Press, 1975.

234

Jones, Francis P. *History of the Sinn Fein Movement and the Irish Rebellion of 1916.* New York: P. J. Kenedy, 1921.

Kee, Robert. *The Green Flag: The Turbulent History of the Irish National Movement.* New York: Delecorte Press, 1972.

Kenny, Herbert A. *Literary Dublin: A History.* Dublin: Gill and MacMillan, 1974.

Krause, David. "Sean O'Casey and the Higher Nationalism: The Desecration of Household Gods." In *Theater and Nationalism in Twentieth-Century Ireland,* ed. by Robert O'Driscoll, Toronto: University of Toronto Press, 1971.

Kung, Hans., Conger, Yves O., and O'Hanlon, Daniel, S. J. In *Council Speeches of Vatican II.* Glen Rock, N.J.: Paulist Press, 1964.

Landis, Judson R. *Sociology: Concepts and Characteristics.* Belmont, Calif.: Wadsworth Publishing Co., 1977.

Laqueur, Walter Z., ed. *The Middle East in Transition: Studies in Contemporary History.* New York: Frederick A. Praeger, 1958.

Lauer, Robert H. *Perspectives on Social Change.* Boston: Allyn and Bacon, Inc., 1973.

Lenski, Gerhard. *Power and Privilege: A Theory of Social Stratification.* New York: McGraw-Hill Co., 1966.

Lieberson, Goddard. *The Irish Uprising, 1916-1922.* New York: MacMillan Co., 1960.

Loftus, Richard J. *Nationalism in Modern Anglo-Irish Poetry.* Madison and Milwaukie: University of Wisconsin Press, 1964.

Mansbach, Richard W., ed. *Northern Ireland: Half a Century of Partition.* New York: Facts on File, Inc., 1973.

Mansergh, Nicholas. *The Irish Question: 1840-1921.* 3rd ed. Toronto: George Allen and Unwin, Ltd., 1975.

MacEoin, Gary. *Northern Ireland: Captive of History.* New York: Holt, Rienhart and Winston, 1974.

MacGiolla Choille, Breandan. *Intelligence Notes: 1913-1916.* Dublin: Government Publication Office, 1966.

MacManus, Sean. *The Story of the Irish Race: A Popular History of Ireland.* New York: The Devin-Adair Co., 1967.

Marcus, David. "The Irish Mode." *Poetry of Ireland.* Nendeln/Liechtenstein: P. J. Madden, 1970.

Marx, Karl, and Engels, Friedrich. *Ireland and the Irish Problem: A Collection of Writings.* New York: International Publishers, 1945.

McCaffrey, Lawrence J. *Ireland from Colony to Nation State.* Englewood Cliffs, N. J.: Prentice-Hall, Inc., 1979.

McCann, Eamon. *War in an Irish Town.* Middlesex, Eng.: Penguin Books, Inc., 1974.

Moore, George. "Literature and the Irish Language." In *Ideals in Ireland,* pp. 45-51. Edited by Lady Augusta Gregory. New York: Lemma Publishing Corporation, 1973.

Nettl, J. P. *The Soviet Achievement.* New York: Harcourt, Brace and World, Inc., 1967.

O'Brien, Conor Cruise. *States of Ireland.* Bungay, Suffolk, England: The Chauser Press, 1974.

O'Donaghue, D. J., ed. *Poems of James Clarence Mangen.* Century ed. London: A. H. Bullen, 1972.

O'Driscoll, Robert. *Theatre and Nationalism in Twentieth-Century Ireland.* Toronto: University of Toronto Press, 1971.

O'Farrell, Patrick. *Ireland's English Question.* New York: Schocken Books, 1971.

Parenti, Michael. *Power and the Powerless.* New York: St. Martin's Press, 1978.

Peterson, Arnold. *Capitalism is Doomed: Socialism is the Hope of Humanity.* New York: New York Labor News Co., 1952.

Rapoport, David. "Politics of Atrocity." In *Terrorism: Interdisciplinary Perspectives.* Edited by Yonah Alexander and S. M. Finger. New York: The John Jay Press, 1977.

Robb, John D. A. *New Ireland: Sell Out or Opportunity?* n. p. 1961.

Rose, Richard. *Governing Without Consensus: An Irish Perspective.* London: Faber and Faber, Ltd., 1971.

Severn, Bill. *Irish Statesman and Rebel: The Two Lives of Eamon De Valera.* New York: Ives Washburn, Inc., 1970.

Sorokin, Pitirim A. *Hunger as a Factor in Human Affairs.* Gainsville, Fla.: University Press, 1975.

Strauss, Eric. *Irish Nationalism and British Democracy.* New York: Columbia University Press, 1951.

Uris, Jill and Leon. *Ireland, A Terrible Beauty.* New York: Bantam Books, 1978.

Uris, Leon. *Trinity.* Garden City, N.Y.: Doubleday and Co., 1976.
Utley, T. E. *Lessons of Ulster.* London: J. M. Dent and Sons, 1975.

Journals

"An Independent Ulster: What Can It Offer Industry?" *Ulster: Voice of the Ulster Defence Assiociation* 2 (n. d.): 4 - 5.
"Andy Tyrie Speaks to Guardian." *Ulster: Voice of the Ulster Defence Assiociation* 2 (n. d.): 14.
"The Archbishop Goes and Comes." *Orange Standard* (May, 1980): 6.
"Are Americans Financing the IRA?" *Protestant Telegraph* (February 27, 1982): 11 - 12.
Arnlis, Peter. "Job Bias Against Catholic School Leavers." *An Phoblacht/Republican News* (September 13, 1980): 3.
Aunger, Edmund A. "Religion and Occupational Class in Northern Ireland." *Economic and Social Review* 7 (1975 - 1976): 4.
Barrington, Donal. "Violence in Ireland." *Furrow* (February, 1970): 67 - 70.
Beattie, W. "The Spirit of Anti-Christ." *Protestant Telegraph* (November 2, 1981): 4.
—— "The Visit of the Pope to the U. K. in 1982 Must be Resisted." *Protestant Telegraph* (May 2, 1981): 8.
Beeson, Trevor. "The Impotence of the Churches." *Christian Century* 89 (September 13, 1972): 888.
—— "Northern Ireland: Can Order Come Out Of Chaos?" *Christian Century* 91 (July 17, 1974): 720 - 724.
"Betraying the Protestant Faith and the Reformation." *Protestant Telegraph* (September 19, 1981): 11.
"Beyond the Religious Divide." *Ulster: Voice of the Ulster Defence Association* (n. d.): 5.
"Blood, Sweat, Tears and Talk." *Orange Standard* (June, 1980): 4.
Boserup, Anders. "Power in a Post-Colonial Setting: The Why and Whither of Religious Confrontation in Ulster." *Bulletin For Peace Proposals* (August, 1969): 62.
Bowden, Tom. "The IRA and the Changing Tactics of Terrorism." *Political Quarterly* 47 (October-December, 1976): 427.

Boyd, Andrew. "The Success of the Peace People." *Nation* 235 (April 16, 1977): 454.

Brady, John, S. J. "Pluralism in Northern Ireland." *Studies: An Irish Quarterly Review* 57 (Summer, 1978): 89.

"Breaking the Deadlock." *Peace By Peace* (May 8, 1981): 1.

Cahill, Kevin M. "America and Ulster: Healing Hands." *Foreign Policy* 37 (Winter, 1979 - 1980): 87.

"Call For Cooperation." *Peace By Peace* (April 9, 1982): 1.

Cameron. "Arms and the South." *Combat: Journal of the Ulster Volunteers* 4 (December, 1980): 3.

——"False Images of a Divided People." *Combat: Journal of the Ulster Volunteers* 4 (n. d.): 6.

"Cardinal Worships With Protestants." *Orange Standard* (June, 1980): 4.

"In Civilian Raiment." *Orange Standard* (November, 1980): 4.

"Comment: Employment and the Want of It." *Orange Standard* (May, 1980): 4.

"Comment." *Orange Standard* (June, 1980): 5.

"Connolly's Words and the Morality of the Freedom Fight." *An Phoblacht/Republican News* (May 12, 1979): 5.

Corrigan, Mairead. "Create the Politics of Friendship." *Peace By Peace* (April 4, 1980): 1.

——"Paisley and Provos Make Northern Ireland 'No Go' Area For Industry." *Peace By Peace* 6 (December 11, 1981): 1.

"Death On the Border." *Ulster: Voice of the Ulster Volunteers* (November, 1980): 6.

Doob, Leonard W., and Foltz, William J., "The Belfast Workshop: An Application of Group Techniques To a Destructive Conflict." *Journal of Conflict Resolution: Research on War and Peace Within Nations* 18 (June, 1974): 247.

——"The Impact of a Workshop Upon Grassroots Leaders in Belfast." *Journal of Conflict Resolution: Research on War and Peace Within Nations* 18 (June, 1974): 247.

Easthope, Gary. "Religious War in Ireland." *Sociology: Journal of the British Sociological Association* 10 (September, 1976): 446.

"EEC Weakened Bonds With Dominions." *Orange Standard* (April, 1981): 3.

"Eire Protestants' Good Citizenship Earns '12th' Praise." *Orange Standard* (August, 1980): 3.

"Eire Workers for Delorean." *Orange Standard* (April, 1981): 2.

Elmen, Paul. "Special Report." *Christian Century* 87 (February 3, 1971): 170.

Engel, Norbert Paul. "European Court Slams Irish Law on Divorce Ban." *Orange Standard* (June, 1970): 2.

Evason, Eileen. "Northern Ireland's Peace Movement: Some Early Reflections." *Community Development Journal* (April, 1977): 180.

"The Failure of the Provisional IRA." *Ulster: Voice of the Ulster Defence Association* 2 (April, 1979): 1.

"Fears for the Future in Border Areas: Provos Have Death List—DUP Claim." *Orange Standard* (May, 1980): 1.

"Fighting for Peace." *Peace By Peace* 11 (June 5, 1981): 1.

"£ 400 Million Damage." *An Phoblacht/Republican News* (September 20, 1980): 6.

Gans, Herbert. "The New Egalitarianism." *Saturday Review* (May 6, 1972): 43 - 46.

"Ghettoes Increase as Protestants Bear Brunt of Intimidation." *Orange Standard* (October, 1981): 8.

Gilhooley, James. "On the Road to Drogheda." *Commonweal* 104 (March 18, 1977): 180.

Graham, Ivor. "Those Secret Talks." *Ulster: Voice of the Ulster Defence Association* (August 1, 1981): 10 - 11.

Greenhill, Anne. "The 'Free' State – And All That." *Ulster: Voice of the Ulster Defence Association* (August, 1980): 8 - 9.

Hayes, Peter, "Deep Sea Docks Dispute: Low Pay and Casual Labour Keeps Workers Out." *An Phoblacht/Republican News* (September 6, 1980): 8.

Hickey, Neil. "The Battle for Northern Ireland: How TV Tips the Balance." *TV Guide* (September 26-October 2, 1981): 1.

"History Repeating Itself? Three Steps to Anarchy." *Ulster: Voice of the Ulster Defence Association* (November, 1980): 1.

"Housing Problems." *Protestant Telegraph* (May 2, 1981): 9.

Hume, John. "The Irish Question: A British Problem." *Foreign Affairs* 58 (Winter, 1979 - 1980): 303.

"Independence – No Other Solution." *Ulster: Voice of the Ulster Defence Association* (October, 1981): 4 - 6.

239

"Inter-Church Discussion." *Orange Standard* (November, 1980): 8.

"IRA Terrorism Exposed." *Ulster: Voice of the Ulster Defence Association* (June 6, 1981): 6 - 7.

"Ireland." *Political Quarterly* 43 (April-June, 1972): 8.

Kennedy, R. Scott, and Klotz-Chamberlin, Peter. "Northern Ireland's Guerrillas of Peace." *Christian Century* 304 (August 31, 1977): 746.

Kingston, William. "Northern Ireland – The Elements of a Solution." *Political Quarterly* 43 (April-June, 1972): 202.

— — "Northern Ireland – If Reason Fails." *Political Quarterly* 44 (January, 1973): 32.

Komorita, S. S. "Concession-Making and Conflict Resolution." *Journal of Conflict Resolution: Research on War and Peace Between and Within Nations* 16 (December 4, 1973): 746 - 747.

Laffan, Michael. "The Unification of Sinn Fein in 1917." *Irish Historical Studies* 17 (March, 1971): 353.

"London and Northern Ireland." *Peace By Peace* (August, 1980): 6.

Long, S. E. "The Economics of Common Sense." *Orange Standard* (October, 1980): 3.

— — "Mixed Marriages." *Orange Standard* (April, 1982): 6.

— — "Mixed Marriages: Rome Maintains Strict Rigidity." *Orange Standard* (May, 1980): 2.

"Massive IRA Propaganda Machine Funded by British Government" *Ulster: Voice of the Ulster Defence Association* (September, 1981): 1.

Mawhinney, Edgar. "A Strange Kind of Peace." *Ulster: Voice of the Ulster Defence Association* (September, 1978): 1.

McAuley, Richard. "Insight Into Imperialism." *An Phoblacht/ Republican News* (September 13, 1980): 10.

McDonagh, Enda. "Violence and Political Change." *Furrow* (February 29, 1978): 86 - 87.

Mc Dowell, Michael. "Northern Ireland: A Protestant Perspective." *Visitor* (February 3, 1980): 6.

McGill, Paul. "R. C. Church 'No' to Education Integration." *Orange Standard* (July, 1980): 7.

McGrail, Michael, S. J. "A Civil Rights Movement for Protestants?" *Orange Standard* (March, 1981): 1.

"McKee Hits Trades Council." *Protestant Telegraph* (May 2, 1981): 11.

McKeown, Archie. "The Shipyard." *Ulster: Voice of the Ulster Defence Association* (July, 1979): 5.

McKeown, Michael. "The Christian Conscience." *Furrow* (September, 1973): 588.

McMeekin, Derek G. "In God's Name Call Off This Fast." *Orange Standard* (May, 1981): 7.

"The Moderate Voice." *Peace By Peace* (September 18, 1981): 4.

"Modern History Background." *Christian Century* 88 (February, 1971): 4.

Moore, Robert. "Race Relations in the Six Counties: Colonialism, Industrialism, and Stratification in Ireland." *Race* 14 (1972): 36.

" 'Murder' the Provo's Answer to Segregation." *Combat: Journal of the Ulster Volunteers* 4 (n. d.): 1.

Murphy, Dervla. "A Return." *Ulster: Voice of the Ulster Defence Association* 2 (n. d.): 16 - 17.

"Murder is a Mortal Sin Say Irish Bishops." *London Tablet* (November, 1981).

National Council for Civil Liberties of Great Britain. *Bulletin of Peace Proposals* (September 29, 1971).

"No Surrender." *Protestant Telegraph* (July 11, 1981): 1, 11.

"No Surrender on Peacemaking." *Peace By Peace* 7 (April 3, 1981): 1.

"NORAID Dossier." *Combat: Journal of the Ulster Volunteers* 4 (n. d.): 1 - 2.

"Northern Ireland Charged With Prisoner Maltreatment." *Matchbox* (Summer, 1978): 1.

O'Brien, Conor Cruise. "Hands Off." *Foreign Policy* 37 (Winter, 1979): 102 - 104, 110.

Paisley, Ian. "The Case for Capital Punishment for Terrorist Murder." *Protestant Telegraph* (October 3, 1981): 7.

—— "Jesuitical Trick to Overthrow the Protestant Throne." *Orange Standard* (September, 1980): 3.

—— "Paisley Spells It Out." *Protestant Telegraph* (January, 1980): 2 - 8.

—— "Pray Against the Pope's Visit." *Protestant Telegraph* (October 3, 1981): 2.

——"Protestant Britain Now the Paymaster of Papist Europe." *Protestant Telegraph* (April 1979): 6 - 7.
——"Rome's Two Faces." *Protestant Telegraph* (August, 1981): 1.
"Paisley Warns Prior Against Power Sharing." *Protestant Telegraph* (February 27, 1982): 5.
"Peace People Press On." *Peace By Peace* (August 21, 1981): 1.
"Peoples' Democracy Manifesto." *Socialist Republic: Paper of Peoples' Democracy* 4 (n. d.): 3.
"Petition Against the Pope's Visit." *Protestant Telegraph* (December 12, 1981): 6.
"Popery in St. Anne's." *Protestant Telegraph* (February 6, 1981): 12.
Power, Jonathan. "Can the Peace People Bring an Irish Peace?" *Encounter* 48 (March, 1977): 16.
"Priests and Terrorism." *Orange Standard* (April, 1981): 1.
"Priests in the IRA Service." *Ulster: Voice of the Ulster Defence Association* 2 (July 19, 1979): 3.
"Primate Criticizes Hunger Strikes." *Orange Standard* (November, 1980): 8.
"Pro Mundi Vita Document." *Furrow* (September, 1973): 570.
"Protestant Revival in Meath, Kildare." *Orange Standard* (November, 1980): 5.
"Protestant-Roman Catholic Attitudes on Ulster Options." *Orange Standard* (August, 1981): 4.
"Protestants Experience Bias in Housing Programs." *Orange Standard* (October, 1981): 7.
Redmond, Mary. "Constitutional Aspects of Pluralism." *Studies: An Irish Quarterly Review* 57 (Spring-Summer, 1978): 44.
Roberts, David A. "The Orange Order in Ireland: A Religious Institution?" British Journal of Sociology 22 (September, 1971): 275.
"Roman Catholic Church Backs IRA Hunger Strikers." *Protestant Telegraph* (June 20, 1981): 9.
"Roman Catholic Birthrate." *Orange Standard* (February, April, 1980): 7.
"Roman Catholic Dissent and the Dangers." *Orange Standard* (April, 1980): 7.

"Roman Catholic Hierarchy 'Bigoted, Brutal'." *Orange Standard* (October, 1981): 8.

"Roman Catholic Hypocrisy." *Protestant Telegraph* (October 3, 1981): 9.

"Rome — The Dragon on Our Streets." *Protestant Telegraph* (August 8, 1981): 1.

Rose, Richard. "On Priorities of Citizenship in the Deep South." *Journal of Politics* 38 (May, 1976): 260.

"The Rush to Rome." *Orange Standard* (March, 1980): 8.

Ryan, Liam. "Church and Politics: The Last Twenty Years." *Furrow* (January, 1979): 17.

Schelling, Thomas C. "An Essay on Bargaining." *American Economic Review* (June, 1956): 278.

"Sectarianism: The Enemy Within the Gates." *Ulster: Voice of the Ulster Defence Association* 2 (April, 1979): 3.

Senior, Alan. "A House Divided." *Peace By Peace* (May 8, 1981): 7.

— — "Masters of Garbage." *Peace by Peace* (June 5, 1981): 7.

Sigelman, Lee, and Simpson, Miles. "A Cross-National Test of the Linkage Between Inequality and Political Violence." *Journal of Conflict Resolution: Research of War and Peace Between and Within Nations* 21 (March, 1977): 106.

Smyth, Martin. " 'No' to Visit by Pope to Britain," *Orange Standard* (November, 1981): 1.

"Southern Irish Begging Bowl Economy." *Ulster: Voice of the Ulster Defence Association* (August, 1981): 12 - 15.

"Struggle on All Fronts." *An Phoblacht/Republican News* (May 12, 1979): 5.

"Support for Negotiated Independence Grows." *Ulster: Voice of the Ulster Defence Association* (August, 1981): 24.

"A Surfeit of R. C. Talk." *Orange Standard* (November, 1981): 5, 8.

"31,278 Fermanagh and South Tyrone Roman Catholics Vote for the Murder of Protestants." *Protestant Telegraph* (September 5, 1981): 1 - 2.

"Towards a New North." *Peace By Peace* (September 5, 1980): 5.

"UDA Plans for Ulster Independence." *Ulster: Voice of the Ulster Defence Association* 2 (April, 1979): 2.

"Ulster After a Year of Thatcher Rule." *Orange Standard* (June, 1980): 1.

243

"Ulster a Key to its Own Future." *Orange Standard* (April, 1980): 6.
"Ulster Works Independently." *Ulster: Voice of the Ulster Defence Association* 2 (n. d.): 10 - 13.
"Vatican in Secret Moves to Fix Pope's Visit to Britain." *Protestant Telegraph* (January, 1980): 9.
"The Voice of Ulster." *Orange Standard* (May, 1979): 8.
"Violence Solves Nothing." *Peace By Peace* (November 27, 1981): 1.
Watson. "Beware Thy Neighbour." *Combat: Journal of the Ulster Volunteers* 4 (n. d.): 2.
— — "The Church and Terrorism." *Combat: Journal of the Ulster Volunteers* 4 (n. d.): 4.
"Who Gets Housing Priority?" *Orange Standard* (November, 1980): 5.
"Why? Britain's Strange Attitude to Our Security Situation." *Orange Standard* (September, 1981): 8.
"Will Protestant Truth Conquer?" *Orange Standard* (May, 1980): 3.

Official Publications

An Industrial and Occupational Profile of the Two Sections of the Population of Northern Ireland: An Analysis of the 1971 Population Census. Fair Employment Agency for Northern Ireland.
British Information Services. *Northern Ireland.* London: Central Office of Information, May, 1975.
Encyclical Letter: Mater et Magistra, Christianity and Social Progress. By Pope John XXIII, trans. by W. J. Gibbons, S. J., Glen Rock, N. J.: Paulist Press, 1962.
Encyclical Letter: *Pacem in Terris, Peace on Earth.* By Pope John XXIII, trans. by Vatican Polyglot Press, Washington, D. C.: National Catholic Welfare Conference, 1963.
Great Britain. Her Majesty's Stationary Office. *Report of the Commission on Disturbances in Northern Ireland,* Cnd., 532, 1969.
— —*Report of the Commission on Legal Procedures to Deal With Terrorist Activities in Northern Ireland, 1972.*
— — *Report of the Housing Executive Corporate Planning Department on the Northern Ireland Housing Survey, 1975.*
Northern Ireland Report. Belfast: Public Information Office, 1975.

244

National Conference of Catholic Bishops. *Matrimonia Mixta.* Canon 1061, Sec. 7.

Official texts promulgated by the Ecumenical Council. *Documents of Vatican II: 1963 - 1965.* New York: The Guild Press, 1966.

"Politics and the Church." In *The Documents of Vatican II.* Western Printing and Lithographing Co., 1966.

Reed, Edward. ed. *Pacem in Terris/Peace on Earth: Proceedings of an International Convocation on the Requirements of Peace,* sponsored by the Center for Democratic Institutions. New York: Pocket Books, Inc., 1965.

Report of Amnesty International. London: Amnesty International Publications, 1980.

Report of the Committee on National and International Affairs to the General Assembly of the Presbyterian Church on Christians in a Situation of Conflict. Belfast: Church House Publications, 1973.

——*Pluralism in Ireland.* Belfast: Church House Publications, 1977.

Report of the Peace People Charitable Trust Report on the Period From Their Establishment to March 31, 1978. Belfast.

Report on Sex in Marriage: Love-Giving, Life-Giving. Washington, D. C.: Archdiocese of Washington, 1968.

Republic of Ireland. *Bunreacht Na heiremann, Constitution of Ireland.* Dublin: Government Publications, 1942.

——Department of Foreign Affairs. *Facts About Ireland.* Dublin: Irish Printers, Ltd., 1978.

——Industrial Development Authority. *Ireland: The Most Profitable Industrial Location in the EEC.* Dublin: Colorman Ltd., 1978.

——Industrial Development Authority. *IDA Industrial Plan: 1977 - 1980.* Richview: Brown and Nolan Ltd.

Newspapers

"Civil War Still Possible, O'Brien Warns." *Cork Examiner,* April 14, 1979.

O'Neill, Liam, and Martin, Peter. "Unionist Interests Guaranteed by Fina Gael." *Cork Examiner,* February 19, 1979, pp. 1 - 2.

" 'No Pleasure in Vote' Says Peace Leader." *Sunday Times,* April 1, 1979, p. 6.

"Secret File Was Lost in the Post." *Belfast Telegraph*, May 11, 1979, pp. 1, 4.
"Senator Kennedy Calls for Talk by All Parties to Promote Unification of Ireland." *Times*, October 21, 1971.

Other Sources

Information in a letter to the author from Jim Watson of Belfast, March 17, 1981.
Information in a letter to the author from Joseph McVeigh of the Peace Studies Institute, Manhattan College, N.Y., October 19, 1980.
Information in a letter to the author from Sam Duddy of the Ulster Defence Association, Belfast, January, 1980, and June 21, 1980.
Carroll, Terrance George. "Political Activists in Disaffected Communities: Dissidence, Disobedience and Rebellion in Northern Ireland." Ph. D. dissertation. Carlton University, 1975.
Coogan, Tim Pat. "Troubles in Northern Ireland." Portland, Oregon, 1981. A public statement to the Irish National Caucus.
Crowley, Michael. University College, Cork, Ireland. Interview, May 10, 1979.
Donaghy, Tom. The Peace People Community, Bledheim, Belfast. Interview, May 10, 1979.
Downey, James E. "Conflict and Crime in Northern Ireland." Ph. D. dissertation. Bowling Green University, 1978.
Duddy, Sam. Ulster Defence Association Headquarters, Belfast. Interview, May, 1979.
"The Easter Rising." BBC Home Service Production, No. 5328. Narrated by Robin Holmes.
Feeney, Edward Vincent. "From Reform to Resistance: A History of the Civil Rights Movement in Northern Ireland." Ph. D. dissertation. University of Washington, 1974.
Gallinagh, Patrick. St. Patrick's Church, Belfast. Interview, May 12, 1979.
Goldberg, Gerald. Address to the Cork Peace Council, Central Hall, Cork, Ireland, May 1, 1979.
Graham, William. The *Belfast Telegraph*, Belfast. Interview, May 13, 1979.

246

Hajda, Jan. "Sociology of Intellectuals." Lecture to a graduate seminar, Portland State University. October, 1978.

Hajda, Jan, and Travis, Robert. "Causes and Consequences of Powerlessness." Portland State University, Portland, Oregon, 1978. (Mimeographed).

Hourani, Benjamin. "On Global Man." 2nd Futurology Symposium, Cincinnati, Ohio, July, 1974. (Mimeographed)

Hurwitz, Cecil. Cork Peace Council, Cork, Ireland. Interview, April 26, 1979.

"Irish Culture During Rebellion." Center for Cassette Studies. No. 27278.

Malcolm Jr., Douglas. "Conflict Regulation vs Mobilization: The Dilemma of Northern Ireland." Ph. D. dissertation. Columbia University, 1975.

McAuley, Richard. Provisional Sinn Fein Headquarters, Belfast, Northern Ireland. Interview, May 11, 1979.

McLachlan, Peter. The Peace People Community at Bledheim in Belfast, Northern Ireland. Interview, May 10, 1979.

Palmer, Shirley Adams. "The Parliament of Northern Ireland: A General Systems Approach to Conflict." Ph. D. dissertation. Ohio State University, 1976.

Points, Samuel, Bishop. The Palace in Cork, Ireland. Interview, June, 1979.

Sloan, George. Cork Peace Council, Cork, Ireland. Interview, May 1, 1979.

Williams, Betty. A statement on the troubles in Northern Ireland. Cork Peace Council, Cork, May 1, 1979.

VIRGINIA E. GLANDON

ARTHUR GRIFFITH AND THE ADVANCED-NATIONALIST PRESS IRELAND, 1900–1922

American University Studies, IX (History), vol. 2
339 pages   hardcover $ 33.–
ISBN 0-8204-0041-6

This book focuses upon the role of Arthur Griffith, Ireland's controversial journalist-statesman, and his fellow journalists in the context of the advanced-nationalist press, during the Irish Renaissance: 1900–1922. It evaluates the contributions to the national cause of Griffith and others and contrasts their goals for Ireland, as seen in their newspapers. It reveals the great diversity of opinion among advanced nationalists – a diversity which precluded a united front as they sought to win freedom from English rule. It assesses Griffith's long struggle, first as a journalist and later as a statesman, to unite the Irish behind his plan for an independent Irish state – and why he failed to hold the new nation together as head of its Provisional Gouvernment in 1922. An index of Irish newspapers which circulated in Ireland during the period surveyed is included.

Virginia E. Glandon teaches Irish History at the University of Missouri, Kansas City. She has lived and worked in Ireland, on and off, during summer vacations since 1971 and has published a number of scholarly articles on Irish topics, both in Irish and American journals. She participates at the national and regional levels in the American Committee for Irish Studies and is a member of the Irish-American Cultural Institute.

PETER LANG PUBLISHING, INC.
34 East 39th Street, USA-New York, NY 10016
Jupiterstrasse 15, CH-3015 Berne